# Communications
# in Computer and Information Science     1171

*Commenced Publication in 2007*
Founding and Former Series Editors:
Phoebe Chen, Alfredo Cuzzocrea, Xiaoyong Du, Orhun Kara, Ting Liu,
Krishna M. Sivalingam, Dominik Ślęzak, Takashi Washio, Xiaokang Yang,
and Junsong Yuan

More information about this series at http://www.springer.com/series/7899

Calebe Bianchini · Carla Osthoff ·
Paulo Souza · Renato Ferreira (Eds.)

# High Performance Computing Systems

19th Symposium, WSCAD 2018
São Paulo, Brazil, October 1–3, 2018
Revised Selected Papers

 Springer

*Editors*
Calebe Bianchini 🆔
Mackenzie Presbyterian University
São Paulo, Brazil

Paulo Souza 🆔
University of São Paulo
São Paulo, Brazil

Carla Osthoff 🆔
National Laboratory for Scientific
Computing
Rio de Janeiro, Brazil

Renato Ferreira
Federal University of Minas Gerais
Belo Horizonte, Brazil

ISSN 1865-0929        ISSN 1865-0937   (electronic)
Communications in Computer and Information Science
ISBN 978-3-030-41049-0        ISBN 978-3-030-41050-6   (eBook)
https://doi.org/10.1007/978-3-030-41050-6

This Springer imprint is published by the registered company Springer Nature Switzerland AG
The registered company address is: Gewerbestrasse 11, 6330 Cham, Switzerland

# Preface

The XIX Symposium on High Performance Computing Systems (WSCAD 2018) in São Paulo, promoted by the Brazilian Computer Society (SBC), is one of the most important Brazilian events supported by the Special Committee on Computer Architecture and High-Performance Processing (CEACPAD). CEACPAD promotes this computing area by running activities that integrate theoretical and practical approaches. Therefore, WSCAD promotes these activities by introducing new scientific, technical, and educational breakthroughs in high-performance computing systems to researchers, students, and developers from academia and industry. In 2018, WSCAD was the largest Brazilian national event in this area, allowing the integration and exchange of experiences of its participants, guided by the latest developments in high-performance computing and computer architecture in Brazil and worldwide.

WSCAD 2018 had six distinguished keynote speakers, including leading researches in computer architectures and high-performance computing. WSCAD was also proud to offer several technical sessions in a three-day event: the main track, Undergraduate Research Workshop (WIC), Workshop on Education in Computer Architecture (WEAC), Doctorate and Master's Thesis Contest (CTD), and Workshop on Heterogeneous Computing (WCH). In addition to these technical sessions, there was also the traditional Marathon of Parallel Programming and three short courses. The main speeches addressed topics related to the importance of processors in the security of computational solutions, the behavior of users in an important Brazilian high-performance computing platform, big data applications and deep neural networks, optimizations in parallel codes for supercomputers, and software that facilitate the development of neural network inference on heterogeneous parallel platforms. This edition invited 24 of the best papers from WSCAD 2018, each having submitted an extended version addressing the topic of the conference and containing at least 30% new content regarding any previously published paper, after which 12 papers were selected for publication.

The WSCAD 2018 website (http://wscad.sbc.org.br/2018/) provides access to the talks at the meetings and photos of the activities. The website (http://wscad.sbc.org.br/edicoes/index.html) also gives information on latest events. This book contains the best papers from WSCAD 2018. We would like to thank the entire Organizing Committee and chairs of WSCAD 2018 for their time, dedication, and hard work. We thank Mackenzie Presbyterian University for welcoming WSCAD 2018 and all its attendants, offering kindly an infrastructure at São Paulo. We thank SBC and CEACPAD for their trust and support. We thank the agencies FAPESP, CAPES, and CNPq, and our sponsors Google, Intel, and Laniaq for their financial support. We thank all keynote speakers who donated their time and shared their experiences. Finally, we would like to thank the authors of the selected papers, the reviewers of all tracks, and all attendants for actually being part of WSCAD 2018.

December 2019

Calebe Bianchini
Paulo Souza
Carla Osthoff
Renato Ferreira

# Organization

## General Chairs

Calebe Biachinni     Mackenzie Presbyterian University, Brazil
Paulo Souza     University of São Paulo, Brazil

## Program Committee Chairs

Carla Osthoff     National Laboratory for Scientific Computing, Brazil
Renato Ferreira     Federal University of Minas Gerais, Brazil

## Program Committee

| | |
|---|---|
| Alfredo Goldman | University of São Paulo, Brazil |
| Alvaro de la Ossa Osegueda | University of Costa Rica, Costa Rica |
| Andrei Tchernykh | Scientific Center for Research and High Education, Mexico |
| Carlos Jaime Barrios Hernández | Industrial University of Santander, Colombia |
| Celso Mendes | University of Illinois at Urbana-Champaign, USA |
| Cesar De Rose | Pontifical Catholic University of Rio Grande do Sul, Brazil |
| Claude Tadonki | PSL University, France |
| Cristiana Bentes | State University of Rio de Janeiro, Brazil |
| Daniel Cardoso Moraes de Oliveira | Federal Fluminense University, Brazil |
| Domingo Gimenez | Universidad de Murcia, Spain |
| Edson Norberto Cáceres | Federal University of Mato Grosso do Sul, Brazil |
| Esteban Meneses | Costa Rica Institute of Technology, Costa Rica |
| Francieli Zanon Boito | French National Institute for Computer Science and Applied Mathematics, France |
| George Teodoro | Federal University of Minas Gerais, Brazil |
| Gilberto Javier Díaz Toro | Industrial University of Santander, Colombia |
| Gonzalo Hernandez | University of Santa Maria, Chile |
| Harold Enrique Castro Barrera | University of Los Andes, Colombia |
| Isidoro Gitler | National Polytechnic Institute, Mexico |
| Jairo Panetta | Technological Institute of Aeronautics, Brazil |
| Jean Francois Mehaut | University of Grenoble Alpes, France |
| Jesus Carretero | University Carlos III of Madrid, Spain |
| João Lourenço | NOVA University of Lisbon, Portugal |
| Jose Nelson Amaral | University of Alberta, Canada |

| Laércio Lima Pilla | French National Centre for Scientific Research, France |
| Leonel Sousa | University of Lisbon, Portugal |
| Liliana Barbosa | University of Guadalajara, Mexico |
| Lucas Cordeiro | The University of Manchester, UK |
| Luiz Angelo Steffenel | University of REIMS Champagne-Ardenne, France |
| Luiz Manuel Rocha Gadelha Junior | National Laboratory for Scientific Computing, Brazil |
| Maria Pantoja | Californa Polytechnic State University, USA |
| Mario Antonio Ribeiro Dantas | Federal University of Juiz de Fora, Brazil |
| Nicolas Wolovick | National University of Cordoba, Argentina |
| Philippe Navaux | Federal University of Rio Grande do Sul, Brazil |
| Radu Prodan | University of Klagenfurt, Austria |
| Rodrigo de Rosa Righi | Universidade do Vale do Rio dos Sinos, Brazil |
| Siang Wun Song | State University of São Paulo, Brazil |
| Veronica Gil-Costa | National University of San Luis, Argentina |

# Contents

# Cloud Computing

# An Interference-Aware Strategy
# for Co-locating High Performance
# Computing Applications in Clouds

Maicon Melo Alves[1,2](✉)🔘, Luan Teylo[1]🔘, Yuri Frota[1]🔘,
and Lúcia Maria de A. Drummond[1]🔘

[1] Fluminense Federal University, Niterói, Brazil
{mmelo,luanteylo,yuri,lucia}@ic.uff.br
[2] Petroleo Brasileiro S. A. - Petrobras, Rio de Janeiro, Brazil

**Abstract.** Cross-interference may happen when applications share a common physical machine, affecting negatively their performances. This problem occurs frequently when high performance applications are executed in clouds. Some papers of the related literature have considered this problem when proposing strategies for Virtual Machine Placement. However, they neither have employed a suitable method for predicting interference nor have considered the minimization of the number of used physical machines and interference at the same time. In this paper, we present a solution based on the Iterated Local Search framework to solve the Interference-aware Virtual Machine Placement Problem for HPC applications in Clouds (IVMP). This problem aims to minimize, at the same time, the interference suffered by HPC applications which share common physical machines and the number of physical machines used to allocate them. Experiments were conducted in a real scenario by using applications from oil and gas industry and applications from the HPCC benchmark. They showed that our method reduced interference in more than 40%, using the same number of physical machines of the most widely employed heuristics to solve the problem.

## 1 Introduction

High Performance Computing (HPC) applications are typically executed in dedicated datacenters. However, in the past few years, cloud computing has emerged as an attractive option to run these applications due to several advantages that it brings when compared with a dedicated infrastructure. Clouds provide a rapid provisioning of resources and a significant reduction in operating costs related to energy, software licence and hardware obsolescence [6,15]. Moreover, with the recent increase of the number of cores in modern physical machines, HPC applications can scale up to many cores even when fully allocated to a single physical machine. Consequently, clouds can offer a reasonable service performance for small-scale HPC applications, that can be entirely placed into a single physical machine, thus avoiding the performance penalty usually imposed by the physical network of clouds [8].

C. Bianchini et al. (Eds.): WSCAD 2018, CCIS 1171, pp. 3–20, 2020.
https://doi.org/10.1007/978-3-030-41050-6_1

Despite these advantages, some challenges must be overcome to bridge the gap between performance provided by a dedicated infrastructure and the one supplied by clouds. Overhead introduced by virtualized layer [4] and hardware heterogeneity [7], for example, affect negatively the performance of HPC applications when executed in clouds. In addition, the absence of a high-performance network can prevent synchronous and tightly-coupled HPC applications from being satisfactorily executed in this environment [12]. Besides these problems, the performance of HPC applications can be particularly affected by resource sharing policies usually adopted by cloud providers. In general, one physical server can host many virtual machines holding distinct applications [5]. Although virtualization layer provides a reasonable level of resource isolation, some shared resources, like cache and main memory, cannot be sliced over all applications running in the virtual machines. As a consequence, these co-located applications can experience mutual interference, resulting in performance degradation [8,9].

Some works, such as [3,8–10,16], and [5] proposed Virtual Machine Placement (VMP) strategies to avoid or, at least, minimize the effect that interference imposes in co-located HPC applications. Some of those works used a static matrix of interference or proposed a naive procedure to determine it. Other works, even proposing more general methods to determine interference, considered just one kind of shared resource, the Shared Last Level Cache (SLLC), or adopted an approach that evaluates only general characteristics of HPC applications. However, as discussed in [2], all of these methods are not suitable for determining the interference because this problem is directly related to the amount and similarity of concurrent access to SLLC, DRAM (Dynamic Random Access Memory) and virtual network. Moreover, although some of those works, [8] and [9], have also considered to reduce the number of used physical machines when trying to minimize interference, none of them treated both problems together.

In this work, we present a solution based on the Iterated Local Search (ILS) framework to solve the Interference-aware Virtual Machine Placement Problem for Small-scale HPC Applications in clouds (IVMPP). This multi-objective problem, whose the mathematical formulation can be found at [1], aims to minimize, at the same time, (i) the interference experienced by small-scale HPC applications, *i.e.*, HPC applications that are small enough to run on a multicore machine in a reasonable amount of time, and (ii) the number of physical machines used to allocate them. To predict the interference level experienced by co-located applications, we used a quantitative and multivariate model originally presented in [2]. This model takes into account the amount of access to SLLC, DRAM, and virtual network, besides the similarity among applications access profiles, to estimate interference with a reasonable prediction error. This model is a step forward for the cross-interference problem since it treats this problem from a multivariate and quantitative perspective. Unlike other strategies proposed in the related literature, this model evaluates the amount of access to shared resources instead of considering general and subjective characteristics of HPC applications. Besides that, the model assumes that the interference problem is influenced by more than one factor to deal with its multivariate nature.

Our proposed VMP strategy was evaluated by using a set of instances created from real-life HPC applications. We compared our strategy with the most widely used heuristics to minimize the number of machines in clouds and with the Multi-Dimensional Online Bin Packing (MDOBP), a heuristic proposed in [8], whose goal is to minimize the interference among co-located HPC applications. It is worth to state that we compared our work with MDOBP, because, among the related works, this proposal is the only one that tackles, jointly, both minimization of interference and minimization of used physical machines. Concerning the work described in [1], this paper brings new analysis between our proposal and an exact approach in order to evaluate the quality of solutions given by our strategy. In addition, we describe, in details, the VND (Variable Neighborhood Descent) method used to execute the local search phase on the used metaheuristic.

## 2   Basic Assumptions

In this work, we assume that the allocation of one application to a physical machine is equivalent to the allocation of all virtual machines, holding that application, to the same physical machine. Besides that, we assume that all physical machines have the same hardware configuration, *i.e.*, they are equipped with the same amount of CPU and main memory.

As mentioned before, we used in our proposed VMP strategy the model introduced in [2] for predicting interference experienced by applications that share a common physical machine. This model relies on the amount of accumulated access to (i) SLLC, (ii) DRAM and (iii) virtual network[1]. This accumulated access, which is the sum of applications individual access, represents the total pressure which all co-located applications put in a given shared resource. Notice that an application individual access can be easily obtained by using performance monitoring tools. From the applications accumulated access, the model estimates the level of interference experienced by the set of co-located applications. This interference level is defined as the average slowdown presented by all applications allocated to the same physical machine. In this paper, the *slowdown* of one application is particularly defined as the percentage of additional time spent by this application when it is executed concurrently with other ones. For example, suppose that the execution times of two applications, namely A1 and A2, when executed in a dedicated physical machine, were equal to 60 and 80 s, respectively. Suppose also that both applications, when executed concurrently in that physical machine, spent 100 s. In this case, the slowdown of applications A1 and A2 would be, respectively, 67% and 25%. This percentage represents how much additional time these applications need to complete their executions when allocated to the same physical machine. Thus, the interference level between both applications would be 46% which means that these two applications would

---

[1] In the context of this work, the amount of access to SLLC and DRAM are measured in terms of millions of references per second (MR/s), while the access to virtual network is expressed as the number of megabytes transmitted per second (MB/s).

experience, on average, 46% of mutual interference when allocated to the same physical machine.

## 3  Mathematical Formulation of IVMPP

Let $M$ be the set of physical machines available in a cloud environment and $A$ the set of applications to be allocated to it. We define the total amount of main memory and number of CPUs provided by each physical machine as $Mem$ and $Cpu$, respectively. Similarly, the amount of CPU and main memory required by an application $i \in A$ is defined as $m_i$ and $c_i$, respectively. It is worth mentioning that, in this work, we assume that all physical machines have the same hardware configuration, i.e., they are equipped with the same amount of CPU and main memory.

Moreover, we define $\gamma_Q$ as the interference level experienced by a subset of applications $Q \subseteq A$ when allocated to a same physical machine and $\omega$ as the maximum interference level that can be reached on each physical machine. We now define a binary variable $X_{i,j}$ for each $i \in A$ and $j \in M$ such that $X_{i,j}$ is equal to 1 if and only if application $i$ is allocated to the physical machine $j$, and equal to 0, otherwise. In addition, we define a binary variable $Y_j$ for each $j \in M$ such that $Y_j$ is equal to 1 if and only if the physical machine $j$ is being used, i.e., if there is, at least, one application allocated to it. $Y_j$ is equal to 0 if no application is allocated to $j$. This problem can be formulated as the integer programming problem described in Eqs. (1) to (8). The objective function defined in Expression 1 seeks for minimization of the sum of interference levels presented in each physical machine and the number of machines used to allocate all applications. Remark that the sum of interference levels, which is used to measure the overall interference of the cloud environment, was normalized with respect to the maximum sum of interference levels that can be reached in our environment

Besides that, we normalized the number of used machines concerning the total number of physical machines available in the cloud environment. As both objectives were normalized between 0 and 1, we can use the weight $\alpha$ to determine the relevance of each objective. Therefore, when $\alpha$ is set to 1 the objective function prioritizes the minimizing of the sum of interference levels, and when $\alpha$ is close to 0 the function minimizes the number of used physical machines. Thus, this parameter can be adjusted to reach a desirable trade-off between both objectives. Constraints described in Eq. 2 ensure that each application is entirely allocated to just one physical machine. Inequalities defined in (3) and (4) enforce that the total amount of CPU and main memory available in physical machines are not exceeded. In Inequalities (5) we defined constraints to guarantee that a physical machine is used if and only if it holds, at least, one single application. As all physical machines permutation yield feasible solutions, we added a set of constraints, defined in (6), that eliminates symmetry by establishing an order at which machines shall be used in the cloud environment. At last, constraints described in (7) and (8) define the binary and integrality requirements on the variables.

$$min\left(\left\{\frac{\sum\limits_{j\in M}\left[\sum\limits_{Q\subseteq A}\left(\prod\limits_{i\in Q}X_{i,j}\right).\gamma_Q\right]}{\omega.\sum\limits_{j\in M}Y_j}\right\}.\alpha+\left(\frac{\sum\limits_{j\in M}Y_j}{|M|}\right).(1-\alpha)\right) \quad (1)$$

$$\sum_{j\in M}X_{i,j}=1, \forall i\in A \quad (2)$$

$$\sum_{i\in A}X_{i,j}.m_i\leq Mem.Y_j, \forall j\in M \quad (3)$$

$$\sum_{i\in A}X_{i,j}.c_i\leq Cpu.Y_j, \forall j\in M \quad (4)$$

$$X_{i,j}\leq Y_j, \forall i\in A, \forall j\in M \quad (5)$$

$$Y_{j+1}\leq Y_j, \forall j=\{1...|M|-1\} \quad (6)$$

$$X_{i,j}\in\{0,1\}, \forall i\in A, \forall j\in M \quad (7)$$

$$Y_j\in\{0,1\}, \forall j\in M \quad (8)$$

## 4   Multistart Iterated Local Search for the IVMPP Problem

The classic VMP problem is classified as an NP-Hard problem [14]. So, IVMPP, that is a variant of VMP, can also be classified as an NP-Hard problem. For this sort of problem, exact procedures have often proven to be incapable of finding solutions in a reasonable time. Therefore, we propose in this work a solution based on the Iterated Local Search (ILS) metaheuristic which employs a multistart approach to explore larger areas of the search space.

In order to present the proposed algorithm, we need to introduce some additional notation. We define a placement solution $s = \{(a1, m1), (a2, m2), ...\}$ as the set of 2-tuples $(a, m)$ representing that the application $a$ is allocated to physical machine $m$. Moreover, we define $Z(s)$ as the normalized sum of interference levels predicted for solution $s$. As previously described, we used the prediction model originally proposed in [2] to calculate the interference level experienced by applications allocated to a single physical machine.

In addition, we define $M(s)$ as the normalized number of physical machines used in $s$, and $E_{CPU}(s)$ and $E_{MEM}(s)$ as the percentage of amount of CPU and main memory exceeded in solution $s$, respectively. A solution is considered feasible if and only if $E_{CPU}(s)$ and $E_{MEM}(s)$ are equal to zero. We define in Eq. 9 a cost function $f : \mathbb{S} \to \mathbb{R}$, where $\mathbb{S}$ is the set of all possible solutions. This function $f(s)$ attempts to minimize the sum of levels of interference and the number of used machines. In addition, $f(n)$ penalizes, in accordance with parameter $\lambda$, unfeasible solutions, which use more CPU and memory than the available amount in the environment.

---

**Algorithm 1.** *ILSivmp*

---

    **Input:** $A, M, \beta, iterMaxILS, iterMaxMultiStart$
    **Output:** $s^*$
1: $s^* = \emptyset$; $f(s^*) = \infty$; $i = 1$; $j = 1$;
2: **while** $i \leq iterMaxMultiStart$ **do**
3:     $s = ConstructivePhase(A, M, \beta)$;
4:     **repeat**
5:         $\overline{s} = VariableNeighborhoodDescent(s, A, M)$;
6:         **if** $(f(\overline{s}) < f(s^*))$ **then**
7:             $s^* = \overline{s}$;
8:             $j = 1$;
9:         **else**
10:           $j = j + 1$;
11:         **end if**
12:         $s = Perturbation(\overline{s}, j)$;
13:     **until** $j \leq iterMaxILS$
14:     $i = i + 1$;
15: **end while**
16: **return** $s^*$

---

Our proposed solution, called *ILSivmp*, is described in Algorithm 1. For each iteration of the *Multistart Loop* (lines 2 to 15), the algorithm executes the procedure *ConstructivePhase* (line 3) to create a new solution to be submitted to the ILS. Then, *ILS Loop* (lines 4 to 13) performs a local search in the neighborhood of the current solution through *VariableNeighborhoodDescent* (VND) method (line 5). Both VND and *ConstructivePhase* are described in detail later.

After executing VND, the *ILSivmp* evaluates the quality of the current solution $\overline{s}$ (line 6). If $\overline{s}$ represents an improvement on the best current solution $s^*$, it is set as the actual best solution and the counter $j$ is reset to 1 (lines 7 and 8). Otherwise, the counter $j$ is incremented (line 10). Then, the algorithm executes the procedure *Perturbation* (line 12) that applies a perturbation on the current solution in order to escape from local optima. *Perturbation* executes $j$ random movements of three classical local search movements for the original VMP problem: *Move1*, *Move2* and *Swap1*. Heuristics *Move1* and *Move2*, move, respectively, one and two applications to another used physical machine, while *Swap1* performs one swap operation, *i.e.*, it swaps two applications between two distinct physical machines. Furthermore, this procedure also adds a new physical machine to the solution, before executing the last perturbation (*i.e.*, when $j$ is equal to *iterMaxILS*) of a given initial solution (*i.e.*, solution created by *ConstructivePhase*).

$$f(s) = Z(s).\alpha + M(s).(1 - \alpha) + E_{CPU}(s).\lambda + E_{MEM}(s).\lambda \qquad (9)$$

Algorithm 2 presents the *ConstructivePhase*, called in line 3 of Algorithm 1. Firstly, the algorithm sorts the list of applications in decreasing order (line 1) by considering the following sequence: (i) amount of accesses to SLLC, (ii) amount of requested CPU and main memory, and (iii) amount of accesses to virtual network and DRAM. Next, the algorithm inserts one physical machine into the set of used machines (lines 2 and 3). Then, the procedure executes *Allocation Loop* (lines 4 to 20) that basically performs the selection of two applications from the list of sorted applications and selection of a physical machine to allocate them. The process of selecting this pair of applications is described as follows. Firstly, the algorithm creates the sets of applications *First* and *Last* that are composed, respectively, of the first and last $N_a$ elements of the sorted list of applications (lines 5 to 7). This number of applications is defined by the parameter $\beta$ that is used to control the degree of randomness of this constructive phase. Next, the algorithm selects, randomly, applications $i$ and $j$ from *First* and *Last*, respectively (line 8). By selecting applications from the head and tail of the sorted list, this process aims to co-locate applications with complementary access profiles and amount of requested resources, thus resulting in a low interference level. After selecting this pair of applications, the best physical machine to allocate them is chosen among the set of physical machines with enough resources to allocate both applications. The method selects the best machine by considering two metrics. These metrics are obtained from the following vectors of resources (CPU and main memory): (i) remaining resources of the physical machine ($\overrightarrow{REM}$), (ii) requested resources ($\overrightarrow{REQ}$) and (iii) remaining resources after allocating requested resources ($\overrightarrow{RAF}$). Each of these vectors has two dimensions, corresponding to the normalized amount of CPU and main memory. The first metric, called *alignment factor*, was also used in [8], and is calculated as the angle between vectors $\overrightarrow{REQ}$ and $\overrightarrow{REM}$. This factor is used to evaluate the shape of the exploitable volume of resources, allowing to assess whether required and remaining resources are complementary to each other. The other metric, called *residual factor*, is equal to the length of vector $\overrightarrow{RAF}$ and is used to assess the size of exploitable volume of resources, *i.e*, it measures the amount of resources left in the physical machine after the allocation of the requested resources. This second metric is proposed as a tiebreaker for the first metric, *i.e.*, for cases with the same alignment factor, the residual factor is used to select the physical machine which will result in the smallest resource wastage.

After calculating those metrics, the *ConstructivePhase* chooses the physical machine with the smallest alignment and residual factors (in this order) to allocate applications $i$ and $j$ (line 10). However, if none of the used physical machines has available resources to allocate applications $i$ and $j$, the *ConstructivePhase* uses a new physical machine from $M$ to allocate them (lines 12 to 14). This approach aims to reduce the number of used machines because it takes new machines only when it is absolutely necessary. Moreover, if none of physical machines is capable of allocating that pair of applications, the method chooses randomly a physical machine to hold them (line 16). At last, both applications $i$ and $j$ are allocated to the selected physical machine and removed from the sorted list of applications (lines 18 and 19). Notice that unfeasible solutions can be generated by this constructive method. However, their corresponding costs are very high due to the penalty applied in the proposed cost function.

---

**Algorithm 2.** *ConstructivePhase*

---
  **Input:** $A$,$M$,$\beta$
  **Output:** $s$
 1: $App = Sort(A)$;
 2: $Used = Used \cup \{m_1\}$;
 3: $M = M\backslash\{m_1\}$;
 4: **while** $App \neq \emptyset$ **do**
 5:     $N_a = \lceil \beta.|App| \rceil$;
 6:     $First =$ first $N_a$ elements of $App$;
 7:     $Last =$ last $N_a$ elements of $App$;
 8:     *Choose randomly applications* $i \in First$ *and* $j \in Last$;
 9:     **if** There is $m \in Used$ with enough resources to allocate $i$ and $j$ **then**
10:         *Choose the best one to allocate* $i$ *and* $j$;
11:     **else if** $M \neq \emptyset$ **then**
12:         *Pick up any* $m \in M$
13:         $Used = Used \cup \{m\}$;
14:         $M = M\backslash\{m\}$;
15:     **else**
16:         *Choose randomly* $m \in Used$;
17:     **end if**
18:     $s = s \cup \{(i,m),(j,m)\}$;
19:     $App = App\backslash\{i,j\}$;
20: **end while**
21: **return** $s$

---

At last, Algorithm 3 presents the VND method. This method executes iteratively these classical local search movements for the original VMP problem: the *Move1*, *Swap1*, and *Move2*, in this order. As we adopted the strategy of first improving, these heuristics stop executing upon improving the current solution. In addition, the VND halts when no improvement is achieved in these neighborhoods.

## 5   Experimental Tests and Results

We carried out experiments to assess our proposal concerning its ability for reducing the sum of interference levels, while keeping a low number of used machines. Moreover, we executed additional experiments to verify the optimality of solutions of our proposal, by comparing them with the ones given by an exact procedure.

At first, we compared our VMP strategy with some of the most employed heuristics to minimize the number of used machines: Best Fit (BF), First Fit (FF), Worst Fit (WF), Best Fit Decreasing (BFD), First Fit Decreasing (FFD) and Worst Fit Decreasing (WFD). Since these greedy algorithms have shown to be effective for solving this problem in previous works [9], they were also used as a baseline here, in our experiments. In this way, we could assess the ability

---

**Algorithm 3.** *VND*

---

    **Input:** $s, A, M$
    **Output:** $\bar{s}$
1:  $M1 = S1 = M2 =$ True;
2: **while** $M1$ or $S1$ or $M2$ **do**
3:     $M1 = S1 = M2 =$ False;
4:     $s' = Move1(s, A, M)$;
5:     **if** $(f(s') < f(s))$ **then**
6:         $s = s'$;
7:         $M1 =$ True;
8:     **end if**
9:     **if** (**not** $M1$) **then**
10:         $s' = Swap1(s, A, M)$;
11:        **if** $(f(s') < f(s))$ **then**
12:            $s = s'$;
13:            $S1 =$ True;
14:        **end if**
15:     **end if**
16:     **if** (**not** Mov1 **and not** Swa1) **then**
17:         $s' = Move2(s, A, M)$;
18:        **if** $(f(s') < f(s))$ **then**
19:            $s = s'$;
20:            $M2 =$ True;
21:        **end if**
22:     **end if**
23: **end while**
24: $\bar{s} = s$;
25: **return** $\bar{s}$

---

of our strategy on reducing interference, while using a small number of physical machines.

After that, we compared our solution with the Multi-Dimensional Online Bin Packing (MDOBP) [8], the closest VMP work related to our proposal, since it aims to minimize the interference among co-located HPC applications. At last, we compared our solution with an exact approach in order to evaluate our proposal with respect to its capability of finding near-optimal solutions. All tests were executed in a Itautec MX214 server equipped with two Intel Xeon X5675 3.07 GHz processors and 48 GB of main memory. Moreover, all codes were compiled with GCC (Gnu C Compiler) version 4.9.2. All presented results are average of 10 execution.

To accomplish this experimental evaluation, we created a set of instances for the IVMPP problem by considering two real-life HPC-applications from petroleum industry: MUFITS (Multiphase Filtration Transport Simulator) [13] and PKTM (Pre-stack Kirchhoff Time Migration) [11]. MUFITS, a petroleum reservoir simulator, is a CPU-intensive application that exercises low-medium lateral communication among their processes. PKTM is a seismic migration method that provides a subsurface image from earth. This application is also CPU-intensive, but, unlike MUFITS, it is an embarrassing parallel application which means that computing processes do not exchange information among themselves.

Besides using both real applications, we tested applications from HPCC, a widely adopted benchmark to evaluate HPC systems. HPCC provides seven kernels in total, but, three of them, are just synthetic kernels used to naively measure memory and communication bandwidth. Therefore, we considered kernels that represent real HPC applications or operations commonly employed in scientific computing: PTRANS, HPL, DGEMM and FFT. As PKTM, DGEMM is also an embarrassing parallel application, while HPL, a CPU-intensive application, exchange data among their computing pairs. PTRANS is a high cache-intensive application, it achieved the highest SLLC access rate of all applications considered in our workload, while FFT is the one which achieved the highest communication rate, using around 50% of the maximum network bandwidth available in our system.

An instance for the IVMPP is composed of (i) the set of applications to be allocated in the cloud environment and (ii) the number of physical machines available in that environment. For each application, the amount of individual access to SLLC, DRAM and virtual network, and the normalized amount of requested CPU and main memory are also given as input to the problem. In this work, we considered that all physical machines available in the cloud environment has the same hardware configuration, *i.e.*, they have the same amount of CPU and main memory. As the amount of requested resources are normalized with respect to the total amount of resources available in physical machines, we could abstract this latter information from the IVMPP instance. Thus, if one application requires 0.5 of CPU, it is requesting 50% of the total amount of CPU available in the physical machine. Notice that this approach prevents the VMP strategy from being concerned about the absolute number of cores or amount of main memory available in the physical machines.

We created 100 instances for the IVMPP, where the number of applications at each instance varied from 5 to 50 (interval of 5). More specifically, we generated 10 instances with 5, 10, 15, 20, 25, 30, 35, 40, 45 and 50 applications. Those instances were generated by selecting some applications from the workload randomly. It is worth mentioning that an application can appear more than once in a same instance. In addition, for all instances, the number of machines available in the cloud environment was set as the total number of applications to be allocated. From this approach, we can evaluate whether *ILSivmp* sacrifices the minimization of physical machines in favor of the minimization of interference. Indeed, by adopting this configuration, *ILSivmp* has the option to spread out the applications, using all physical machines, in order to fully avoid interference in the cloud environment.

## 5.1   Comparing *ILSivmp* and Heuristics

To evaluate our proposal concerning its capacity to reduce interference while using a small number of physical machines, we devised the following two metrics. In the first one, we determined the percentage of test cases where our solution achieved a *strictly smaller sum of interference levels* than the one reached by the heuristic. Concerning the minimization of interference, this metric allows to quantify the number of test cases where our solution outperformed the tested heuristic. In the second metric, we calculated the percentage of cases where our proposal used a *smaller or equal number of physical machines* than the one used by the heuristic. By using this metric, we expect to evaluate the number of test cases where our solution achieved the minimal number of physical machines needed to allocate all applications in the cloud environment.

Note that, when comparing with a single heuristic, the best trade-off between minimizing interference and the number of physical machines is achieved when both metrics, reach, simultaneously, 100% of evaluated instances. In this hypothetical scenario, *ILSivmp* would reduce interference for all instances, while keeping, at least, the same number of used physical machines given by the heuristic. Concerning *ILSivmp*, the input parameter $\alpha$, which allows to control the relevance of each objective, was varied from 0.00 to 1.00 (interval of 0.10). By varying this parameter, we can verify the behavior of *ILSivmp* with respect to minimizing both interference and number of physical machines. The remaining input parameters of *ILSivmp* were defined from an empirical evaluation. So, parameters $\beta$, $\lambda$, *iterMaxILS* and *iterMaxMultistart* were fixed in 0.4, 0.5, 10 and 50, respectively. As *ILSivmp* is a non-deterministic algorithm, we repeated the execution of each instance until reaching a coefficient of variation smaller than 2%. Moreover, we restricted the execution time of *ILSivmp* in all cases to 15 s.

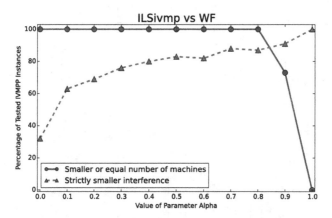

**Fig. 1.** ILSivmp against WF for minimizing the number of used physical machines

The best trade-off between reducing interference and number of used machines was achieved when $\alpha$ was equal to 0.70. Result of the comparison between *ILSivmp* and WF is presented in Fig. 1. The results of comparison with the other heuristics were similar. Our proposal has achieved a smaller or equal number of used machines in 100% of instances for all heuristics, besides reaching a strictly smaller interference in 88% of instances.

However, it is worth mentioning that the heuristic achieved the best interference levels only when it also used a greater number of physical machines than our solutions. This behaviour is expected since interference can really be reduced by allocating applications to more physical machines. In those cases, the heuristic penalized the minimization of physical machines to achieve a lower sum of interference levels. In short, in those cases, heuristic solutions were not better than our solutions. In only 2 instances, which represents 2% of all tested cases, all heuristics (except for WF) indeed outperformed our solution by achieving a smaller sum of interference levels while using the same number of machines indicated by our proposal. More specifically, heuristics FF and BF, when solving instance "IVMPP_5.5", reached a smaller sum of interference levels than *ILSivmp*. This same behavior can be observed for heuristics FFD, BFD and WFD when solving the instance "IVMPP_40.7". Even so, the difference between the sum of interference levels, in both cases, was smaller than 1%.

In order to verify the accuracy of the results achieved in those experiments, we conducted an additional evaluation in a real scenario by using the same set of physical machines previously described. We selected five instances where *ILSivmp* and the heuristics achieved the same number of physical machines. So, by allocating applications according to the placement given by *ILSivmp* and to the heuristic that achieved the smallest interference, we calculated the real sum of interference levels reached in practice. Results show that our strategy, even

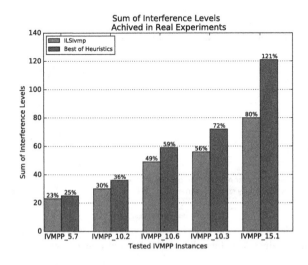

**Fig. 2.** Sum of interference levels achieved in a real scenario

using the same number of physical machines of the other heuristic, reduced the sum of interference levels up to 41%, as presented in Table 2. Moreover, it is worth mentioning that the difference between the predicted sum of interference levels and the one achieved in real experiments was, in average, around 8%. The highest difference between the sum of interference levels achieved by our solution and the one reached by heuristics occurred when they solved the instance "IVMPP_15.1". In such case, *ILSivmp* reached a sum of interference levels 41.25% smaller than FF, the best greedy heuristic in this case.

*ILSivmp* outperformed FF in that case because it co-located applications with complementary access profiles, as can be seen in Fig. 3. For example, our solution placed "PTRANS.I1.P6", a high access rate application, in a dedicated physical machine ("PM2"), thus, avoiding a possible cross-interference. On the other hand, heuristic FF, unlike our proposal, allocated "PTRANS.I1.P6" together with "PTRANS.I1.P4" and "DGEMM.I1.P2", leading to an interference level equal to 32.83%. This high interference level stems from the fact that those applications put a high pressure on the three shared resources.

Besides that, FF achieved a high interference level in the physical machine "PM1", around 46%, because it co-located applications that resulted in accumulated access scores equal to 0.28, 0.42 and 1.23 for SLLC, DRAM and virtual network, respectively. Conversely, our solution avoided to allocate, in the same physical machine, two applications "FFT.I2.P4" because this application presents the highest access rate for the virtual network.

Furthermore, we could observe that the difference between the sum of interference levels achieved by our solution and the greedy heuristics tended to increase with the rising of the number of applications. For example, our solution achieved a sum of interference levels 2% smaller than the heuristics solutions when solving instance "IVMPP_5.7". On the other hand, for instance "IVMPP_15.1", which has 10 times more applications than "IVMPP_5.7', this difference raised to 41%. In fact, as a higher number of applications incurs in a larger amount of placement combinations and our solution explores several distinct combinations of co-locations, it is expected, for those cases, that *ILSivmp* achieves smaller sums of interference levels solutions than the ones greedily found by the heuristics. Those results allowed to confirm conclusions drawn from offline experiments. *ILSivmp* was really able to reduce the level of interference experienced by HPC applications without increasing the number of physical machines needed to allocate them in cloud environments.

## 5.2   Comparing *ILSivmp* and MDOBP

Results described in the previous section showed that our solution was able to reduce interference even using a small number of physical machines. However, we acknowledge that, unlike our proposal, those heuristics seeks only for the minimization of the number of used machines. So, to fairly evaluate our proposal, we compared it with a VMP strategy aware of interference and number of used physical machines. This VMP strategy, called MDOBP (Multidimensional Online Bin Packing), was proposed in [8].

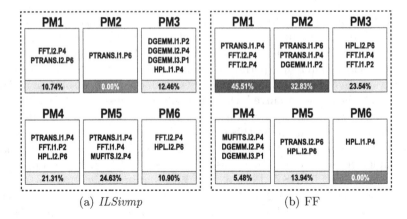

|  | PM1 | PM2 | PM3 |
| --- | --- | --- | --- |
|  | FFT.I2.P4<br>PTRANS.I2.P6 | PTRANS.I1.P6 | DGEMM.I1.P2<br>DGEMM.I2.P4<br>DGEMM.I3.P1<br>HPL.I1.P4 |
|  | 10.74% | 0.00% | 12.46% |

|  | PM4 | PM5 | PM6 |
| --- | --- | --- | --- |
|  | PTRANS.I1.P4<br>FFT.I1.P2<br>HPL.I2.P6 | PTRANS.I1.P4<br>FFT.I1.P4<br>MUFITS.I2.P4 | FFT.I2.P4<br>HPL.I2.P6 |
|  | 21.31% | 24.63% | 10.90% |

(a) *ILSivmp*

|  | PM1 | PM2 | PM3 |
| --- | --- | --- | --- |
|  | PTRANS.I1.P4<br>FFT.I2.P4<br>FFT.I2.P4 | PTRANS.I1.P6<br>PTRANS.I1.P4<br>DGEMM.I1.P2 | HPL.I2.P6<br>FFT.I1.P4<br>FFT.I1.P2 |
|  | 45.51% | 32.83% | 23.54% |

|  | PM4 | PM5 | PM6 |
| --- | --- | --- | --- |
|  | MUFITS.I2.P4<br>DGEMM.I2.P4<br>DGEMM.I3.P1 | PTRANS.I2.P6<br>HPL.I2.P6 | HPL.I1.P4 |
|  | 5.48% | 13.94% | 0.00% |

(b) FF

**Fig. 3.** Interference levels break down per physical machine for placement given by *ILSivmp* and FF when solving IVMPP_15.1

At first, MDOBP classifies each HPC application according to its communication pattern. Then, based on these classes, the algorithm decides where each virtual machine, holding an application, should be allocated. Tightly-coupled synchronous HPC applications, for example, are always allocated to a dedicated physical machine. On the other hand, for the remaining classes of HPC applications, the VMP strategy seeks for the minimization of the number of physical machines, also observing acceptable interference criteria. Thus, depending on the class of the HPC application, MDOBP focuses on fully avoiding interference or minimizing the number of used physical machines.

Unlike our proposal, MDOBP employs an online approach, *i.e.*, it promptly allocates a virtual machine to a physical one upon its request. Consequently, the sequence (order) at which the applications appear in the instance influences the behavior of MDOBP. Our solution, on the other hand, has a global and complete view of the problem. To workaround this issue in the MDOBP case, we generate, for each IVMPP instance, 50.000 different sequences of application. Then, we selected the sequence at which MDOBP achieved the smallest sum of interference levels. We tested both *ILSivmp* and MDOBP over a set of instances containing 50 applications, that is the highest number of applications in all instances. The number of physical machines in the instances was also 50. Concerning our proposal, the input parameter $\alpha$ was set to 1.0 so that *ILSivmp* prioritizes the minimization of interference.

As can be seen in Table 1, *ILSivmp* was able to outperform MDOBP in terms of interference in all tested instances, using the same number of physical machines. In fact, MDOBP just tries to fully avoid interference or attempts to keep interference within bounds when minimizing the number of physical machines, while *ILSivmp* treats both problems at the same time.

**Table 1.** Comparing ILSivmp ($\alpha = 1.0$) with MDOBP.

| Instance | ILSivmp $\alpha = 1.0$ | | | MDOBP | | Difference between interference levels |
|---|---|---|---|---|---|---|
| | Sum of interference levels | std | Number of used hosts | Sum of interference levels | Number of used hosts | |
| IVMPP_50.1 | 20.48% | 0.01 | 38 | 24.05% | 38 | 3.57% |
| IVMPP_50.2 | 21.37% | 0.01 | 33 | 28.40% | 33 | 7.03% |
| IVMPP_50.3 | 25.15% | 0.01 | 33 | 37.07% | 33 | 11.92% |
| IVMPP_50.4 | 28.80% | 0.01 | 36 | 38.68% | 36 | 9.88% |
| IVMPP_50.5 | 28.00% | 0.02 | 36 | 33.67% | 36 | 5.67% |
| IVMPP_50.6 | 24.22% | 0.01 | 33 | 28.47% | 33 | 4.25% |
| IVMPP_50.7 | 27.24% | 0.01 | 33 | 34.42% | 33 | 7.18% |
| IVMPP_50.8 | 24.60% | 0.01 | 36 | 32.30% | 36 | 7.70% |
| IVMPP_50.9 | 20.64% | 0.01 | 34 | 30.67% | 34 | 10.03% |
| IVMPP_50.10 | 36.77% | 0.01 | 32 | 44.58% | 32 | 7.81% |

### 5.3   Comparing *ILSivmp* with an Exact Approach

As presented in the previous section, *ILSivmp* achieved good solutions in a reasonable execution time, spending less than 15 s to solve each instance, when compared with other heuristics from the related literature. In spite of those satisfactory results, there is no guarantee that our proposal has achieved the best solution for any of the tested IVMPP instances, since metaheuristics, although can often find good solutions with less computational effort than exact approaches, do not guarantee that a globally optimal solution can be found. So, to have another parameter of solution quality, *ILSivmp* was also compared with *EXACTivmp*, a naive exact procedure for solving IVMPP, in a sample of small instances.

*EXACTivmp* enumerates all possible solutions and selects the one with the smallest cost. This sort of procedure, also known as exhaustive or direct search, evaluates each possible solution of a discrete problem to determine the optimal one. As this exact approach executes an exhaustive search on the space of possible solutions, the computational time of this method grows exponentially with the size of instance being solved. In the context of IVMPP, the size of instance is related to the number of applications to be allocated in the cloud environment. Thus, the greatest the number of applications in the instance, the higher the execution time of *EXACTivmp* is. Due to its computational complexity, *EXACTivmp* was just used to solve small instances which could be solved within 12 h time limit. Therefore, we considered instances with 5, 6, 7 and 8 applications, where instances with 6 to 8 applications were exclusively created for this analysis and were not considered in our previous experiments. To solve instances with 8 applications, we implemented a parallel version of *EXACTivmp* that was executed with 12 processors. It is worth mentioning that we have tried to solve instances with 9 applications. However, even using 12 processors, the exact procedure was not able to solve this kind of instance in less than 24 h.

**Table 2.** Results achieved by *ILSivmp* and *EXACTivmp* when solving a set of instances

| Number of Applications | Instance | EXACTivmp | | ILSivmp | | Gap |
|---|---|---|---|---|---|---|
| | | Cost | Time (s) | Cost | Time (s) | |
| 5 | IVMPP_5.1 | 0.123759 | 0 | 0.123788 | 0 | 0.02% |
| | IVMPP_5.2 | 0.128015 | 0 | 0.128015 | 0 | 0.00% |
| | IVMPP_5.3 | 0.128016 | 0 | 0.128016 | 0 | 0.00% |
| | IVMPP_5.4 | 0.128427 | 0 | 0.128427 | 0 | 0.00% |
| | IVMPP_5.5 | 0.127375 | 0 | 0.127398 | 0 | 0.02% |
| | IVMPP_5.6 | 0.132018 | 0 | 0.132083 | 0 | 0.05% |
| | IVMPP_5.7 | 0.132136 | 0 | 0.132205 | 0 | 0.05% |
| | IVMPP_5.8 | 0.130486 | 0 | 0.130486 | 0 | 0.00% |
| | IVMPP_5.9 | 0.126877 | 0 | 0.126885 | 0 | 0.01% |
| | IVMPP_5.10 | 0.135305 | 0 | 0.135305 | 0 | 0.00% |
| 6 | IVMPP_6.1 | 0.107733 | 0 | 0.107735 | 0 | 0.00% |
| | IVMPP_6.2 | 0.157338 | 0 | 0.157345 | 0 | 0.00% |
| | IVMPP_6.3 | 0.117550 | 0 | 0.117617 | 0 | 0.06% |
| | IVMPP_6.4 | 0.110082 | 0 | 0.110082 | 0 | 0.00% |
| | IVMPP_6.5 | 0.105597 | 0 | 0.105597 | 0 | 0.00% |
| | IVMPP_6.6 | 0.120686 | 0 | 0.120686 | 0 | 0.00% |
| | IVMPP_6.7 | 0.153522 | 0 | 0.153522 | 0 | 0.00% |
| | IVMPP_6.8 | 0.152300 | 0 | 0.152312 | 0 | 0.01% |
| | IVMPP_6.9 | 0.121506 | 0 | 0.121684 | 0 | 0.15% |
| | IVMPP_6.10 | 0.112187 | 0 | 0.112190 | 0 | 0.00% |
| 7 | IVMPP_7.1 | 0.134135 | 16 | 0.134153 | 0 | 0.01% |
| | IVMPP_7.2 | 0.139690 | 16 | 0.139690 | 0 | 0.00% |
| | IVMPP_7.3 | 0.141633 | 16 | 0.141645 | 0 | 0.01% |
| | IVMPP_7.4 | 0.132102 | 16 | 0.132105 | 0 | 0.00% |
| | IVMPP_7.5 | 0.173459 | 16 | 0.173459 | 0 | 0.00% |
| | IVMPP_7.6 | 0.137693 | 16 | 0.137714 | 0 | 0.02% |
| | IVMPP_7.7 | 0.129884 | 16 | 0.129889 | 0 | 0.00% |
| | IVMPP_7.8 | 0.106974 | 16 | 0.106994 | 0 | 0.02% |
| | IVMPP_7.9 | 0.134610 | 16 | 0.134610 | 0 | 0.00% |
| | IVMPP_7.10 | 0.135761 | 16 | 0.135770 | 0 | 0.01% |
| 8 | IVMPP_8.1 | 0.152632 | 111 | 0.152638 | 0 | 0.00% |
| | IVMPP_8.2 | 0.125171 | 111 | 0.125364 | 0 | 0.15% |
| | IVMPP_8.3 | 0.124114 | 111 | 0.124148 | 0 | 0.03% |
| | IVMPP_8.4 | 0.114537 | 110 | 0.114578 | 0 | 0.04% |
| | IVMPP_8.5 | 0.119423 | 110 | 0.119555 | 0 | 0.11% |
| | IVMPP_8.6 | 0.117526 | 112 | 0.117544 | 0 | 0.02% |
| | IVMPP_8.7 | 0.156977 | 112 | 0.157014 | 0 | 0.02% |
| | IVMPP_8.8 | 0.117246 | 112 | 0.117263 | 0 | 0.01% |
| | IVMPP_8.9 | 0.154842 | 112 | 0.154864 | 0 | 0.01% |
| | IVMPP_8.10 | 0.130006 | 110 | 0.130008 | 0 | 0.00% |

As can be seen in Table 2, *ILSivmp* obtained good solutions with small gaps, around 0.02% in average. Moreover, for some instances ("IVMPP_7.9" and "IVMPP_5.2", for example), our solution and the exact procedure achieved exactly the same cost. Thus, for that cases, *ILSivmp* was able to reach the optimal solution for the problem. Those experiments were repeated 10 times and the coefficient of variation, for all cases, was less than 0.18%. At last, we acknowledge that this evaluation is not enough to assess the capability of our proposal on reaching optimal or, at least, near-optimal solutions. However, we claim that those results, together with the previous experiments, indicate that our solution is indeed capable of giving good solutions for the IVMPP.

## 6    Conclusion and Future Work

In this work, we presented a solution based on the Iterated Local Search (ILS) framework to solve the Interference-aware Virtual Machine Placement Problem for Small-scale HPC Applications in clouds (IVMPP). Experiments conducted in a real scenario, with real HPC applications, showed that our proposal reduced interference by more than 40%, while keeping the same number of physical machines given by the most employed heuristics for the problem. Besides that, in comparison with MDOBP, the closest approach found in literature to solve VMP, *ILSivmp* reduced the interference levels in 7.51%.

We conclude that the performance of small-scale HPC applications executed in clouds can be improved when the virtual placement strategy considers complementary access profiles in co-allocation, minimizing consequently the cross-application interference. To decide the placement of virtual machines, our strategy needs to know in advance the set of applications that should be allocated in the cloud. Although this offline approach can be used in practice by accumulating a given number of requests before performing placement decisions, we expect to propose an online version of our approach which allocates virtual machines as they arrive. But, before implementing this online approach, we need to determine in what extent the live migration of virtual machines would affect the execution of HPC applications on clouds.

Besides that, although our strategy requires the execution profile of applications, in some scenarios like in private clouds, the users/providers may know the execution profile of some applications. Besides that, our proposal could evolve to profile application during its execution on cloud environment. At last, remark that our solution was not implemented and tested in a real cloud scenario. In order to prove our point, we implemented and tested our strategy in a virtual environment which is the basis of cloud computing. As future work, we expect to test our strategy in a commercial cloud.

## References

1. Alves, M., Teylo, L., Frota, Y., Drummond, L.: An interference-aware virtual machine placement strategy for high performance computing applications in clouds.

In: XIX Simpósio em Sistemas Computacionais de Alto Desempenho (WSCAD 2018), Brazil (2018)

2. Alves, M.M., de Assumpção Drummond, L.M.: A multivariate and quantitative model for predicting cross-application interference in virtual environments. J. Syst. Softw. **128**, 150–163 (2017)

3. Basto, D.T.: Interference aware scheduling for cloud computing. Master's thesis, Universidade do Porto (2015)

4. Chen, L., Patel, S., Shen, H., Zhou, Z.: Profiling and understanding virtualization overhead in cloud. In: 44th International Conference on Parallel Processing (ICPP), pp. 31–40. IEEE (2015)

5. Chen, L., Shen, H., Platt, S.: Cache contention aware virtual machine placement and migration in cloud datacenters. In: 24th International Conference on Network Protocols (ICNP), pp. 1–10. IEEE (2016)

6. El-Gazzar, R., Hustad, E., Olsen, D.H.: Understanding cloud computing adoption issues: a Delphi study approach. J. Syst. Softw. **118**, 64–84 (2016)

7. Gupta, A., et al.: Evaluating and improving the performance and scheduling of HPC applications in cloud. IEEE Trans. Cloud Comput. **7161**(c), 1 (2014)

8. Gupta, A., Kale, L.V., Milojicic, D., Faraboschi, P., Balle, S.M.: HPC-aware VM placement in infrastructure clouds. In: International Conference on Cloud Engineering (IC2E), pp. 11–20. IEEE (2013)

9. Jersak, L.C., Ferreto, T.: Performance-aware server consolidation with adjustable interference levels. In: Proceedings of the 31st Annual Symposium on Applied Computing, pp. 420–425. ACM (2016)

10. Jin, H., Qin, H., Wu, S., Guo, X.: CCAP: a cache contention-aware virtual machine placement approach for HPC cloud. Int. J. Parallel Program. **43**(3), 403–420 (2015)

11. Melo Alves, M., da Cruz Pestana, R., Alves Prado da Silva, R., Drummond, L.M.A.: Accelerating pre-stack Kirchhoff time migration by manual vectorization. Concurr. Comput.: Pract. Exp. **29**(22), 1–20 (2017)

12. Netto, M.A., Calheiros, R.N., Rodrigues, E.R., Cunha, R.L., Buyya, R.: HPC cloud for scientific and business applications: taxonomy, vision, and research challenges. ACM Comput. Surv. **1**(1) (2017)

13. Otto, C., Kempka, T.: Prediction of steam jacket dynamics and water balances in underground coal gasification. Energies **10**(6), 739 (2017)

14. Pires, F.L., Barán, B.: A virtual machine placement taxonomy. In: 15th International Symposium on Cluster, Cloud and Grid Computing (CCGrid), pp. 159–168. IEEE/ACM (2015)

15. Tsuruoka, Y.: Cloud computing-current status and future directions. J. Inf. Process. **24**(2), 183–194 (2016)

16. Yokoyama, D., Schulze, B., Kloh, H., Bandini, M., Rebello, V.: Affinity aware scheduling model of cluster nodes in private clouds. J. Netw. Comput. Appl. **95**, 94–104 (2017)

# Automatic Minimization of Execution Budgets of SPITS Programs in AWS

Nicholas T. Okita[1(✉)], Tiago A. Coimbra[1], Charles B. Rodamilans[1,2], Martin Tygel[1], and Edson Borin[1,3]

[1] Center for Petroleum Studies (CEPETRO), University of Campinas (UNICAMP), Campinas, Brazil
nicholas.okita@ggaunicamp.com, tgo.coimbra@gmail.com, mtygel@gmail.com
[2] Computing and Informatics Department (FCI), Mackenzie Presbyterian University (MPU), São Paulo, Brazil
charles.rodamilans@mackenzie.br
[3] Institute of Computing (IC), University of Campinas (UNICAMP), Campinas, Brazil
edson@ic.unicamp.br

**Abstract.** Cloud computing platforms offer a wide variety of computational resources with different performance specifications for different prices. In this work, we experiment how Spot instances and Availability Zones on the Amazon Web Services (AWS) could be utilized to reduce the processing budget. Not only that, but we propose instance selection algorithms in AWS to minimize the execution budget of programs implemented using the programming model Scalable Partially Idempotent Task System (SPITS). Our results show that the proposed method can identify and dynamically adjust the virtual machine types that offer the best price per performance ratio. Therefore, we conclude that our algorithms can minimize the budget given a long enough execution time, except in situations where the startup overhead caused the budget difference or in a short period execution.

**Keywords:** Cloud-computing · Auto-scaling · Economics

## 1 Introduction

The Infrastructure as a Service (IaaS) is a business model known by the users of the leading cloud computing service providers, such as Amazon Web Services (AWS) from Amazon, Azure from Microsoft, and Google Cloud Platform. In this model, the users can instantiate virtual machines with different hardware configurations, for example, the number of processing cores and amount of RAM, and set it up with their software stack.

On AWS, for example, there are three ways to acquire a virtual machine instance [4]. The first one is called On-Demand instances, in which the consumer

Supported by Petrobras, Fapesp, CNPq, and CAPES.

C. Bianchini et al. (Eds.): WSCAD 2018, CCIS 1171, pp. 21–36, 2020.
https://doi.org/10.1007/978-3-030-41050-6_2

pays for the resource utilization for as long as they have used it (with its price usually given in USD per hour). The second is called Reserved instances, in which the consumer pays upfront for the resource utilization for an extended period (e.g., months or years), offering thirty to sixty percent savings when compared to On-Demand instances [1]. At last, there are Spot instances, which behave the same way as On-Demand instances, however with volatile prices; usually up to three times lower than their On-Demand counterparts. To acquire a Spot instance the user must select the maximum value to be paid per hour, if this value is higher than the current price and there are resources available, then the cloud provider will let the user use the instance; otherwise, the request will not be fulfilled and, unless it is canceled, will be put on hold until it can be completed. The three ways mentioned above have different prices for different instances. Therefore, there lies an optimization problem: the choice of the best virtual machine configuration for the lowest price.

Furthermore, AWS offers its services in many regions in the world, with each area having multiple availability zones; allowing better reliability since the user can choose different datacenters to execute their code. These zones are connected by low latency links that allow the processes to communicate between themselves. Similarly to how there are different prices related to different hardware configurations, there is also a price difference for instances in different availability zones and regions.

In this work, we explore how to minimize the expenses of high-performance programs implemented using the Scalable Partially Idempotent Task System (SPITS) programming model [2] in computing cloud machines. The advantages provided by SPITS rely on dynamic resource provisioning and fault tolerance. Such mechanisms can minimize the unavailability risks and, also, enabling the utilization of new Spot Instances. With these mechanisms, we implement a method that can replace low performance per price instances with higher performing ones. Throughout the experiments, we see that the method can dynamically adjust the instances executing a high-performance seismic processing program in a way that only high performance per price instances are part of the processing cluster in the end.

This paper is an extended version of the work presented in [6]. In the previous work, we have implemented an algorithm to minimize the execution costs on the cloud. For the current work, we will further discuss how to improve that algorithm with new instance selection strategies, where we show the limitations and also solutions to the open problems of the work to be extended.

## 2   Related Work

Amazon Web Services offers their unused resources as Spot instances. To use them, the client inputs the maximum value that should be paid per hour, then the provider itself decides which clients will use the Spot instance. When the provider requires that resource, it sends an alert to the client and after a predetermined period, the Spot instance is terminated.

The *HotSpot* tool [7] tries to reduce the processing budget on Spot instances by moving the application to an instance that offers the best cost-benefit at that moment. The migration decision compares the price of stopping the usage of the Spot instance and then creating a new one against how much savings are expected in the new Spot Instance. The application migration between instances happens using containers. Furthermore, HotSpot allows the usage of both On-Demand and Spot Instances and simplifies the cost-benefit calculation using an equation considering the VM usage (for example, CPU utilization).

The *SpotOn* [8] automatically selects and configures the Spot Instances to execute the task, not only that, but it also chooses the fault tolerance mechanism (checkpoint or replication) that is acceptable when the provider terminates an instance. This tool only replaces a Spot instance after a termination by the provider has happened.

Wan et al. [9] proposed a dynamic bidding and resource management algorithm to reduce the Spot instance budgets. It works in two timescales, the first responsible for determining the bidding, instance rental and job dispatch policy, while the second is responsible for instance allocation in a finer granularity. The greatest advantage of this work is that it does not require any statistical information either of the Spot prices or the workload that will be processed. While they did theoretically prove the algorithm, it was only tried through simulations and assumes that all Virtual Machines are homogeneous (that is, they have the same OS and hardware configuration), still missing further studies in heterogeneous scenarios.

Briefly, when using the computational cloud, based on Spot instances, the client has to accept some risks, for example:

(i) Risk of Spot instance unavailability, such uncertainty is related to the lack of available resources from the provider, which starts to claim the Spot instances back to be used as Reserved and On-Demand instances or even their usage.

(ii) Risk of provider region unavailability, it occurs due to communication failure and, therefore, the impossibility of accessing the Spot instance.

(iii) Risk of price volatility, i.e., price oscillation, in which some of the instances can become worse choices than other ones, and similarly, with price decreases, some Spot instances can become better choices.

The present work addresses and tries to reduce costs associated with price volatility. Therefore, such a reduction in prices allows us to have a more optimized budget.

Our proposal uses the target program performance information (which is sent periodically, with its frequency defined by the user) to choose instances that offer the best performance per price more precisely.

## 3 Tools and Methodology

We use the SPITS programming model and its runtime [2] to implement a high-performance program that estimates the parameters of the Non-hyperbolic

Common Reflective Surface operator, or simply, NCRS method [3]. The details of this implementation are out of scope for this paper since it is only used as an example to run the experiments.

The NCRS program is compiled using the gcc compiler in its version 5.4.0 with the compiling flag *-O3*, while the runtime is executed using Python version 3.5.2. The program input is a seismic dataset of approximately 1.3 GB.

Table 1 shows the instances used on the experiments. Their choice is based on the NCRS program execution on a smaller section of the data set with 200 MB. The optimization column refers to what type of application these instances are better suited for, according to Amazon themselves.

**Table 1.** Selected AWS instances

| Instance type | vCPUS (number of virtual cores) | RAM (GB) | Price (USD/h) | Optimization |
|---|---|---|---|---|
| c4.4xlarge | 16 (Xeon E5-2666 v3 Haswell) | 30 | 0.796 | Compute |
| c4.8xlarge | 32 (Xeon E5-2666 v3 Haswell) | 60 | 1.591 | Compute |
| c5.4xlarge | 16 (Xeon Platinum 8124 3GHz) | 32 | 0.680 | Compute |
| c5.9xlarge | 36 (Xeon Platinum 8124 3GHz) | 72 | 1.530 | Compute |
| c5.18xlarge | 72 (Xeon Platinum 8124 3GHz) | 144 | 3.060 | Compute |
| d2.4xlarge | 16 (Xeon E5-2676 v3 Haswell) | 122 | 2.760 | Storage |
| d2.8xlarge | 36 (Xeon E5-2676 v3 Haswell) | 244 | 5.520 | Storage |
| m4.4xlarge | 16 (Xeon E5-2676 v3 Haswell) | 64 | 0.800 | General Usage |
| m4.10xlarge | 40 (Xeon E5-2676 v3 Haswell) | 160 | 2.000 | General Usage |
| m5.4xlarge | 16 (Xeon Platinum 8175 2.5GHz) | 64 | 0.768 | General Usage |
| m5.12xlarge | 48 (Xeon Platinum 8175 2.5GHz) | 192 | 2.304 | General Usage |
| m5.24xlarge | 96 (Xeon Platinum 8175 2.5GHz) | 384 | 4.608 | General Usage |
| r4.4xlarge | 16 (Xeon E5-2686 v4 Broadwell) | 122 | 1.064 | Memory |
| r4.8xlarge | 32 (Xeon E5-2686 v4 Broadwell) | 244 | 2.128 | Memory |
| r4.16xlarge | 64 (Xeon E5-2686 v4 Broadwell) | 488 | 4.256 | Memory |

To configure each instance, a 20 GB storage device of the type Provisioned IOPS (or io1) with a performance of a thousand input/output operations per second (IOPS) is attached; it comes configured with a custom Ubuntu 16.04 virtual machine image, with a few packages installed (namely, *awscli, binutils, cloud-utils, efs-utils, gcc, make, python3-pip, sshpass, unzip and zip*) and a copy of the input dataset.

The program and its results are stored in the Amazon Elastic File Storage (EFS), which is a filesystem that can be shared between different instances; similar to an NFS server but already configured by Amazon. To compute the budget we disregard both the EFS and io1 storage device prices.

The instance selection algorithm is implemented in Python 3.6 in the AWS Lambda platform. The algorithm is responsible for starting and terminating Spot instances based on the instance performance per price ratio, which is computed by dividing an instances performance measurement by its price. We try three different approaches on how to handle instance replacements.

In the three approaches, we consider that the instances id and type, some sort of performance measurement and its standard deviation are stored. The standard deviation of the performance of the instances is considered so that instances that are too close in performance to the best ones are not replaced. The procedure shown in Algorithm 0 shows how the instance replacement logic works when using this data structure to store instances information.

On our first approach, we replace the Spot instance that has the worst performance per price measurement with a new Spot instance of the type that has the best performance per price measurement. To do that, we implement Algorithm 1, which has a list of the current running instance tuples as its input, sorted by the "perf" attribute. The performance measurement chosen for this algorithm is the ratio of performance per cost, therefore to apply the approach replacement we simply call the replacement procedure from Algorithm 0 replacing the first instance from the list (with the lowest performance per cost ratio) with the last instance from the list (with the highest performance per cost ratio).

Secondly, in Algorithm 2, we replace a group of instances instead of only one Spot instance at a time. Therefore it renews the $P$ percentage instances that have worst performance per price measurement with new Spot instances of the type with the best performance per price measurement. Its implementation is very similar to Algorithm 1, except, it also has $P$ as an input and a loop to replace the $P$ percentage first instances in the list with the instance in the last position.

Lastly, in Algorithm 3, we take into consideration the instances performance, by creating a new measurement that uses both normalized performance (that is, how this instance performs in comparison to the fastest Spot instance in the group) and normalized cost per performance (that is, how expensive this instance is in contrast to the Spot instance that would provide the best budget in the group). The goal of this approach is to select VM types that offer a good cost vs performance trade-off. Similarly to the second approach, we replace a percentage $P$ of instances that offer the lowest values of this new measurement with the one that offers the highest. However, instead of a single instance tuples list for input, it has two instance tuples lists (one that has its performance measurement as performance per dollar, while the other has its performance measurement the raw performance of the instance). Those two instance tuples lists are used to create a third one, with a weighted cost and performance measurement. Then it follows the same procedure as Algorithm 2, but has its performance measurement set as that new weighted measurement.

## 4 Experimental Results

In this section, we present an analysis of the application budget and performance in different instances and then how the method performs when minimizing the budget.

### 4.1 Spot Instances

Briefly, Spot instances are a budget-effective option for tasks that are currently flexible to run on, as well as for applications that can be stopped. For example,

**Algorithm 0.** Replaces an old instance with a new one

1: # inst is the tuple:
2: (inst. id, inst. type, a perf. measurement (perf), its std.deviation (std))
3: # This procedure is called to replace an old instance with a newer one
4: # The replacement only happens after their performance is compared
5: **procedure** REPLACEINSTANCE($inst_{old}$, $inst_{new}$)
6:    **if** $inst_{old}.type \neq inst_{new}.type$ **then**
7:       **if** $inst_{old}.perf + inst_{old}.std < inst_{new}.perf - inst_{new}.std$ **then**
8:          $z \leftarrow$ availability zone with smallest price for instance $inst_{new}.type$
9:          starts a new instance of type $inst_{new}.type$ in $z$
10:         terminates instance with id $inst_{new}.id$

**Algorithm 1.** Instance selection algorithm

1: # The list must be sorted by performance ratio
2: L: List of running instances (inst. id, inst. type, perf. ratio, perf. std)
3: **procedure** INSTANCE SELECTION($L$)
4:    replaceInstance($L[0], L[len(L)]$)

**Algorithm 2.** Instance selection algorithm

1: # The list must be sorted by performance ratio
2: L: List of running instances (inst. id, inst. type, perf. ratio, perf. std)
3: P: Percentage of instances to be replaced
4: **procedure** INSTANCE SELECTION($L, P$)
5:    $lim = max(len(L) * P, 1)$
6:    **for** $i$ in 0 to $lim$ **do**
7:       replaceInstance($L[i], L[len(L)]$)

**Algorithm 3.** Instance selection algorithm

1: # Both lists sorted by id
2: $L_{usd}$: List of running instances with perf defined as performance per dollar
3: $L_{sec}$: List of running instances with perf defined as the actual performance
4: P: Percentage of instances to be replaced
5: **procedure** INSTANCE SELECTION($L_{usd}, L_{sec}, P$)
6:    $cost_{max} = max(L_{usd}.perf)$
7:    $perf_{max} = max(L_{perf}.perf)$
8:
9:    # Generates new list of tuples with perf as the weighted performance + cost
10:   $L_{final} = \{\}$
11:   $lim = L_{sec}$
12:   **for** $i$ in 0 to $lim$ **do**
13:      $inst.id = L_{usd}[i].id$ ; $inst.type = L_{usd}[i].type$
14:      $inst.perf = \frac{L_{usd}[i].perf}{ratio_{max}} + \frac{L_{sec}[i].perf}{perf_{max}}$ ; $inst.std = \frac{L_{usd}[i].std}{ratio_{max}} + \frac{L_{sec}[i].std}{perf_{max}}$
15:      $L_{final}$.insert(inst)
16:   $L_{final}$.sort($perf$)
17:
18:   $lim = max(1, len(L_{final}) * P)$
19:   **for** $i$ in 0 to $lim$ **do**
20:      replaceInstance($L_{final}[i], L_{final}[len(L_{final})]$)

Spot instances are suitable for data analysis, batch jobs, background processing, and optional tasks. Thus, for such tasks, we propose the structure that we describe as follows.

**Efficiency Frontier:** We have used the idea of a Pareto efficiency frontier to select instances that offer the best performance, the best budget, or a combination of these measurements in [5]. Let $p_x$ and $q_x$ be the execution time of VMs $p$ and $q$, and $p_y$ and $q_y$ be the budget. The Pareto frontier $\mathbb{P}$ consists of the set of instances $\mathbf{p} = (p_x, p_y)$ in $\mathbb{D}$, for which no instance $\mathbf{q} = (q_x, q_y)$ in $\mathbb{D}$ has both lower execution time $(q_x < p_x)$ and, at the same time, lower cost $(q_y < p_y)$ than the ones of instance $\mathbf{p}$. Which can be mathematically defined by

$$\mathbb{P} = \{\mathbf{p} \in \mathbb{D} : \{\mathbf{q} \in \mathbb{D} : (q_x < p_x) \wedge (q_y < p_y) \wedge \mathbf{p} \neq \mathbf{q}\} = \emptyset\}. \qquad (1)$$

The instances in a subset $\mathbb{P}$ are the ones with the best performance per price ratio. Although, it is essential to keep in mind that the choice of the points can vary through time, depending on the current VM price, the experiment being performed, and the first instances pool. To find the Pareto frontier, we need to find the points that belong to $\mathbb{P}$, defined by Eq. 1. In words, an instance point $\mathbf{p}$ belongs to $\mathbb{P}$, if no instance-point $\mathbf{q}$ in $\mathbb{D}$ has both better performance $(q_x < p_x)$ and, at the same time, lower cost $(q_y < p_y)$ than the ones of instance $\mathbf{p}$.

To plot the Pareto frontier we execute a performance test for the instances in Table 1. Using the data set and configurations as described by the "Tools and Methodology" section, however approximately 85% smaller than the original one. This test was performed five times and the time and budget median values for each instance are shown in Fig. 1.

Figure 1 shows the On-Demand instances as blue squares, while the Spot instances are shown as orange triangles. Notably, Spot instances are around three times less expensive than their On-Demand equivalent, for no performance impact. Additionally, note that the bad instance selection can increase dramatically both budget and execution times, for example, when comparing the instance d2.4xlarge On-Demand with the c5.18xlarge Spot, the Spot instance is around seven times faster and seventeen times less expensive.

The Pareto frontier, in this case, was defined by three different virtual machine instances, both in On-Demand and Spot cases, which means that they were the best choice to execute the program, offering the best combinations of performance and price. Notice that using more instances result in changes in this frontier. However, the idea of this section is to show that Spot instances offer budget reductions, as long as the program has fault tolerance mechanisms, because there is the possibility of instance termination by the provider.

## 4.2 Availability Zones

When the user creates a Spot instance, they are given the possibility of selecting an availability zone. As previously explained, while a region is geographically isolated from another (and so is their communication), an availability zone is

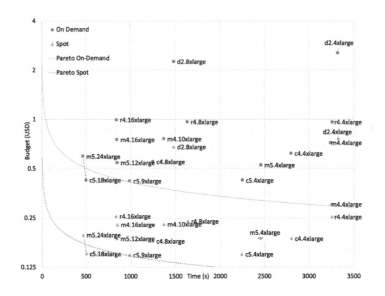

**Fig. 1.** Budget and execution time of each instance

connected to another one by a low latency network. Therefore, after choosing a region, it is possible to execute parallel processes in multiple availability zones since there is communication between instances in different zones.

Instances in different availability zones have different Spot market prices from each other, therefore changing where the instance is processing becomes another point that needs attention for budget minimization. Figure 2 shows the c5.18xlarge instance price oscillation in different availability zones in a certain period.

As shown by Fig. 2, a good availability zone choice can reduce the budget when compared to a naïve choice in any other availability zone. For example, on April 6th of 2018, the availability zone us-east-1f had a price around forty percent smaller than zones us-east-1c for the same instance.

## 4.3   Instance Selection Algorithm

This subsection shows the results of a few experiments on how the different algorithms proposed in the Methodology subsection perform in the budget reduction task. For these experiments, we have configured the time between instance replacements as three minutes and the percentage of instances to be replaced (P) as twenty percent. Furthermore, the available instances are restricted to those shown in Table 1 while the total number of instances is set to fifteen. The initial instance pool is simply one instance of each type shown in Table 1.

Additionally, to evaluate the performance of the algorithms we need a baseline to compare. The baseline considers the naïve case scenario, in which the customer simply creates their cluster from the instances in Table 1. Since this

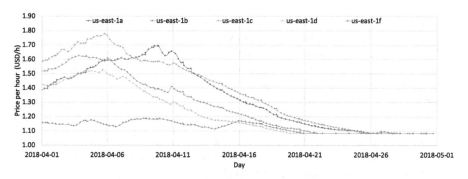

**Fig. 2.** Price oscillation of instance *c5.18xlarge* in different availability zones

is the target to beat, we call it the worst case scenario. It is to be noted that even this scenario already uses Spot instances, it could be made even worse by considering On-Demand instances.

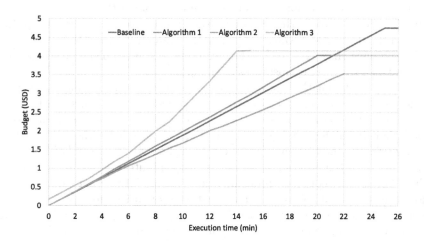

**Fig. 3.** Budget comparison for different selection algorithms

In Fig. 3 the softer line shows the price after the execution finished (to simplify comparison among the different techniques), while the darker line shows how the budget increased overtime. Notably, all proposed algorithms achieve budgets below the baseline. Not only that, but all of them also achieve lower execution times.

Even though both Algorithm 3 and Algorithm 1 choose instances that have a higher price per hour, the total budget is still smaller than the baseline, due to them finishing the execution earlier. Algorithm 2, on the other hand, choose instances that provide lower price per hour than the baseline, while also finishing earlier and, therefore, offering a lower budget.

As expected, all techniques provide a lower budget than the baseline. Surprisingly, all of them are also able to provide a lower execution time.

Briefly, Algorithm 3 achieved the lowest execution time of them, however, it also has the highest budget (not considering the baseline). Algorithm 2 has the lowest budget, with the longest execution time. At last, Algorithm 1 offered a budget similar to Algorithm 3, but with a longer execution time. The explanation of how each algorithm achieves their results will be shown in the next subsections.

**Algorithm 1:** This subsection discusses how Algorithm 1 performs as shown in Fig. 3. Algorithm 1 is the basic idea behind all three techniques, replacing only one instance at a time considering the performance per price, aiming the lowest overall budget.

Figure 4 shows the timespan for each VM instance used during the execution, from the moment of its initialization to its termination. The instances of types *c5.18xlarge* and *c5.9xlarge* were the ones that the algorithm choose that would provide the best budget minimization. Two more important points to be highlighted for all timespan figures is that the first *c5.4xlarge* instance represents the Job Manager, and the one minute gap is due to the initialization time that each instance took to start reporting its existence to the algorithm.

In Fig. 4 it is notable that instances that are not optimized for computing tasks are the first to be terminated, while the compute optimized instances are always the ones that get created. For example, instances of family d2 are the first one to be replaced by instances of the family c5.

Not only that, but the instances selected as the best performance per price are more expensive than average, making this method more expensive than the baseline until the twenty minutes mark in Fig. 3. However, as briefly mentioned earlier, they are higher performing instances, therefore, even though they have a higher price per hour, they finish the task earlier causing a smaller budget.

Finally, since the program takes only twenty minutes to execute, an interval of three minutes to replace each instance becomes too large. That can be verified in Fig. 4 in which there were still many instances of the original pool present at the end of the execution. In a longer execution, the program would have only the most cost effective instances processing in the end.

**Algorithm 2:** This subsection discusses how the Algorithm 2 performs as shown in Fig. 3. Algorithm 2 works very similarly to Algorithm 1, but instead of replacing only one instance it replaces a group of instances, specifically a percentage $P$ of the current running instance pool defined by the user.

Similarly to Figs. 4 and 5 shows how long each instance stayed on, from the moment of its initialization to its termination. In this experiment, the instances type *c5.9xlarge* was preferred when choosing which instance would provide the best budget minimization.

Again, the instances that are not optimized for computing task are replaced first. This means that at that moment, the compute optimized instances have a better price for the performance when compared to other types. However, this does not necessarily hold for all times, since we are dealing with Spot instance,

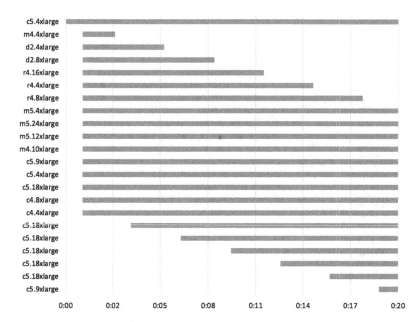

**Fig. 4.** Timespan that each instance type was alive during the execution of the seismic program while using instance selection Algorithm 1

at other times a different type of instance can offer better performance for its price, even when compared to the compute optimized ones.

When comparing with Fig. 4, it is notable that the previous method preferred different instances than the one preferred in this experiment. Considering that these experiments were executed in different days (Fig. 4 comes from results from November 19th of 2018, while Fig. 5 comes from results from November 18th of 2018) this could mean simply different prices for each instance.

Furthermore, it is noticeable that this experiment is able to replace all instances, ending the execution with only a *c5.18xlarge* Spot instance and fourteen *c5.9xlarge* Spot instance (the first *c5.4xlarge* is an On-Demand instance for the Job Manager). This is the major reason that this approach is the one that requires the smallest budget to run, as seen in Fig. 3.

**Algorithm 3:** At last, this subsection discusses how the Algorithm 3 performs as shown in Fig. 3. Algorithm 3 has a different approach from the previous two algorithms, while it does replace a percentage of instances like Algorithm 2, it takes in consideration the instances performance and not only the price. Therefore we do not expect it to have the lowest budget, but we do expect to select a performance vs budget trade-off.

Again, similarly to Figs. 4 and 6 shows how long each instance stayed on, from the moment of its initialization to its termination. In this experiment, the instance type *m5.24xlarge* was preferred. As previously explained, this algorithm also considers the instance performance when selecting which is the best instance

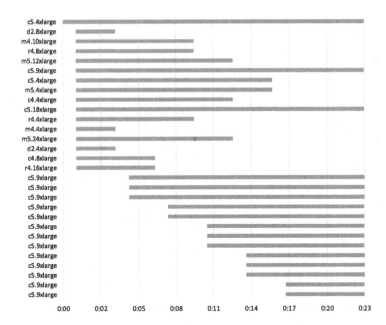

**Fig. 5.** Timespan that each instance type was alive during the execution of the seismic program while using instance selection Algorithm 2

to execute the program. The reason for this selection can be verified by Fig. 1, which depicts that the instance *m5.24xlarge* performs around 10% faster than instance *c5.18xlarge* while being around 25% more expensive. Remembering that the heuristic selects instance in the Pareto frontier set.

The execution conclusions are similar to the ones obtained from Algorithm 2. The selection script can converge to a single type of instance which is deemed the best combination of performance and price per performance at the execution moment. With this convergence it is able to give satisfactory results, as seen in Fig. 3, in which this method is the fastest by a relatively large margin without sacrificing the budget.

**General Remarks:** The budget spent when using instance selection algorithms was smaller than the baseline of executing the program using all instances types. It is to be noted that the algorithms would be able to present an even further budget reduction with a more computational costly input data set, as the budget lost by the initialization time and convergence time would become more negligible.

Further discussing initialization and convergence times. The first is around three minutes for our experiment configurations, including booting the machine, running a few scripts that are used to report the performance and reading the data set, which is the reason for the choice of three minutes interval to call the replacement algorithm. The latter is the time that the algorithm takes to replace

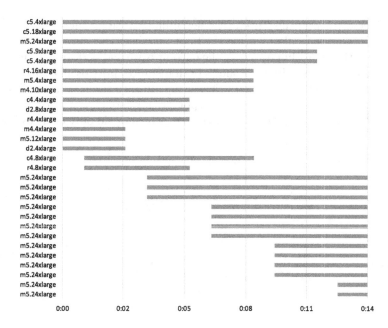

**Fig. 6.** Timespan that each instance type was alive during the execution of the seismic program while using instance selection Algorithm 3

all sub-optimal instances by optimal ones, which can vary from a few minutes to hours, given the percentage of instances being replaced and the interval between replacements. In our experiments, replacing one instance at a time every three minutes it would take around forty minutes to replace fourteen sub-optimal instances; while replacing twenty percent of sub-optimal instances every three minutes requires only around fifteen minutes.

After the instance selection pool achieves a converged state, it will continue the execution with only the optimal instances, not applying further replacements.

**Criticism and Limitations:** The main limitation of the proposed algorithm is related to the way it chooses new instances, which significantly affect the final budget. This limitation occurs when we keep the optimal Spot instances and terminate all sub-optimal ones. Since the algorithm only uses information available to the current instance pool, when the selection ends up with only one type of instance, then no further replacements will be made, since it will not replace Spot instances of the same kind. Therefore, if the pool is made of only one Spot instance type, and this instance type has a price increase, then the customer will end up paying more. Or, even worse, the algorithm would not be able to deal with all instances being terminated by the provider, ending up without any worker processing the task.

Another problem reported in the algorithm happens with high price oscillations. To clarify, let's consider that two instances have the same performance, when we replace a Spot instance every few minutes, the instance pool may not converge, because it would override the Spot instances that have just been created because the algorithm uses only the current price and performance information of the Spot instance. Figure 7 shows both instances price oscillation throughout seven hours in a day, changing prices every three to seven minutes. Furthermore, we highlight that in the current Spot pricing model, the price change in minutes does not happen, since the price that is being paid only changes hourly.

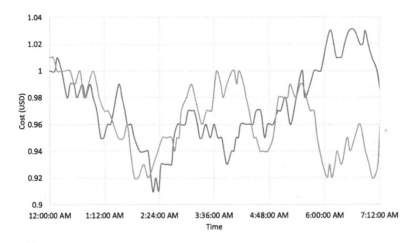

**Fig. 7.** Fabricated price oscillation of two instances used to stress test the algorithms

## 5   Discussion

Following, we discuss how instance selection matters and the instance selection algorithm. Figure 1 shows how vital an acceptable Spot instance selection is since there is a performance difference of multiple times when comparing a right instance choice (as *c5.18xlarge*) against a bad one (as *d2.4xlarge*) for the program being executed. If the user uses Spot instances, then the already significant difference can become even more substantial, namely, in our experiments, the On-Demand *d2.4xlarge* instance was around seven times slower and seventeen times more expensive than the *c5.18xlarge* Spot instance. Additionally, with the availability zone price differences in the Spot market (as seen in Fig. 2, we can get even better reductions from a right zone choice).

At last, with the knowledge that instance selection matters when minimizing the computing final budget, the problem that remains is how to select the best instances when there are so many options available. To tackle this problem, we implement instance selection algorithms that select which instances process the most tasks for the minimal price. In Fig. 3 it is noticeable that the proposed algorithms can process a given data set in less time and with a smaller budget when compared to a naïve execution.

# 6  Conclusions

The computing cloud service offers a wide variety of virtual machine configurations for the users, enabling the execution of high-performance code with great flexibility. However, bad virtual machine instance choices can lead to budgets over the necessary and slower processing speeds. Therefore, to be able to effectively minimize the budget when executing high performance computing applications on the cloud it is necessary to avoid these bad choices.

To verify the price per performance ratio and how to dynamically select the instances that provide the best budget minimization we execute a high-performance seismic processing program in different groups of virtual machine instances.

In the experiments, it was notable that the right instance choice guarantees performance up to seven times higher at a lower price, especially when using Spot Instances. Also, with the price differences in the availability zone in the Spot market, we can achieve even more significant budget-reductions when migrating to other available zone.

To demonstrate our premises, we implemented and evaluated three algorithms of automatic Spot instance selection that makes usage of the instant performance measurement of the application. These algorithms' objective is to optimize the execution budget and does not need any previous information about the program or the instances themselves. The algorithm explores the price variation in availability zones when choosing instances, always opting for the zone with the lowest price, and it was able to converge to the best instance type and obtain a budget inferior to that of a naïve execution with all instances.

At last, these results show that a good instance selection algorithm can reduce the execution budget of a high-performance program in the computing cloud, considering that this program allows the possibility of migration between virtual machines and availability zones, namely fault tolerance and dynamic provisioning, as is the case for programs implemented with the SPITS programming model.

**Acknowledgments.** This work was possible thanks to the support of Petrobras, CNPq (313012/2017-2), and Fapesp (2013/08293-7). The authors also thank the High-Performance Geophysics (HPG) team for technical support.

# References

1. Amazon: Amazon EC2 Reserved Instances pricing. https://aws.amazon.com/ec2/pricing/reserved-instances/pricing/ (2019). Accessed 03 May 2019
2. Borin, E., Benedicto, C., Rodrigues, I.L., Pisani, F., Tygel, M., Breternitz, M.: PY-PITS: a scalable Python runtime system for the computation of partially idempotent tasks. In: 2016 International Symposium on Computer Architecture and High Performance Computing Workshops (SBAC-PADW) (2016). https://doi.org/10.1109/SBAC-PADW.2016.10
3. Fomel, S., Kazinnik, R.: Non-hyperbolic common reflection surface. Geophys. Prospect. **61**(1) (2012). https://doi.org/10.1111/j.1365-2478.2012.01055.x

4. Li, Z., et al.: Spot pricing in the cloud ecosystem: a comparative investigation. J. Syst. Softw. **114**, 1–9 (2016). https://doi.org/10.1016/j.jss.2015.10.042
5. Okita, N., Coimbra, T., Rodamilans, C., Tygel, M., Borin, E.: Using SPITS to optimize the cost of high-performance geophysics processing on the cloud. In: First EAGE Workshop on High Performance Computing for Upstream in Latin America. EAGE Publications BV (2018). https://doi.org/10.3997/2214-4609.201803077
6. Okita, N., Rodamilans, C., Coimbra, T., Tygel, M., Borin, E.: Otimização automática do custo de processamento de programas SPITS na AWS. In: Anais da Trilha Principal do XIX Simpósio em Sistemas Computacionais de Alto Desempenho (WSCAD 2018), pp. 196–207, SBC (2018)
7. Shastri, S., Irwin, D.: Hotspot: automated server hopping in cloud spot markets. In: Proceedings of the 2017 Symposium on Cloud Computing. ACM (2017)
8. Subramanya, S., Guo, T., Sharma, P., Irwin, D., Shenoy, P.: SpotOn: a batch computing service for the spot market. In: Proceedings of the Sixth ACM Symposium on Cloud Computing. ACM (2015)
9. Wan, J., Gui, X., Zhang, R.: Dynamic bidding in spot market for profit maximization in the public cloud. J. Supercomput. **73**(10), 4245–4274 (2017). https://doi.org/10.1007/s11227-017-2007-9

# Analysis of Virtualized Congestion Control in Applications Based on Hadoop MapReduce

Vilson Moro⬤, Maurício Aronne Pillon⬤, Charles Christian Miers⬤, and Guilherme Piêgas Koslovski$^{(\boxtimes)}$⬤

Graduate Program in Applied Computing, Santa Catarina State University, Florianópolis, Brazil
vilson.moro@edu.udesc.br,
{mauricio.pillon,charles.miers,guilherme.koslovski}@udesc.br

**Abstract.** Among the existing applications for processing massive volumes of data, the Hadoop MapReduce (HMR) is widely used in clouds, having above all internal network flows of different volume and periodicity. In this regard, providers have the challenge of managing data centers with a wide range of operating systems and features. The diversity of algorithms and parameters related to TCP constitutes a heterogeneous communication scenario prone to degradation of communication-intensive applications. Due to total control in the data center, providers can apply the Virtualized Congestion Control (VCC) to generate optimized algorithms. From the tenant's perspective, virtualization is a transparently performed. Some technologies have made possible to develop such virtualization. Explicit Congestion Notification (ECN) is a technique for congestion identification which acts by monitoring the queues occupancy. Although promising, the specialized literature lacks on a deep analysis of the VCC impact on the applications. Our work characterizes the VCC impact on HMR on scenarios in which there are present applications competing for network resources using optimized and non-optimized TCP stacks. We identified the HMR has its performance substantially influenced by the data volume according to the employed TCP stack. Moreover, we highlight some VCC limitations.

**Keywords:** Virtualized Congestion Control · Hadoop MapReduce · TCP

## 1 Introduction

One of the key aspects of Infrastructure-as-a-Service (IaaS) clouds is the manageability and malleability provided to its tenants. Specifically, a virtual machine (VM) can be of several flavors, composed by different configurations of memory,

---

Supported by UDESC/FAPESC, developed on LabP2D.

C. Bianchini et al. (Eds.): WSCAD 2018, CCIS 1171, pp. 37–52, 2020.
https://doi.org/10.1007/978-3-030-41050-6_3

storage, and CPU. Above all, the client has the control over the operating system (OS) installed on the VM, being able to install and update: applications, libraries, and OS kernel. Specifically, focusing on Transmission Control Protocol (TCP), two scenarios are relevant due to the heterogeneity of its configurations [10]: *(i)* The maintenance complexity and dependencies of specific software versions are limiting factors for VMs updating. OSs with non-optimized TCP do not incorporate the latest advances on algorithms related to congestion control and avoidance; and *(ii)* Optimized settings related to temporary buffers, slow-start, selective acknowledgment, and so on may circumvent the fairness originally aimed by congestion control algorithms.

Algorithms for congestion control aid in the recovery of the performance in the occurrence of bottlenecks, while congestion avoidance algorithms act in the prediction of eventual losses [3]. Traditionally, TCP controls and avoids congestion at the endpoints of the network [9], without native support of the network core equipment. Several versions of TCP have been proposed to optimize traffic performance in data centers (DCs) [1,21] by changing the interpretation of binary feedback originally conceived. In some cases, the core network participates by offering packet tags with alerts of possible bottlenecks [4]. In fact, it is in the interest of the provider to circumvent the problem imposed by the heterogeneous scenario of congestion control algorithms, qualifying the service offered to their customers. Possible solutions include the provision of communication resources (bandwidth and configuration of switches) [12,19,20,22] and dynamic routing queue configuration [10]. However, the techniques listed tend to underuse communication resources or to have high management complexity [17]. In this context, Virtualized Congestion Control (VCC) was proposed as an alternative to standardize non-optimized TCP algorithms [5,8]. In summary, the providers have administrative access to the virtual switches or VM hypervisors responsible for routing the packets between the tenants' VMs. Thus, a virtualization layer can intercept non-optimized traffic and handle, when necessary, to meet the requirements of the updated DC protocols. Although promising, the specialized literature lacks on a deep analysis of the VCC impact on the final applications.

Originally, VCC was analyzed with synthetic charges indicating the efficacy for scenarios aiming at equity of sharing and maximization of use in bottlenecks for mostly long flows [5,8]. However, actual communication loads of applications traditionally run on clouds DCs have not been analyzed. Specifically, applications based on HMR have communication flows with characteristics different from those originally studied [1,18]. Thus, the aim of the present work is to analyze the applicability of VCC to HMR applications. Our main contributions are: *(i)* Analysis of the execution time of HMR, using real execution traces, in heterogeneous scenarios using VCC; *(ii)* Discuss the perceived impact on HMR regarding the configuration of the marking on the switches queue; and *(iii)* Correlate the dropped packets in the switches with the total execution time. Our experimental analysis indicates applications based on HMR have a considerable impact when executed on VCC-based environments[1].

---

[1] This paper is a revised and expanded version of [14].

## 2   Motivation and Problem Definition

### 2.1   Data Flow in Hadoop MapReduce

HMR framework is widely used, both for structured and unstructured data processing. The optimization of HMR data communication is realized by scheduling processing on servers close to the data to be processed. The main server, called *Master*, takes a metadata view of the entire file tree of the system and manages the distribution of the tasks to the servers which will process the data (*Workers*). The *Master* monitors the execution in *Workers* and defines the tasks each one will execute, either the *map* or *reduce*. It is important to note that 33% of the execution time of HMR is attributed to the TCP-based communication tasks [4], motivating the accomplishment of this work. Above all, HMR clusters present a data locale dependency, overloading switches and generating congestion during different stages of execution [18]. Specifically regarding the TCP perspective, the HMR flows suffer with switches queues and packets dropped, which triggers retransmissions on TCP congestion control algorithms.

Applications based on partitioning, processing, and aggregation of information, such as HMR, carry control data sensitive to latency, as well as flows for data synchronization. Thus, latency-sensitive flows compete with background traffic. Analyzing the occupation of the switches queues, it is possible to note HMR flows larger than 1 MB have low multiplexing rate and consume a large portion of the available bandwidth [1], inducing the increased of the latency for the others flows. DCs are designed for high throughput and low latency. However, commonly used switches have shared memory-based architectures. Thus, when multiple flows converge to the same interface, the storage space in queues can be totally consumed, leading to drop packets.

### 2.2   TCP Congestion Control in DCs with Multiple Clients

Originally, because TCP is based on binary feedback [3], it only changes its mode of transmission in the occurrence of segment loss. In the absence of losses, the transmission window is increased, while in the occurrence, it is decreased [7,9]. Specifically, congestion is perceived when a timer is terminated or when a set of duplicate ACKs are received by the sender. Although efficient in the scenarios originally proposed (mainly related to communication over networks with distinct configurations and capacities), the algorithms are unable to detect and control the previously listed scenario for HMR, common in DCs [1].

The Explicit Congestion Notification (ECN) technique, an extension of the TCP/IP stack, has modified the feedback received by the TCP sender, *i.e.*, packet loss is eventually replaced by a warning of the possible occurrence of congestion. Based on this warning, the sender can preventively reduce the volume of traffic data, mitigating queuing on the intermediate switches. As for the protocols, the implementation of this mechanism was accomplished through the introduction of 2 bits in the network layer: ECN-Capable Transport (ECT) and Congestion Experienced (ECE). The first one indicates the equipment is capable of conveying congestion notification, while the second one signals a congestion situation is happening. In the transport layer of destination, when the notification is identified, the next segment is marked to inform the congestion situation. Upon receiving the notification, the sender reduces the congestion window to avoid loss of segments, and informs its action to the receiver via the bit Congestion Window Reduced (CWR).

The packets experiencing congestion are marked by the intermediate switches. For this, a constant monitoring of the switching queues is performed, triggering actions according to the parameters previously defined. In this context, configurations of Random Early Detection (RED) [21] can be applied by specifying: *(i)* The maximum bandwidth of the link (bytes/s); *(ii)* The minimum, maximum and snapshot size (to meet bursts) of the queue (bytes); *(iii)* The average packet size; *(iv)* The tolerance for the snapshot size of the packet queue; and *(v)* The drop packet probability (from 0.0 to 1.0).

When the packet is received and remains below the minimum specified, no marking occurs. However, packets which are between the minimum and maximum thresholds are marked according to the reported probability. Finally, packets above the maximum threshold are dropped. It is a fact ECN allowed a better sharing of communication resources in DCs [2]. However, the effective application requires uniformity of the algorithms, *i.e.*, the servers must understand the meaning of the markings realized by the network core. Usually, this requirement is not take into account in cloud DCs, in which each tenant can execute different TCP algorithms. Also, several versions of OSs do not have support enabled by default for ECN [11]. Thus, while DC implements mechanisms to optimize traffic, the settings applied on VMs may be conflicting with the ideal scenario.

Although the TCP congestion control algorithms have been improved by the specialized literature, it is evident that a multi-tenant DC network carries flows originated from distinct and competitive versions. Moreover, as HMR is a network-based paradigm, the final performance of an HMR-based application is directly influenced by the TCP congestion control objective (*e.g.*, fairness, low latency, high throughput), even when executed by distinct tenants.

## 3   Virtualized Congestion Control (VCC)

The VCC consists in creating a translation layer for the TCP used by VMs in order to translate it to an optimized/recognized version used in the DC [5,8]. In this way, the communication occurs using the TCP version selected by the provider. It is worthwhile to mention, no changes are needed on the endpoint hosts. Two approaches to VCC implementation have recently been proposed. AC/DC [8] implements VCC in virtual switches, obtaining a fine granularity in the control. Thus, algorithms can be selected for different types of flows, *e.g.*, Cubic for external flows to DC and Data Center TCP (DCTCP) for internal flows. Due to the control is implemented in the virtual switch datapath [16], all traffic can be monitored. [5] implemented VCC directly in the hypervisor of VMs. In both, the perception of congestion is obtained through network core marked packets. Figure 1 presents the canonical architecture for VCC.

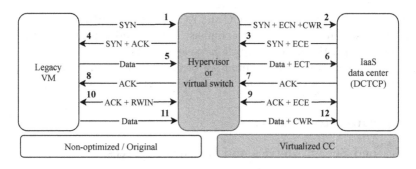

**Fig. 1.** Example of VCC usage.

When a non-optimized (or legacy) application establishes a connection (Fig. 1), the hypervisor (or virtual switch) monitors the exchange of packets and includes the information necessary for non-optimized traffic to be recognized by the network as traffic capable of supporting ECN. Initially, non-optimized TCP application sends a packet requesting connection (1), which is intercepted (2) to append the support information ECN. The recipient responds by confirming the establishment (3, ECE). Again, the packet is intercepted to notify the sender with a synchronization acknowledgment (4). It is important to note, the confirmation sent to the sender with non-optimized TCP algorithm does not have the information about ECN, which was removed by the virtualizer. The data sending starts (5), being intercepted to add the bit ECT, informing this flow is capable of conveying congestion information (6). Subsequently, the recipient acknowledges the received packet (7). The sender receives packet recognition from the hypervisor (8). In case of possible occurrence of congestion in the DC network, the *ECE* bit is activated (9). When congestion occurs, the sender with an optimized algorithm is forced to reduce the sending of data through the bottleneck of the receiving window (10), performed by the hypervisor. Finally, the sender continues to send data (11) to the hypervisor that transfers the data and the window size set to the recipient (12).

In order to induce the host transmission deceleration with non-optimized TCP without applying an intrusive technique, the congestion control is applied over the Receiver Window (RWND). The information internally measured by the algorithm in VM over the congestion window, congestion Window (CWND), remains unchanged. Natively, TCP checks $min(cwnd, rwnd)$ to identify the amount of data which ca be transmitted. On VCC, the value of RWND is changed to represent the correct value of CWND calculated by the virtualization algorithm, based on ECN.

AC/DC mechanism source code was not found available to the community. Thus, [5] was selected for our analysis (Sect. 4). VCC was implemented in Linux by a patch to the hypervisor core. In short, a set of intermediate buffers were created for each TCP connection, *i.e.*, the hypervisor monitors the communication of the VMs. In order to differentiate non-optimized flows and ECN

configurations, the capabilities of VCC and ECN are activated directly by manipulating the *sysctl*. It is important to emphasize the described implementation is
a proof of concept. However, the authors have demonstrated the computational
overhead does not impact on the final performance of the communications, *i.e.*,
the implementation can be used for controlled experimental analysis [5].

## 4 Experimental Analysis

### 4.1 Testbed Setup, Metrics and Execution Traces

The experiments aim to analyze the impact of VCC on the execution of HMR
applications when executed on VM using non-optimized TCP. Data traffic in
HMR was emulated by MRemu [15] using traces of HiBench benchmarking in a
cluster consisting of 16 servers. MRemu only emulates the HMR traffic (using
Mininet [13]), not performing the data processing. Our experimental testbed is
composed of 16 VMs interconnected by a 1 Gbps Dumbbell topology (2 switches
with 8 VMs each). Dumbbell topology was chosen to simplify the representation
of the network bottlenecks. Background traffic was ingested using *iperf* tool,
setting the number of communicating TCP pairs in order to represent multiple
tenants disputing the communication capabilities. The *iperf* servers are connected to *Switch 1* while clients are connected to *Switch 2* (data source). As
for the physical host, MRemu and Mininet were executed on a computer with
OS GNU/Linux Ubuntu 14.04, AMD Phenom II X 4 core processor, and 8GB
RAM. The VMs originally executed the TCP *New Reno*.

To analyze the results, four metrics were collected: *(i)* Elapsed time to run
HMR; *(ii)* Number of dropped packets on switches; *(iii)* Switches queue occupation; and *(iv)* Amount of background traffic. The first metric represents the
view of the tenant, while the other metrics provide data to do the analysis
of the dropped packets and queue formation in switches from traffic of non-
optimized TCP, virtualized, or optimized (IaaS provider perspective).

### 4.2 Experimental Scenarios

Three TCP configurations were used in our experimental scenario: *(i)* TCPVM:
HMR using non-optimized TCP, without support for ECN; *(ii)* TCPDC: HMR
using TCP optimized by the DC, support enable for ECN; and *(iii)* VCC: HMR
using Virtualized Congestion Control (VCC). Background traffic was executed
with TCPDC on all presented scenarios, and HMR was executed on TCPVM,
TCPDC, and VCC. ECN and RED switches configurations were based on two
configurations from the bibliography (Table 1) [1,5]. The first configuration,
RED1, the values of *min* and *max* are close, therefore, with no margin of ade-
quacy. In addition, the *prob* parameter is set to mark 100% of packets, forcing
the rapid reduction of traffic. The configuration identified as RED2, there is a
suitability interval established between the values *min* and *max*. This interval
allows the matching of the traffic according to the congestion notification by
marking packets. Still, there is a difference in the maximum queue size.

**Table 1.** RED settings for marking packets in the *switch* queues.

| Configuration | min | max | limit | burst | prob |
|---|---|---|---|---|---|
| RED1 | 90000 | 90001 | 1 M | 61 | 1.0 |
| RED2 | 30000 | 90000 | 400 K | 55 | 1.0 |

Regarding to the volume of data transferred between the pairs (Client/Server), responsible for the production of background TCPs traffic, two scenarios are analyzed. Scenario 1 was based on unlimited background load and there are 3 sets of experiments (2, 4, and 8 pairs), in which is performed a gradual increase in the number of pairs, and each communicating pair sent the maximum allowed by the application (and bottleneck). Scenario 2 was planned to have a controlled background traffic, using TCP load from 2 MB to 32 GB, and 4 pairs. We run each scenario 10 rounds, the presented graphs comprise mean, standard deviation, and variability of the data.

### 4.3   Result Analysis

The first analysis focuses on the impact of the chosen TCP, and the two configurations of RED, tenant's perspective. Thus, the elapsed time of HMR execution was observed, considering smaller the time than better is the result.

**Scenario 1.** Figure 2 shows the HMR execution results. Figure 2(a) indicates TCPDC has the smallest values, regardless of the number of concurrent pairs and RED configuration. TCPVM is most susceptible to the configuration difference of RED. For example, at 8 pairs, the mean time with RED1 was reduced from 535 s to 213 s using RED2. In this case, we identified the importance of proper RED configuration to the application behavior. The greatest peculiarity of the results was the behavior of VCC, which obtained results compatible with the other protocols when analyzed with 2 pairs, both RED1 and RED2. Using 4 pairs, it remained competitive only with RED1, and proved inefficient with 8 pairs. Using 8 pairs, while HMR/TCPDC using RED1 gets an average time of 84 s, VCC gets 2153 s. Worst results were obtained using RED2, reaching to 2234 s. Different from the results initially obtained with VCC [5,8], the analyzed HMR applications undergo a considerable overhead at run time. Moreover, the application of VCC is influenced by the ECN and RED configurations, information that is abstracted from the tenants. On the other hand, background traffic (Fig. 2(b)) is practically the same, regardless of which TCP protocol was chosen (when the configuration is RED1). RED2 behavior differs only when 2 pairs are used. *Iperf* reaches values close to 130 MB/s using TCPDC/TCPVM, and 120 MB/s using VCC. The lower throughput identified using RED2 was from packet conservative marking, *i.e.*, due to the wide marking interval, the TCP emitters have a conservative behavior, reducing the data sending in order

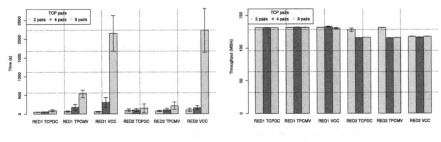

(a) HMR execution time.          (b) Throughput of background traffic.

**Fig. 2.** HMR execution time and throughput of background.

to avoid congestion. Finally, the background traffic is independent of the HMR execution time.

The second approach is the analysis in the provider's perspective. In this case, the observation is in the traffic of the switches, through the occupation of the queues. Figures 3 and 4 resume the results for *Switches* 1 and 2, respectively. Specifically, Figs. 3(a) to 4(f) axis $x$ presents the probability of occurrence and, axis $y$ the accumulated value of the queues (expressed as CDF - Cumulative Distribution Function). The tendency of queuing behavior in the switches is the higher the number of TCP pairs, than greater the number of queues. This behavior was noted in all the scenario variations for the TCPVM protocols and VCC, the only exception was Fig. 3(a) and (d) which are all similar. TCPDC and RED2 protocols, regardless of the switch, 2 pairs presents a larger queue occurrence values than 8 pairs, indicating the total occupancy (400000 bytes) and holding sharing equity (indicated by the throughput, Fig. 2(b)).

We also counted the number of dropped packets in each scenario (Fig. 5(a) and (b)). The smallest losses are with the TCPDC protocol, regardless of the number of pairs or switch. *Switch 1* (connecting HMR and *iperf* servers), the number of dropped packets using RED2 is greater than the number dropped by RED1, both for TCPVM and for VCC. *Switch 2* (connecting HMR and *iperf* clients), the highlight is the high number of packets dropped by VCC to 8 pairs, regardless of RED configuration adopted. Finally, it is important to note that approximately 75% of the data flows transmitted in the analyzed HMR applications carry a maximum of 7 MB, being 10 MB the largest volume transmitted. The volume is less than originally analyzed in VCC [5, 8], being susceptible to the impact of the ECN mark. The queues occupation in the switches indicated the RED configuration is directly related to the application. Even if we control the queue occupation, the volume of dropped packets (Fig. 5(a) and (b)), especially for *Switch 2*) is abusive to VCC when compared with TCPDC.

In summary, the analysis has shown VCC application is promising for pursuing fairness in a heterogeneous environment, such as clouds (presented by the background throughput on Fig. 2(b)). However, the use of VCC for HMR applications requires the proper configuration of the switches queues, a task

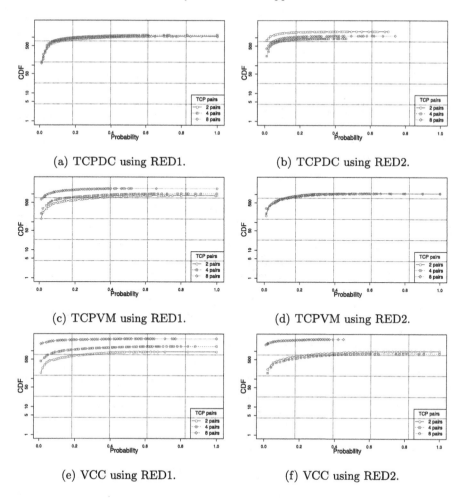

(a) TCPDC using RED1.   (b) TCPDC using RED2.

(c) TCPVM using RED1.   (d) TCPVM using RED2.

(e) VCC using RED1.     (f) VCC using RED2.

**Fig. 3.** Queue occupation on *Switch 1*.

commonly performed by the providers because it is needed administrative access
to configure it [10,17].

**Scenario 2.** This scenario uses 4 ECN-aware TCP pairs to generate background
traffic while HMR is being executed. Figure 6 presents the HMR execution time
for RED1 configuration, and Fig. 6(a) reveals that there is no direct correlation
between background load and HMR execution time when ECN is used for all
nodes (including HMR). In turn, Fig. 6(b) summarises results for HMR without
ECN support. Background traffic with loads between 1 GB and 32 GB induced
an overhead on HMR execution time. When applying the VCC (Fig. 6(c)), the
problem is soften for background loads between 1 MB and 256 MB. However,
a high variation is observed on all other scenarios, justified by the switches

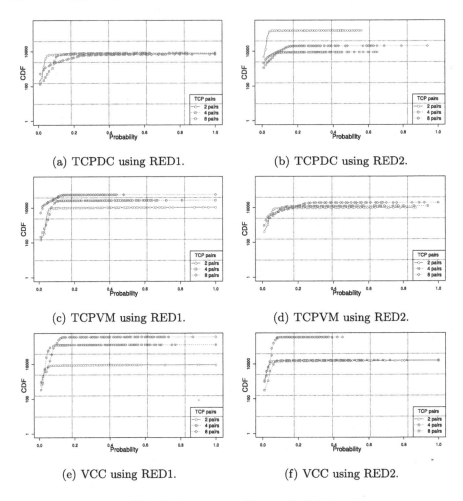

(a) TCPDC using RED1.          (b) TCPDC using RED2.

(c) TCPVM using RED1.          (d) TCPVM using RED2.

(e) VCC using RED1.            (f) VCC using RED2.

**Fig. 4.** Queue occupation on *Switch 2*.

queue occupancy. Finally, the results for RED2 configuration are summarized in Fig. 6(d)–(f). The minimum threshold for RED2 configuration is 1/3 of RED1 value, leading to an early packets marking, while the upper-bound limit is $3x$ RED1 configuration, increasing the marking interval. In this sense, the wide marking interval explains the variation observed with RED2 results.

Regarding the dropped packets originated by the introduction of background traffic, Fig. 7(a)–(c) summarize results for RED1 configuration, while results for RED2 configuration are given by Fig. 7(d)–(f). TCPDC with RED1 configuration has the values concentrated between 1900 and 4000 bytes, and smaller background traffic loads (2 MB, 4 MB, and 8 MB) resulted on higher dropped packets. The loss in larger loads is less influenced by the stabilization of the congestion control window, while smaller background loads are more susceptible to aggressiveness in opening the window. TCPVM (Fig. 7(b)) significantly increased

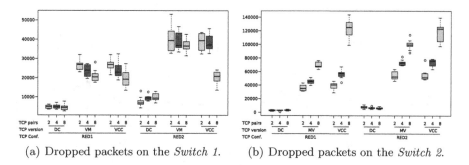

(a) Dropped packets on the *Switch 1*.     (b) Dropped packets on the *Switch 2*.

**Fig. 5.** Dropped packets on *Switches* 1 and 2.

the amount of dropped packet on all background loads. Background loads which are greater than 4 GB, the values remained above 35000 bytes. RED1 configuration and the use of VCC (Fig. 7(c)) decreases the packet dropping occurrence on smaller background traffic (2 MB to 512 MB). On the other hand, it dramatically increases the packet dropping for background loads between 1 GB at 32 GB, when compared to TCPVM scenario. In turn, the dropped packets for TCPDC with RED2 configuration (Fig. 7(d)) oscillated following the increase in background traffic load, with an upper-bound of 10000 bytes, while for TCPVM (Fig. 7(e)) varies from 30000 to 70000 bytes. Using VCC enabled (Fig. 7(f)) the amount of dropped packets is decreased for small background loads.

The last set of data for Scenario 2 is the switches queue occupancy, summarized by Fig. 8. Initially, for RED1 configuration, TCPDC shows a gradual distribution of the queues in relation to the volume of background traffic (Fig. 8(a)), while the TCPVM scenario (Fig. 8(b)) the probability of queue occupancy increased 50% when compared to TCPDC. In addition, the VCC scenario with RED1 configuration (Fig. 8(c)) indicated the concurrent HMR execution time with background loads up to 256 MB, VCC was able to keep the switches queue occupancy just over 5000 bytes, eventually outperforming the TCPDC scenario (for 8 and 16 GB background traffic). Finally, results for RED2 configuration are summarized by Fig. 8(d), (e), and (f) for TCPDC, TCPVM, and VCC. This corroborates what has been previously concluded in Scenario 1; VCC is susceptible to the background traffic load and consequently impacts on the execution time of HMR.

## 5    Related Work

Related work comprises studies on explicit congestion notification, techniques for VCC, characterization and optimization of HMR traffic in DC. Initially, Sally Floyd [6] discusses the use of ECN in TCP. Simulations using New Reno and RED markers indicated the benefits of this feature in congestion control, avoiding losses by anticipating and predicting likely network saturation scenarios. Although disruptive, the implementation of RED on modern operating systems

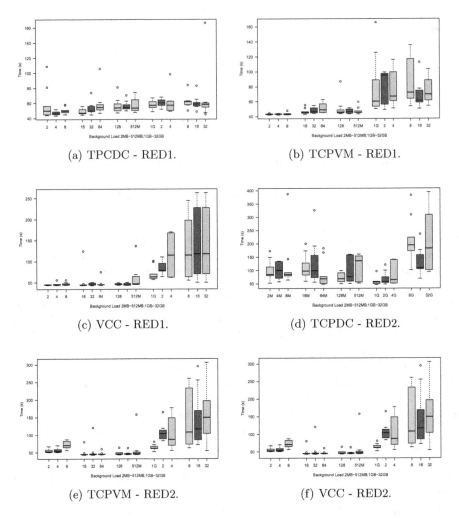

(a) TPCDC - RED1.

(b) TCPVM - RED1.

(c) VCC - RED1.

(d) TCPDC - RED2.

(e) TCPVM - RED2.

(f) VCC - RED2.

**Fig. 6.** HMR execution time with 4 pairs of background traffic.

was recently largely adopted, motivating the present work. Specifically, Kuhlewind *et al.* [11] addresses the historical evolution of ECN in OSs, presenting a view of other ways to congestion prevention and mitigation. In summary, the work indicates the absence of a *de facto* solution to bypass the sharing disparity when multiple algorithms for congestion control are sharing bottlenecks. The present work is based on such assumption. Indeed, we envisage a multi-tenant DC scenario in which multiple users, each one with a private TCP congestion control algorithm, share the data center resources (processing and communication). For instance, the tenants virtual machines or containers can be configured with private TCP options, leading to an unfairness sharing of congested links.

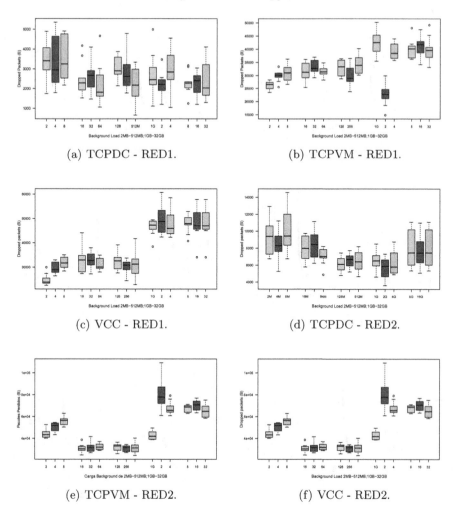

(a) TCPDC - RED1.

(b) TCPVM - RED1.

(c) VCC - RED1.

(d) TCPDC - RED2.

(e) TCPVM - RED2.

(f) VCC - RED2.

**Fig. 7.** Total dropped packets for Scenario 2.

Aware of the diversity of applications running on a cloud DC with out-dated TCP/IP stacks, the specialized literature [5,8] proposed flexibilization in configuration, defining the concept of VCC. This was a key motivator for our performance analysis using HMR applications. Alizadeh *et al.* [1] has identi-fied communication patterns in DC that host HMR: query traffic, background traffic, competing flows of different sizes. Furthermore, Wu *et al.* [21] addresses the congestion traffic caused by incast traffic which occurs when multiple flows converge to the same receiver. We advanced the field by investigated the per-formance impact when running HMR, a real large-scale distributed application. Instead of applying synthetic loads, our experiments were based on traces of HMR execution performed on a real cluster.

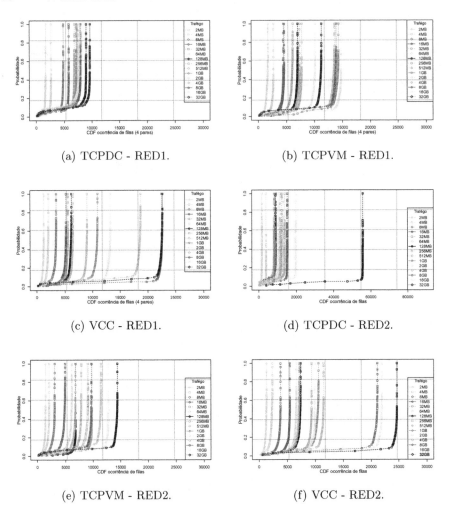

(a) TCPDC - RED1.

(b) TCPVM - RED1.

(c) VCC - RED1.

(d) TCPDC - RED2.

(e) TCPVM - RED2.

(f) VCC - RED2.

**Fig. 8.** Switches queue occupancy for Scenario 2.

Regarding the management of IaaS DCs, Popa and colleagues [17] investigated the tough negotiation when establishing bandwidth allocation policies to ensure a proportionality of network usage, granting a minimum guarantee for the flow of the VM and at the same time to avoid idleness, inducing the high occupation of the network. In turn, Zahavi *et al.* [22] proposes a new abstraction of cloud services, called Link-as-a-Service (LaaS), with isolation between virtualized communication links. The client can choose to introduce in the link the congestion control algorithm that best meets the needs of their application, that is, the decision does not belong to the provider. Both works are examples of how VCC can be combined with bandwidth reservation techniques to provide Quality of Service (QoS) requirements. In our analysis we stressed the HMR application with heavy competitive load causing the worst-case scenario for congestion control. A future work can combine bandwidth reservation techniques to soften the degradation of HMR performance when executed atop VCC-enabled DCs.

# 6 Final Considerations and Future Work

IaaS clouds allow tenants to install and configure their OS according to their hosted applications requirements. Such advent diffused the malleability of VMs, however, resulted in a heterogeneous scenario running on DC. Above all, several clients do not upgrade libraries, modules, and OSs due to technical constraints on legacy applications. Consequently, outdated versions of TCP algorithms for congestion control compete with updated versions in DCs. To mitigate disparity, virtualized congestion control was recently proposed.

The present work investigated the application of VCC in the execution of applications HMR, executed in VMs with non-optimized TCP. The experimental analysis was performed with traces of HMR execution on a dedicated cluster. Analyzing the results, was evidenced the virtualization is directly dependent on the configurations applied in the switches. Above all, experiments following the settings indicated in the literature (referred to as RED1 and RED2) resulted in an impact on the execution time of the HMR applications. The results advanced the TCP congestion control literature by empirically analysing the execution of a trace from a real communication-intensive application atop a VCC-based DC. As a continuity perspective, it is clear that VCC is a promising technology, however, as the results indicated, the definition of optimized RED and ECN configurations are essential and of course a continuum line.

# References

1. Alizadeh, M., et al.: Data center TCP (DCTCP). SIGCOMM Comput. Commun. Rev. **40**(4), 63–74 (2010)
2. Alizadeh, M., Javanmard, A., Prabhakar, B.: Analysis of DCTCP: stability, convergence, and fairness. In: Proceedings of the ACM SIGMETRICS Joint International Conference on Measurement and Modeling of Computer Systems. SIGMETRICS 2011, pp. 73–84. ACM (2011)
3. Chiu, D.M., Jain, R.: Analysis of the increase and decrease algorithms for congestion avoidance in computer networks. Comput. Netw. ISDN Syst. **17**(1), 1–14 (1989)
4. Chowdhury, M., Zaharia, M., Ma, J., Jordan, M.I., Stoica, I.: Managing data transfers in computer clusters with orchestra. SIGCOMM Comput. Commun. Rev. **41**(4), 98–109 (2011)
5. Cronkite-Ratcliff, B., et al.: Virtualized congestion control. In: Proceedings of the 2016 ACM SIGCOMM Conference. SIGCOMM 2016, pp. 230–243. ACM (2016)
6. Floyd, S.: TCP and explicit congestion notification. SIGCOMM Comput. Commun. Rev. **24**(5), 8–23 (1994)
7. Ha, S., Rhee, I., Xu, L.: CUBIC: a new TCP-friendly high-speed TCP variant. SIGOPS Oper. Syst. Rev. **42**(5), 64–74 (2008)

8. He, K., et al.: AC/DC TCP: virtual congestion control enforcement for datacenter networks. In: Proceedings of the 2016 SIGCOMM Conference. SIGCOMM 2016, pp. 244–257. ACM (2016)
9. Jacobson, V.: Congestion avoidance and control. SIGCOMM Comput. Commun. Rev. 18(4), 314–329 (1988)
10. Judd, G.: Attaining the promise and avoiding the pitfalls of TCP in the datacenter. In: Proceedings of the 12th USENIX Conference on Networked Systems Design and Implementation. NSDI 2015, pp. 145–157. Berkeley (2015)
11. Kühlewind, M., Neuner, S., Trammell, B.: On the state of ECN and TCP options on the Internet. In: Roughan, M., Chang, R. (eds.) PAM 2013. LNCS, vol. 7799, pp. 135–144. Springer, Heidelberg (2013). https://doi.org/10.1007/978-3-642-36516-4_14
12. Kumar, P., et al.: : PicNIC: predictable virtualized NIC. In: Proceedings of the ACM Special Interest Group on Data Communication. SIGCOMM 2019, pp. 351–366. ACM (2019)
13. Lantz, B., Heller, B., McKeown, N.: A network in a laptop: rapid prototyping for software-defined networks. In: Proceedings of the 9th ACM SIGCOMM Workshop on Hot Topics in Networks. HotNets-IX, pp. 19:1–19:6. ACM (2010)
14. Moro, V., Pillon, M.A., Miers, C., Koslovski, G.: Análise da virtualização do controle de congestionamento na execução de aplicações hadoop mapreduce. In: Simpósio de Sistemas Computacionais de Alto Desempenho - WSCAD, October 2018
15. Neves, M.V., De Rose, C.A.F., Katrinis, K.: MRemu: an emulation-based framework for datacenter network experimentation using realistic MapReduce traffic. In: Proceedings of the 2015 IEEE 23rd International Symposium on Modeling, Analysis, and Simulation of Computer and Telecommunication Systems. MASCOTS 2015, pp. 174–177 (2015)
16. Pfaff, B., et al.: The design and implementation of Open vSwitch. In: Proceedings of the 12th USENIX Conference on Networked Systems Design and Implementation. NSDI 2015,pp. 117–130 (2015)
17. Popa, L., Kumar, G., Chowdhury, M., Krishnamurthy, A., Ratnasamy, S., Stoica, I.: FairCloud: sharing the network in cloud computing. In: Proceedings of the ACM SIGCOMM 2012 Conference on Applications, Technologies, Architectures, and Protocols for Computer Communication. SIGCOMM 2012, pp. 187–198. ACM (2012)
18. Roy, A., Zeng, H., Bagga, J., Porter, G., Snoeren, A.C.: Inside the social network's (datacenter) network. SIGCOMM Comput. Commun. Rev. 45(4), 123–137 (2015)
19. de Souza, F.R., Miers, C.C., Fiorese, A., Koslovski, G.P.: Qos-aware virtual infrastructures allocation on SDN-based clouds. In: Proceedings of the 17th IEEE/ACM International Symposium on Cluster, Cloud and Grid Computing. CCGrid 2017, pp. 120–129. IEEE Press, Piscataway (2017)
20. Primet, P.V.-B., Anhalt, F., Koslovski, G.: Exploring the virtual infrastructure service concept in Grid'5000. In: 20th ITC Specialist Seminar on Network Virtualization. Hoi An, May 2009
21. Wu, H., Ju, J., Lu, G., Guo, C., Xiong, Y., Zhang, Y.: Tuning ECN for data center networks. In: Proceedings of the 8th International Conference on Emerging Networking Experiments and Technologies. CoNEXT 2012, pp. 25–36. ACM (2012)
22. Zahavi, E., Shpiner, A., Rottenstreich, O., Kolodny, A., Keslassy, I.: Links as a service (LaaS): guaranteed tenant isolation in the shared cloud. In: Proceedings of the 2016 Symposium on Architectures for Networking and Communications Systems. ANCS 2016, pp. 87–98. ACM (2016)

# Performance

# Improving Oil and Gas Simulation Performance Using Thread and Data Mapping

Matheus S. Serpa[1]($\boxtimes$) , Eduardo H. M. Cruz[2] , Jairo Panetta[3] ,
Antônio Azambuja[4], Alexandre S. Carissimi[1], and Philippe O. A. Navaux[1]

[1] Federal University of Rio Grande do Sul, UFRGS, Porto Alegre, Brazil
{msserpa,asc,navaux}@inf.ufrgs.br
[2] Federal Institute of Paraná, IFPR, Paranavaí, Brazil
eduardo.cruz@ifpr.edu.br
[3] Technological Institute of Aeronautics, ITA, São José dos Campos, Brazil
jairo.panetta@gmail.com
[4] Petróleo Brasileiro S.A, Rio de Janeiro, Brazil
antonio.azambuja@petrobras.com.br

**Abstract.** Oil and gas have been among the most important commodities for over a century. To improve their extraction, companies invest in new technology, which reduces extraction cost and allow new areas to be explored. Computing science has also been employed to support advances in oil and gas extraction technologies. Techniques such as computing simulation can be used to evaluate scenarios quicker and with a lower cost. Several mathematical models that simulate oil and gas extraction are based on wave propagation. To simulate with high performance, the software must be written considering the characteristics of the underlying hardware. In this context, our work shows how thread and data mapping policies can improve the performance of a wave propagation model provided by Petrobras, a multinational corporation in the petroleum industry. In our experiments, we are revealing that, with smart mapping policies, we reduced the execution time by up to 48.6% on Intel's multi-core Xeon.

**Keywords:** Oil and gas · Thread mapping · Data mapping

## 1 Introduction

The geophysics of exploration continues to be fundamental to the modern world, seeking to keep up with the demand for energy resources. This effort results in high drilling costs. Thus, the oil and gas industries rely on software focused on high-performance computing (HPC) to reduce risks and make drilling economically viable [16].

---

Supported by Petrobras grant n.° 2016/00133-9.

Typically, these applications are accelerated through systems based on Graphical Processing Units (GPUs). However, the use of systems based on Central Processing Units (CPUs) can also be attractive because of their flexibility, memory capacity, and scalability. With the new multi-core processors, CPUs can be a better choice for large parallel workloads that were previously dominated by GPUs [14, 20].

Multi-core processors are often defined as processors built with a considerable number of cores focused on latency. They offer higher throughput for parallel applications, coupled with improved energy efficiency. Multi-core architectures are present on all the top ten Top-500 computers in November 2018 [10].

With dozens of threads running simultaneously on the same system, synchronization related overhead, for example in maintaining cache consistency, has an even more significant impact on performance. Threads in multithreaded applications, such as those that implement oil and gas simulation applications, share data, forcing them to be moved through inter-chip or intra-chip interconnections, depending on the hierarchy of memory and the location of threads [7].

Threads that communicate intensely have lower communication latencies if placed close to each other. On the other hand, the bandwidth is also shared, which means that the threads will compete for it. On NUMA (Non-uniform memory access) systems, the data present in the main memory can be local or remote, depending on the node where it is stored and the CPU running it. Reading data from a remote memory bank results in higher latencies and more traffic on the interconnections.

This article is a continuation of our previous work [15]. In this previous research work, we showed that geophysics models could be accelerated thanks to a smarter placement of threads and data. The main improvements are: We improve the related work; We use a newer multi-core architecture; We proposed and evaluated an optimized version of the application.

The remaining sections of this paper are organized as follows. Section 2 discusses the related work. Section 3 shows the potential of the geophysical application for mapping. Section 4 describes the architectures, the geophysical application, and the techniques we evaluated. Section 5 provides an evaluation of the performance of different mapping strategies and, finally, Sect. 6 presents conclusions and future work.

## 2 Related Work

Very few works look at the performance implications of thread and data mapping techniques on a geophysics algorithm for multi-core architectures. First, we discuss works that focus on optimize Geophysics applications. Afterward, we present several works that improve other applications performance using thread and data mapping.

## 2.1  Geophysics Applications

Recent architectures, including accelerators and co-processors, have proven to be suitable for geophysics, simulations of hydrodynamics and magnetic flux, surpassing general-purpose processors.

Micikevicius [12] compared the performance of a stencil ported from CPU to GPU. Their version of the stencil running in a GPU achieved an order of magnitude higher than running in a contemporary CPU. They conclude that it is possible to improve their results by using shared memory to reduce communication overhead.

Carrijo Nasciutti et al. [2] analyzed several memory optimizations for 3D stencils running on GPUs. They conclude that techniques such as grid tiling, kernels equipped with spatial and temporal loops, and register reuse improve stencils performance by up to 3.3× compared with the classical stencil formulation.

In Andreolli et al. [1], the authors focused on acoustic wave propagation equations, choosing the optimization techniques from systematically tuning the algorithm. The usage of collaborative thread blocking, cache blocking, register reuse, vectorization, and loop redistribution resulted in significant performance improvements.

Serpa et al. [16] also analyzed several optimization strategies aiming to improve the cache memory usage, vectorization, load balancing, portability, and locality in the memory hierarchy.

Compared to the related work, our paper is the first to analyze the performance implications of thread and data mapping techniques on an oil and gas application.

## 2.2  Thread and Data Mapping

Several papers identify the mapping of threads and data as an effective way to improve the performance of parallel applications and propose new methods to perform the mapping more efficiently.

Tousimojarad and Vanderbauwhede [18] show that the default thread mapping of Linux is inefficient when the number of threads is as large as on a many-core processor and presents a new thread mapping policy that uses the amount of time that each core does useful work to find the best target core for each thread.

Liu et al. [11] propose an approach based on profiling to determine thread-to-core mapping on the Knights Corner architecture that depends on the location of the distributed tag directory, achieving significant reductions in communication latency.

He, Chen, and Tang [9] introduce NestedMP, an extension to OpenMP that allows the programmer to give information about the structure of the tasks tree to the runtime, which then performs a locality-aware thread mapping.

Cruz et al. [5] improve state of the art by performing a very detailed analysis of the impact of thread mapping on communication and load balancing in two many-core systems from Intel, namely Knights Corner and Knights Landing. They observed that the widely used metric of CPU time provides very inaccurate information for load balancing. They also evaluated the usage of thread mapping based on the communication and load information of the applications to improve the performance of many-core systems.

Serpa et al. [17] focus on Intel's multi-core Xeon and many-core accelerator Xeon Phi Knights Landing, which can host several hundreds of threads on the same CPU. Execution time was reduced by up to 25.2% and 18.5% on Intel Xeon and Xeon Phi Knights Landing, respectively.

Different from our approach, these techniques are limited to the algorithm. Our approach can be used in any application running on a NUMA architecture.

## 3     Mapping Potential for an Oil and Gas Application

The oil and gas application we used is based on a wave propagation model. This type of application performs many data accesses. Thus, the mapping of threads and data is a useful technique to optimize the performance of these applications.

In this section, we analyze how thread and data mapping can improve the performance of an oil and gas application.

### 3.1     Impact of Memory Access on Mapping

For data mapping, the amount of memory access from each thread (or NUMA node) to each page is essential. With this information, each page can be mapped to the NUMA node that executes most of the memory accesses for them. The objective of this technique is to reduce the number of accesses to remote memories, which are more expensive than the accesses to local memory. The least exclusivity a page can have is when all threads access the page the same number of times. The biggest exclusivity of a page is when a page is accessed only by one thread, that is, the page is private.

Applications with the largest number of pages with high exclusivity are those with the greatest potential for performance improvements with data mapping considering locality [6]. For example, if there is an application with a large number of private pages. Therefore, by mapping these pages to the NUMA node closest to the threads they access the most, we can reduce the number of accesses to remote memory for these pages. Only the pages that contain the lowest level of exclusivity are not affected by mapping considering locality, so mapping considering load balancing is more appropriate in this case.

Applications with high levels of exclusivity tend to benefit more from data mapping. This is because if a page with high exclusivity is mapped to the NUMA node of the threads that most access the page, the number of accesses to remote memory is reduced. On the other hand, if a page has a low level of exclusivity, the number of accesses to remote memory would be similar, regardless of the NUMA node used to store the page.

## 3.2   Impact of Architectural Topology on Mapping

The difference in memory location between the cores affects data sharing performance [7]. Since parallel applications need to access shared data, the memory hierarchy presents challenges for mapping threads to cores and data to NUMA nodes [19]. Threads that access a large amount of shared data must be mapped to cores close to each other in the memory hierarchy, while data must be mapped to the NUMA node by executing the threads that access them. In this way, the location of memory accesses is improved, which increases performance and energy efficiency. Ideally, the mapping of threads and data should be performed together [4].

For multicore architectures, there are three possibilities for sharing between threads. Threads running on the same core can share data through the L1 or L2 fast caches and have the best sharing performance. Threads that run on different cores have to share data through the L3 cache, which is slower but can still benefit from fast intra-chip interconnection. When threads running share data between physical processors at different NUMA nodes, they need to use inter-chip interconnection, which is slow.

On NUMA systems, the time to access the main memory depends on the core that requested the memory access and the NUMA node that contains the target memory page. If the core and the target memory page belong to the same node, we have access to local memory. On the other hand, if the core and destination memory page belong to different NUMA nodes, we have remote memory access. The accesses to local memory are faster than the accesses to remote memory. By mapping the application threads and data in order to increase the number of local memory accesses compared to remote memory accesses, the average latency of the main memory is reduced.

# 4   Evaluation Methodology

In this section, we show how we evaluate the mapping performance. We present the architecture, the oil and gas application, and the evaluated mapping policies.

## 4.1   Multi-core Architecture

We used one environment to analyze the impact of thread and data mapping. We used a 2-node Broadwell architecture, where each node consists of a 22-core Intel Xeon E5-2699 v4 processor. Each core supports 2-way Simultaneous Multithreading (SMT) and has private L1 and L2 caches, while the L3 cache is shared across all processor cores. We refer to this system as Xeon.

Each experiment was executed 30 times with the number of virtual cores of the architecture (88 threads). The graphs show the average runtime values and the 95% confidence intervals according to the Student's t-distribution [13].

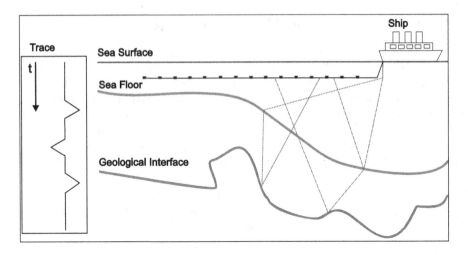

**Fig. 1.** Marine seismic operations at sea.

## 4.2  Oil and Gas Application

During the Petrobras project 2016/00133-9, a modeling program for wave propagation in an anisotropic environment was written. The deduction of partial
differential equations, such as boundary and stability conditions, can be found
in Fletcher et al. [8]. Discretization was performed using finite differences. The
code was written in C and parallelized with OpenMP. We also consider GPUs
and other programming models such as CUDA in a previous work (IJHPCA
2019). Results show that GPUs were 3× faster than multi-core architectures for
geophysics models. However, GPUs have a small global memory size, which limits
our execution parameters, not allowing representative problems being simulated.

The modeling simulates data collection in seismic operations at sea, as in
Fig. 1. From time to time, equipment coupled to the ship emits waves that reflect
and refract from changes in the subsoil environment. Eventually, these waves
return to the sea surface, being collected by specific microphones coupled to
cables towed by the ship. The set of signals received by each headset overtime
constitutes a seismic trace. For each wave emission, the seismic traces of all the
cable headsets are recorded. The ship continues to travel and emit signals over
time.

**Naive Version.** Algorithm 1 shows the main loop of the model. This algorithm
is an example of stencil computation that is commonly used in scientific applications to solve partial differential equations over multidimensional grids. These
computations are point independent because each point is a combination of the
values of the point and its neighbors in the previous iteration, as we show in
Fig. 2. Therefore, the computations are highly parallelizable, and the memory
access behavior presents challenges to optimize the performance.

**Algorithm 1.** Stencil code snippet

```
1: for all timesteps do
2:     for all X points do
3:         for all Y points do
4:             for all Z points do
5:                 3D stencil computation
6:             end for
7:         end for
8:     end for
9:     Time integration
10: end for
```

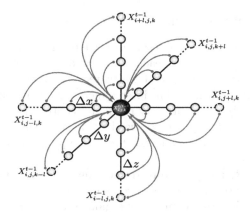

**Fig. 2.** 3D symmetric cross-shaped 7-point stencil. Each $X_{i,j,k}^t$ point is updated with the weighted neighbors $(X_{i\pm1..\ell,j\pm1..\ell,k\pm1..\ell}^{t-1})$ of the previous time-step $(t-1)$.

The code snippet advances the propagation of the time wave at the grid point (cube). The three-dimensional fields are mapped into one-dimensional arrays in the order (x, y, z), that is, x is a direction that changes faster in memory. Every second derivative is invoking the Der2 function. The direction of the derivative is determined by the jump in memory (strideX, strideY, strideZ). The parallelism of the version is immediate, since the propagation in one point of the note is independent of the propagation in any other point of the grid, with each step without time.

**Optimized Version.** We identified that the calculation of the crossed derivatives demanded 76% of the floating-point operations in the naive version. In this sense, we seek to reduce the number of operations to calculate the cross-derivatives by calculating the cross-derivative at xy as the first derivative at y of the first derivative at x. This does not reduce the number of operations in the cross-derivative calculation at one point but reduces the number of operations in the cross-derivative calculation in consecutive y by reusing seven derivatives in x previously calculated from the eight required. As the same reduction occurs in the other cross-derivatives, this suggestion was applied to the calculation of all cross-derivatives.

Initially, the first derivatives in x and y of all points of the grid were calculated and stored. The first derivative at x was used to compute the cross-derivatives at xy and xz, and the first derivative at y to compute the cross-derivative at yz. Then, we reduce the memory gain by storing the first derivative in a circular buffer. The buffer consists of nine xy planes of the complete grid, containing the first derivatives in the nine depths used by Fletcher modeling. At each new depth, only one plane is replaced: the plane of the smallest depth is replaced by the plane of the greatest depth.

### 4.3    Data and Thread Mapping Policies

The goal of mapping is to improve resource usage by organizing threads and data according to a fixed policy, where each approach can enhance different aspects. Some techniques focus on improving locality, reducing cache gaps, remote memory access, and traffic on inter-chip interconnections, while others seek to distribute the load evenly across memory cores and controllers.

The following thread mapping policies have been evaluated:

**Default** (baseline): Linux standard thread mapping focused on load balancing.

**RoundRobin:** RoundRobin thread mapping distributes the threads to the cores in order from 0 to the number of cores minus 1.

**Compact:** Compact thread mapping organizes neighboring threads to closer cores according to the memory hierarchy.

**Scatter:** Scatter thread mapping distributes threads as evenly as possible across the system, which is the opposite of compact.

The following data mapping policies have been evaluated:

**Default** (baseline): Linux standard data mapping, the first-touch data mapping policy, where the page is mapped to the NUMA node of the first core that accessed the page.

**NUMA Balancing:** NUMA Balancing [3] data mapping migrates pages throughout the execution to the NUMA node of the last thread that accessed the page, which is detected by page faults.

**Interleave:** Interleave data mapping distributes consecutive pages to consecutive NUMA nodes.

We have combined some thread and data mapping techniques to show that together they improve performance even more.

## 5    Oil and Gas Application Results

This section presents the results of different thread and data mapping techniques in the geophysical application, following the methodology shown in Sect. 4.

We present the performance and energy results of thread mapping, data mapping, and thread and data mapping for Xeon architecture. We evaluated

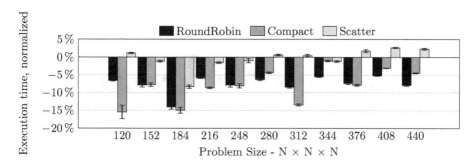

**Fig. 3.** Thread mapping

different input sizes from $120 \times 120 \times 120$ to $440 \times 440 \times 440$, resulting in a total of 11 different input sizes. The CPU experiments were run with the number of virtual cores (Hyper-Threading was activated) of the architectures.

### 5.1 Performance of Naive Version

Figure 3 shows the thread mapping results for the naive version. We show the reduced execution time for the RoundRobin, Compact, and Scatter techniques compared to default Linux thread mapping. For the experiments in this section, we run the application using 88 threads, which is the default in the Xeon processor. The best result for thread mapping was a 15.5% reduction in execution time for a cube of size 120 using a compact thread mapping. In average, the compact thread mapping improves the performance by 8.1%.

Figure 4 shows the results of the data mapping. We analyzed the interleave and NUMA Balancing techniques against first-touch data mapping. The best reduction was 14.7% to size 152 with an interleave data mapping. In average, the performance reduction was 7.9% for interleave and 1.1% for NUMA balancing. The reason NUMA balancing performance is worst as the problem size increase is the number of page migrations. NUMA balancing migrates pages during execution to the NUMA node of the last thread that accessed the page. As expected, it is very costly and limits its performance.

Figure 5 shows the results of mapping both threads and data. We show a subset of the possible combinations because all combinations would generate many bars. We selected the round-robin and scatter thread mappings, and combined them with the interleave data mapping. The best result was 27.3% for a cube of 120 with compact thread mapping and interleave data mapping. The best average reduction was also for compact thread mapping with 15.8%.

### 5.2 Performance of Optimized Version

Figure 6 shows the thread mapping results for the optimized version. The techniques are the same as those analyzed in the naive version.

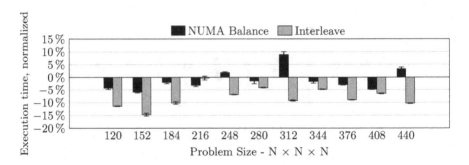

**Fig. 4.** Data mapping

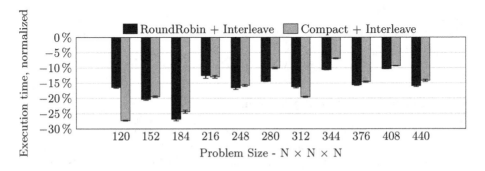

**Fig. 5.** Thread and Data mapping

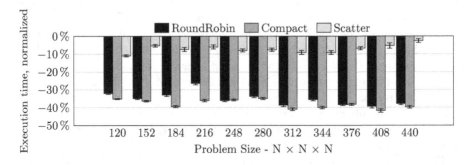

**Fig. 6.** Thread mapping

Using thread mapping alone, the best results were achieved for a cube of size 408, reducing execution time by 41.8% using a compact thread mapping. The average execution time reductions were 35.1% for the round-robin, 38.1% for compact and 7.1% for the scatter. For most of the inputs, round-robin and compact techniques, have almost the same performance. In applications with

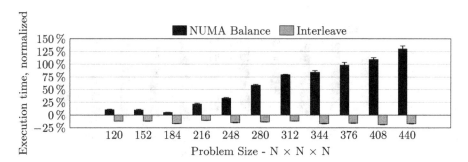

**Fig. 7.** Data mapping

irregular memory access patterns, thread mapping can improve performance by reducing the number of unnecessary thread migrations.

Figure 7 shows the data mapping results for the optimized version. We analyzed the interleave and NUMA Balancing techniques against first-touch data mapping. We also gain using data mapping because, even if applications do not share much data, each thread still needs to access its private data. The best reduction in execution time was 18.7% for size 408 and interleave data mapping. This application has a significant number of shared pages, which, when distributed between nodes by the interleave technique, improve load balancing between memory controllers. NUMA Balancing has the worst results due to high page migration overhead since threads can be migrated to other NUMA nodes during execution.

Figure 8 shows the results for thread and data mapping together. We combine both techniques because, in most applications, the effectiveness of data mapping depends on thread mapping. We show the possibilities of using round-robin and compact thread mapping and interleave data mapping, which was the techniques that perform better for our oil and gas application. The best reductions were 48.6% for an interleave data mapping with compact thread mapping in a cube of 440. Interleave data mapping alone (Fig. 7) was 29.9% worse because default thread mapping migrates threads during execution, unlike the round-robin, compact, and scatter policies that fix the threads on a given core. In average, we improve the performance by 43.5% using mapping techniques.

### 5.3 Comparison Between Different Versions

We test different thread and data mapping techniques in the geophysical application. Figure 9 shows the performance in MSamples of the best mapping for application version evaluated. For the naive version, the best data mapping was interleave, and thread mapping was round robin and compact depending on input size. For the optimized version, the best data mapping was also interleave with a compact thread mapping.

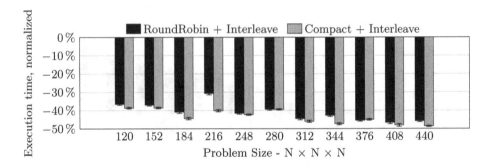

**Fig. 8.** Thread and Data mapping

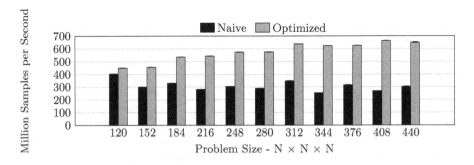

**Fig. 9.** Thread and Data mapping

For the naive version, the best performance was 403 MSamples for a cube of size 120. In average, the performance was 308 MSamples. The naive version recalculates several equations inside the main loop. The optimized version proposes a solution to this problem. For the optimized version, the best performance was 664 MSamples for a cube of size 408, which is 1.7× faster than the naive version. In average, the performance was even better, 576 MSamples.

## 6    Conclusion and Future Work

We evaluated different thread and data mapping policies for two versions of an oil and gas application. The experiments were conducted on an Intel Xeon processor. Furthermore, our approach could be extended to different multi-core and many-core architectures. It works better on NUMA architectures.

The experimental results showed that the execution time was reduced by up to 27.3% for the naive version and 48.6% for the optimized version. The reductions were achieved for compact thread mapping with interleave data mapping. The differences in performance between the two versions are due to the number of private pages of each version. Our optimized version requires more memory due to the cross-derivative buffers and thus, giving mapping techniques more opportunities to improve the performance.

Also, our results showed that for this kind of application, policies that focus on load balancing are better. We also observed that policies that focused on improving memory access locations had better results.

As future work, we intend to modify the source code of the algorithms to enable fine-grain mapping granularity. Other possibilities include dynamic adaptive policies.

# References

1. Andreolli, C., Thierry, P., Borges, L., Skinner, G., Yount, C.: Characterization and optimization methodology applied to stencil computations. In: Reinders, J., Jeffers, J. (eds.) High Performance Parallelism Pearls. Morgan Kaufmann, Boston (2015)
2. Carrijo Nasciutti, T., Panetta, J., Pais Lopes, P.: Evaluating optimizations that reduce global memory accesses of stencil computations in GPGPUs. Concurr. Comput.: Pract. Exp. **31**, e4929 (2018)
3. Corbet, J.: Toward better NUMA scheduling (2012). http://lwn.net/Articles/486858/
4. Cruz, E.H., Diener, M., Alves, M.A., Pilla, L.L., Navaux, P.O.: LAPT: a locality-aware page table for thread and data mapping. Parallel Comput. **54**, 59–71 (2016)
5. Cruz, E.H., Diener, M., Serpa, M.S., Navaux, P.O.A., Pilla, L., Koren, I.: Improving communication and load balancing with thread mapping in manycore systems. In: 2018 26th Euromicro International Conference on Parallel, Distributed and Network-Based Processing (PDP), pp. 93–100. IEEE (2018)
6. Diener, M., Cruz, E.H.M., Navaux, P.O.A., Busse, A., Heiß, H.U.: kMAF: automatic kernel-level management of thread and data affinity. In: International Conference on Parallel Architectures and Compilation Techniques (PACT) (2014). https://doi.org/10.1145/2628071.2628085
7. Diener, M., Cruz, E.H., Alves, M.A., Navaux, P.O., Busse, A., Heiss, H.U.: Kernel-based thread and data mapping for improved memory affinity. IEEE Trans. Parallel Distrib. Syst. **27**(9), 2653–2666 (2016)
8. Fletcher, R.P., Du, X., Fowler, P.J.: Reverse time migration in tilted transversely isotropic (TTI) media. Geophysics **74**(6), WCA179–WCA187 (2009)
9. He, J., Chen, W., Tang, Z.: NestedMP: enabling cache-aware thread mapping for nested parallel shared memory applications. Parallel Comput. **51**, 56–66 (2016)
10. Dongarra, J., Meuer, H., Strohmaier, E.: Top500 supercomputer: November 2018 (2018). https://www.top500.org/lists/2018/11/. Accessed 26 Feb 2019
11. Liu, G., Schmidt, T., Dömer, R., Dingankar, A., Kirkpatrick, D.: Optimizing thread-to-core mapping on manycore platforms with distributed tag directories. In: Asia and South Pacific Design Automation Conference (ASP-DAC) (2015)
12. Micikevicius, P.: 3D finite difference computation on GPUs using CUDA. In: Kaeli, D., Leeser, M. (eds.) Proceedings of 2nd Workshop on General Purpose Processing on Graphics Processing Units, GPGPU-2, pp. 79–84. ACM, New York (2009). https://doi.org/10.1145/1513895.1513905. http://doi.acm.org/10.1145/1513895.1513905
13. Ott, R.L., Longnecker, M.T.: An Introduction to Statistical Methods and Data Analysis. Nelson Education (2015)

14. Serpa, M.S., et al.: Memory performance and bottlenecks in multicore and GPU architectures. In: 2019 27th Euromicro International Conference on Parallel, Distributed and Network-Based Processing (PDP), pp. 233–236, February 2019. https://doi.org/10.1109/EMPDP.2019.8671628

15. Serpa, M.S., Cruz, E.H.M., Panetta, J., Navaux, P.O.A.: Optimizing geophysics models using thread and data mapping. In: 2018 19th Symposium on Computer Systems (2018)

16. Serpa, M.S., et al.: Optimization strategies for geophysics models on manycore systems. Int. J. High Perform. Comput. Appl. **33**(3), 473–486 (2019). https://doi.org/10.1177/1094342018824150

17. Serpa, M.S., Krause, A.M., Cruz, E.H., Navaux, P.O.A., Pasin, M., Felber, P.: Optimizing machine learning algorithms on multi-core and many-core architectures using thread and data mapping. In: 2018 26th Euromicro International Conference on Parallel, Distributed and Network-based Processing (PDP), pp. 329–333. IEEE (2018)

18. Tousimojarad, A., Vanderbauwhede, W.: An efficient thread mapping strategy for multiprogramming on manycore processors. Parallel Comput. Accel. Comput. Sci. Eng. (CSE) Adv. Parallel Comput. **25**, 3–71 (2014)

19. Wang, W., Dey, T., Mars, J., Tang, L., Davidson, J.W., Soffa, M.L.: Performance analysis of thread mappings with a holistic view of the hardware resources. In: IEEE International Symposium on Performance Analysis of Systems & Software (ISPASS) (2012). https://doi.org/10.1109/ISPASS.2012.6189222

20. Witten, I.H., Frank, E., Hall, M.A., Pal, C.J.: Data Mining: Practical Machine Learning Tools and Techniques. Morgan Kaufmann, Burlington (2016)

# SMCis: Scientific Applications Monitoring and Prediction for HPC Environments

Gabrieli Silva$^{(\boxtimes)}$ ⓘ, Vinícius Klôh ⓘ, André Yokoyama ⓘ, Matheus Gritz ⓘ,
Bruno Schulze ⓘ, and Mariza Ferro ⓘ

National Laboratory for Scientific Computing (LNCC), Getúlio Vargas, 333,
Quitandinha, Petrópolis, Rio de Janeiro, Brazil
{gabrieli,viniciusk,andremy,masgritz,schulze,mariza}@lncc.br

**Abstract.** Understanding the computational requirements of scientific applications and their relation to power consumption is a fundamental task to overcome the current barriers to achieve the computational exascale. However, this imposes some challenging tasks, such as to monitor a wide range of parameters in heterogeneous environments, to enable fine grained profiling and power consumed across different components, to be language independent and to avoid code instrumentation. Considering these challenges, this work proposes the SMCis, an application monitoring tool developed with the goal of collecting all these aspects in an effective and accurate way, as well as to correlate these data graphically, with the environment of analysis and visualization. In addition, SMCis integrates and facilitates the use of Machine Learning tools for the development of predictive runtime and power consumption models.

**Keywords:** HPC · Monitoring tools · Energy · Performance

## 1 Introduction

The use of High-Performance Computing (HPC) has become fundamental in order to discover new knowledge and therefore its use has become crucial to scientific research across many research domains. With the current computational power offered by this generation of petaflopic supercomputers, it's possible to perform complex simulations with realism and precision never achieved before. In spite of these advancements, there's a growing number of problems that are not accurate enough or even impossible to perform. Many scientific tasks in areas such as energy industry, materials science, climate and precision medicine are still too complex for the available resources and should benefit from the HPC growth, as expected for the next generation of exascale supercomputing.

Many studies, such as [4,8,29] and [24] consider that one of the greatest barriers to the viability of the exascale processing is the energy consumption of HPC environments. Today's energy costs of supercomputers already reach high values, so reaching the new generation will rely on a lot of effort to considerably increase the processing capacity while reducing energy consumption.

© Springer Nature Switzerland AG 2020
C. Bianchini et al. (Eds.): WSCAD 2018, CCIS 1171, pp. 69–84, 2020.
https://doi.org/10.1007/978-3-030-41050-6_5

To achieve this new generation, tasks such as monitoring applications, environments, performance degradation and energy consumption are indispensable. We need to deepen our understanding of the factors that limit application performance and interfere with energy consumption, and map them to the architectures that represent the current state of the art in high-performance processing.

The most widely used paradigm for determining hardware performance and performance evaluation programs are benchmarks. However, with benchmarks usually only the theoretical peaks of performance are obtained, and it's little informative when determining the real performance of the hardware considering the requirements of applications. Benchmarks, for the most part, do not represent the model of scientific applications, both in terms of the computational requirements that characterize the application, as well as in the reality of the programming language or the size of problems that are executed in an actual research center. Thus, the performance analysis that is truly informative about the real applications is itself another challenge.

With this type of evaluation in mind, an systematic methodology was developed, focused on the requirements of scientific applications [14]. The methodology seeks to identify the objectives of the evaluation and the set of more relevant parameters to be evaluated according to the problem. The applications are cataloged according to computational requirements based on a classification named Motifs [27], used as a reference for the study of scientific applications. The assessments made on the basis of the requirements of the real applications and how they relate to other aspects that influence their performance [13] and energy consumption [14], aiding in discovering the relevant aspects in order to achieve the general improvement of performance and energy consumption. However, to monitor and evaluate a set of parameters, which may change with each evaluation and which may involve aspects of application, architecture, performance, scalability and energy consumption, and how these relate is not to a trivial task.

Another challenge is to define a precise way to collect all these parameters and correlate them for an effective analysis. We have investigated a set of monitoring tools and techniques, briefly described in Sect. 3. However, each one collects a specific set of parameters, which do not always meet the needs of the evaluation, thereby making the experimentation process costly and time-consuming, as it was necessary to combine a set of tools. These challenges motivated the development of a monitoring tool that allows this type of evaluation, with high accuracy and low resource overload. Therefore, this work proposes the SMCis, an application monitoring tool capable of collecting all these aspects efficiently and relate them graphically to an environment developed for analysis and visualization of experimental data.

For monitoring, SMCis uses direct measuring through internal hardware sensors, which is considered the most accurate source of information [11]. Furthermore, the tool uses sampling and the offline approach to collect this data. The motivation for this is presented in Sect. 4. As such, the main contributions of SMCis over other existing monitoring tools are: collecting different aspects of an application (performance and energy) with only one tool; collect and visualise a set of features that vary with each evaluation; monitor applications regardless of the programming language they were written without using the tracing technique, or source code instrumentation; collect, analysis and visualization in only one tool with the ease of using the results directly in Machine Learning (ML).

This paper is organized as follows: Sect. 2 presents a brief discussion of performance and energy analysis. In Sect. 3 we present some background and related works in tools for monitoring performance and energy (direct measuring) and also for predictive modeling (indirect). In Sect. 4 are presented the SMCis, developed to monitor performance and energy and some experiments that demonstrate its use. Finally, in Sect. 6 the conclusion is presented.

## 2  An Analysis of Performance and Energy

A number of collaborative initiatives between government, academy, and industry point to the main challenges and strategic possibilities for achieving exascale processing in HPC environments [1,4,5,20,24,29]. Amongst them, preparing simulations and algorithms that can in fact achieve processing levels for future architectures and energy efficiency. The next generation of supercomputers needs to be developed using approaches where the requirements of the scientific problem guide the computer's architecture and system software design. In addition, these requirements of the scientific problem should guide the orchestration of different energy saving techniques and mechanisms in order to improve the balance between energy savings and application performance. To do this, monitoring applications, environments, performance degradation and energy consumption are indispensable tasks. We need to deepen our understanding of the factors that limit application performance and interfere with energy consumption, and map them to the architectures that represent the current state-of-the-art in high-performance processing.

Evaluating all these aspects, imposes the challenge of defining a precise and effective way to collect and correlate all these parameters. In the methodology used in this work, the parameters to be evaluated can change with each evaluation, but with a focus on the applications, their computational requirements and how they relate to different architectures, problem sizes and energy consumption. After extensive research it was not possible to find a single tool capable of collecting all aspects related to the performance and energy efficiency of the applications and the system. In addition, most tools are focused on monitoring the system as a whole or for creating application profiles. These tools assess the impact that application is having on the environment, but do not provide the percentage of resource consumption for the entire execution of the application. In addition, tools focused on optimization, present an analysis of how each function of the code is consuming resources, but not on energy consumption. Thus, it was often necessary to combine various tools and yet there was the difficulty of obtaining an analysis on how the execution of the application consumes resources by component and power.

In addition, in order to achieve the proposed objectives, it is necessary that the testing methodology obtain precise and refined measurements. A fine granularity in the measurements is necessary to allow the identification of characteristics of an application and how different resources are being used, allowing to identify aspects for power reduction or performance optimization [37]. It is important that the tool used is independent of the implementation language and that it avoids code instrumentation. Scientific applications usually have a numeric core written in a language and frameworks, and communication libraries in another. Thus, the ability to be independent of the implementation language is essential [3]. The instrumentation can modify the behavior of the application, usually due to overload and, for some applications, the time needed to prepare the experiments is too long.

In order to collect energy counters, direct measuring through internal hardware sensors is also used. However, the necessary counters for power and performance profiling may not be available in some settings. As internal sensors are neither a standard feature across hardware nor have its access allowed in some environments (when superuser benefits are required), there is a need, especially in HPC, for indirect power and performance acquisition methods [11]. Indirect measurements cover modeling and simulation techniques for power and performance estimation and prediction. Thus, the Modeling module integrates and facilitates the use of Machine Learning (ML) tools and has been used for the development of predictive runtime and power consumption models. Also, these models are important for energy saving techniques (Dynamic and Frequency Voltage Scaling - DFVS, Throttling, power cap) and must integrate a framework for performance and energy optimization, under development.

The power and energy monitoring tools should also allow the consumption profile with fine granularity. A measurement with a sampling rate of 1 or 2 Hz (samples per second) may not be fast enough to capture small changes in energy consumption, which are important for understanding the behavior of the system and of the application. In addition to the monitoring, another desirable feature is to enable the energy output to be controlled while the application is running. Some researchers point out that in order to reach exascale processing, where the power consumption is a highly restricted resource, techniques based on energy auto adjustment will be needed. But for this, beyond measuring energy consumption with fine granularity, it is necessary to measure the energy consumed by different components and to be able to control it.

In the search for these characteristics to monitor and predict performance and energy consumption in heterogeneous distributed environments, such as HPC, several approaches and monitoring tools have been investigated, which are presented in Sect. 3. For each one, the advantages and limitations for scientific computing in the current and future settings are presented.

## 3   Related Works

There are many tools for monitoring performance and energy, many of which are designed to meet specific goals of research groups and therefore monitor different sets of parameters. In Sect. 3.1 we present some of the analyzed tools, pointing out the advantages and limitations observed. Given the wide scope of the area and the various works that propose its own tools, the related works are restricted to these tools. In addition, the Sect. 3.2 is focused on works that make use of hardware counters and ML to predict performance and power or energy consumption.

## 3.1 Monitoring Performance and Energy

Nagios [16] is an open source tool that uses an online approach to monitor servers, services, applications, and local or remote hosts. In addition, it provides several resources to ensure that systems, applications and services are functioning properly. Its main focus is not on analyzing the performance of a specific application, but on the impact that application is having on the environment by monitoring system performance. According to [25] there is a native plug-in (check_proc) to monitor a specific process in Linux. However, after the unsuccessful attempts to use it, we have developed a plugin for this purpose, with which it is possible to obtain the percentage that the process is using of the CPU, Memory and I/O, while it's being executed [19]. Intel VTune [31] also uses the online approach, provides an analysis of different parameters on the execution of the application.

Nagios and Intel VTune are tools that use the sampling technique for data collection. With Nagios it is difficult to obtain an equilibrium between the sample frequency and the accuracy of the data, since the minimum sampling interval offered by the tool is 10 samples per second, which offers low accuracy. VTune offers a set of modules for different types of analysis, such as Basic Hotspots (which identifies the time spent in a code region) and Memory Access (which obtains information on how the application consumes resources related to memory). For some modules, the tool uses sampling and event tracing simultaneously. However, tracing produces a high overhead for the analysis. Therefore, using the two techniques at the same time may not be the best alternative. With VTune, the sampling interval is very small (at least 1 sample/millisecond), which incurs in high overloads.

TAU [33] and Pablo [30] are tools that make use of both sampling and tracing approaches simultaneously. However, for large parallel applications, the generation of historical data on the execution of the application through tracing will be impractical. The greater the number of processors, the greater the generation of data and, consequently, the greater the complexity of the data generated and its presentation in the visualization tools.

As power and energy became dominant constraints, suppliers developed a variety of packages to measure and control power and energy consumption. These are focused on direct methods to access internal sensors and obtain consumption. Examples are the VTune and NVSMI tools [26]. In order to monitor power with VTune, a specific driver (powerdk) is required, which requires many dependencies and configurations, and after the many attempts to install and use it, success has not been achieved.

NVML [26] is an API developed to monitor and manage NVIDIA GPU device states such as GPU utilization rate, process execution, clock and clock state, temperature and speed, power consumption, and power management. NVSMI allows system administrators to query, with appropriate privileges, the statuses of GPU devices. Its functions are those provided by the NVML library. The sampling rate of the NVSMI on power collection is somewhat low, around 1 million samples per second, which may not be enough to notice changes in the power consumed by applications with a short execution time.

There are solutions that integrate software and hardware in the collection of energy consumption by components [21], such as PowerPack [15] and Power-Mon [7]. Hardware components include, for example, sensors, meters, and circuits, and software components include drivers for various meters and sensors. Although these tools have refined measurements, they use external hardware, which in HPC environments, is a costly task due to the large number of computational nodes, and the cost of acquiring these devices.

External meters, such as Watt's Up Pro [2] and Cray XC30 [21], despite providing power measurements directly, have some limitations. They have low granularity and collect the energy consumption of the entire system, which does not reveal how energy is being consumed by different components, such as the processor and memory.

The direct measurement by means of internal or external sensors is considered the most appropriate technique, since the data are collected more accurately [11]. With the internal sensors, it is not necessary to acquire any external hardware to perform the collection and it is still possible to obtain the consumption per component. However, not all hardware has built-in sensors, and when available, the ways of accessing them and the accuracy of collection may change with each architecture. To overcome this challenge indirect measurement approaches

**Table 1.** Summary of some available performance and power monitoring tools, its respective monitoring approaches and data collection techniques.

| Tool | Performance | Energy | Sampling | Tracing |
|------|-------------|--------|----------|---------|
| Nagios | ✓ | | ✓ | |
| PowerMon | | ✓ | ✓ | |
| Cray XC30 | | ✓ | ✓ | |
| Intel VTune | ✓ | ✓ | ✓ | ✓ |
| PowerPack | | ✓ | ✓ | |
| TAU | ✓ | ✓ | ✓ | ✓ |
| Watt's Up | | ✓ | ✓ | |
| NVSMI | | ✓ | ✓ | |
| Pablo | ✓ | | ✓ | ✓ |
| **SMCis** | ✓ | ✓ | ✓ | |

(modeling techniques) for power and performance estimation and prediction are used.

Table 1 presents the comparative analysis of all the tools mentioned in this section, having different monitoring approaches, data collection techniques and methods for performance and energy measurement.

## 3.2 Predicting Performance and Energy

Performance modeling has been extensively used to understand and predict the performance and energy consumption of scientific applications. A number of approaches for performance modeling rely on analytical modeling to predict the behaviour of an application, such as [6,18,34] and [36]. In other side, a large number of researchers explore the possibility of using ML techniques to obtain this kind of knowledge such as [9,23,34] and [22].

Martínez et al. [23] use ML models to predict and optimize applications based on data collected by performance counters. They propose a specific ML approach tailored for stencil computation using Support Vector Machines and collecting data from two established stencil kernels with help of PAPI and conclude that their performance can be predicted with high precision due to the use of the appropriate hardware counters.

Bhimani et al. [10] propose a tool using ML as its base to predict the overall required time to complete multi-stage scientific data processing applications and using the Linux kernel's *perf* to collect hardware counters, presenting the effectiveness of using perf as well as ML as their conclusion.

Wang et al. [35] focus on power consumption of accelerators such as GPUs. They propose a prediction model based on Support Vector Regression, which can estimate the average runtime power of a given GPU kernel using a set of profiling parameters under different GPU core and memory frequencies. The results show that they can find the optimal GPU frequency settings to save an average of 13.2% energy across those tested GPU kernels.

Ibeid et al. [17] propose a hybrid approach for performance modeling and prediction, which couples analytical and ML model. They validated the approach using a 7-point 3-D stencil code and a fast multipole method code applications. Their results show that the hybrid approach is effective in predicting the execution time.

## 4 The SMCis Tool

As mentioned, SMCis was developed[1] to circumvent the limitations found in other monitoring tools. This tool allows the collection of performance and energy parameters during the execution of the application in different architectures, with high sampling rates and low impact on the consumption of computational resources. In addition, it is easy to use and provides a graphical view of the

---

[1] The SMCis is available in https://github.com/ViniciusPrataKloh/SMCis.

different parameters simultaneously. Although these help overcome many of the challenges presented, when sensors and hardware counters are not available, performance models (for energy and runtime prediction) are required. This was the main motivation to integrate SMCis with Machine Learning, in order to allow performance modeling and make easier to study and develop predictive models for performance and energy.

## 4.1    Methodology to Performance Evaluation

Using the methodology for performance evaluation presented in Fig. 1, the objectives of the evaluation are defined, the parameters to be monitored, for which applications and in which architectures. For this monitoring, which was very costly combining different tools, SMCis was developed.

After monitoring, the tool saves the results in an output file that is used in the evaluation phase of the results. The results can be explored both for performance modeling, where this file is converted to the `.csv` format and could be used in the Weka or *scikit-learn* [28] ML tools, or directly in the SMCis visualization module. These parameters and the performance models to runtime and power consumption prediction will be used in the energy saving framework. The framework, under development, will enable the orchestration of techniques to reach the balance of performance and power consumption of parallel applications. It depends on application characteristics, architectural parameters, runtime node configuration and input data. Based on these initial information, the characterization of the application and architectures available for the job execution will be defined. This information and models would be used by the scheduler to predict the execution time and energy consumption in order to choose the best architecture for the job execution and also the feasibility to select the best frequency, using energy saving techniques.

The SMCis uses the sampling technique and the offline approach, since they were considered the most appropriate for the type of analysis performed. With sampling there is no need to insert instrumentation policies into the code. With the offline analysis of the data, the competition for system resources decreases, because the data resulting from the monitoring are only analyzed in a later stage of the execution of the application.

Taking into account that in HPC environments, external power meters do not provide the desired accuracy, while they are difficult to use, either by the need to acquire the measuring equipment or by the need of physical access, SMCis was developed to monitor energy through internal sensors, present in most architectures of HPC environments. In order to collect the information from these sensors, it is often necessary to use superuser privileges, which is the only limitation for collecting energy consumption with SMCis. As the internal sensors provide information on the system, in the experimental methodology (Fig. 2) an application launcher is used to enable the monitoring of the state of the sensors before and after the execution of the application. In this way, it is possible to calculate the static and dynamic power consumption and the temperature. Static power refers to the consumption of the system and the dynamic to the execution of the application. Figure 2 shows the flowchart of the monitoring modules that compose SMCis (detailed in Sect. 4.2).

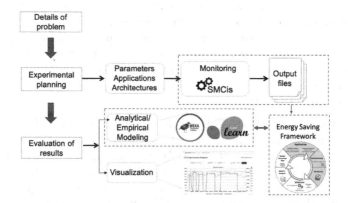

**Fig. 1.** Methodology for performance and power consumption evaluation and the SMCis in it.

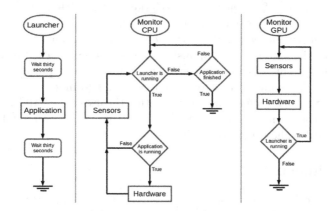

**Fig. 2.** Flowchart of monitoring modules of the SMCis.

## 4.2   SMCis Architecture

The SMCis consists of two monitoring modules, CPU and GPU, and a module for visualization and analysis of experimental data, named GraphCis.

**CPU Monitoring Module:** this module was developed in Python and uses the psutil library [32] to collect the hardware parameters (CPU utilization rate, memory allocated and read/write rate for disk and network). The psutil allows you to collect information on the use of system resources in respect of the application in execution. The module can be configured with adjustable sampling rates according to the need of the experiment, the highest accuracy being at the 10 Hz rate. This precision is given by the fact that the module computes the reading and written rates as the difference between two consecutive monitoring samples. Thus, the interval between the samples should be large enough to detect the read and write flow and small enough to obtain accuracy in the collected data. When the power collection method is activated, IPMItool is used for access to the internal sensors, in which case the sampling rate is limited to the IPMItool rate (1 to 3 Hz).

**GPU Monitoring Module:** This module is similar to NVSMI. However, its main characteristics are: (i) it has been programmed to collect a smaller set of parameters, on the utilization of the GPU cores and memory (total, free, used and time spent with operations of reading and writing in main memory), thus reducing the overhead on the consumption of system resources; (ii) be able to monitor applications with high accuracy, since it has an average sample rate of 500 samples per second. Since this module also collects energy through IPMItool, there is the same limitation of the CPU module in the sampling rate when the power method is activated.

**GraphCis:** This module was developed as a web server, giving users access to experimental data from generation of graphs. The technologies used in its implementation form a set of different frameworks, which are used for the server (Angularjs, jQuery and Node.js), for the generation of graphics templates (Canvas.js) and for the server to be responsive (Bootstrap). Since the Canvas.js templates interpret input data only in the JSON format, the output data generated by the monitoring modules must be serialized in this format.

Next, the Sect. 5 is focused on demonstrating the use of the SMCis monitoring tool and how the results could be analysed in the visualization module and also are being used for the predictive task with ML.

## 5  Experiments

In Sects. 5.1 and 5.2 are presented some experiments to demonstrate the results obtained in the monitoring and prediction tasks. We present the experiment using the monitoring modules in CPU and GPU and the data visualization module. The overhead measurement of collection modules is also presented, demonstrating that SMCis is able to perform monitoring with high sample rates and low overhead. In sequence, the experiments performed with the output files, using a ML tool to develop a runtime prediction model are presented.

All the experiments were performed in a machine with x5650 Intel (R) Xeon CPU with 2 processors (12 cores) at 2.66 GHz, 23 GB of main memory, 32 GB/s of memory band and cache of 12288 KB. Also in 2 Tesla M2050-T20 GPUs, with 1.15 GHz, 3 GB of memory and 448 cores.

The experimental setup for this work is comprised of applications from the NAS Parallel Benchmark suite: Block Tri-diagonal solver (BT), Lower-Upper

Gauss-Seidel solver (LU) and Scalar Penta-diagonal solver (SP) and the Rodinia Benchmark suite: Lower Upper Decomposition (LUD) [12].

## 5.1   Monitoring and Visualization

In this section, only the results with LUD application is used in the graphs. LUD is an algorithm that decomposes a matrix as the product of a triangular matrix and a superior one, making it possible to solve a linear equations system.

**CPU Execution:** Monitoring was started 30 s before the execution of the application and finished 30 s after the application. As mentioned, these intervals were adopted to allow the measurement of static and power consumption, since this information provided by IPMItool refers to the total consumption of the system. Through static consumption it is possible to calculate the dynamic consumption, which is influenced by the execution of the monitored application.

By performing a brief analysis of the monitoring result (Fig. 3, generated using the Graphics environment), it is possible to notice the three execution stages of the application: (i) the matrix is loaded to the main memory, in approximately 30 s and 110 s; (ii) the application executes the decomposition of the matrix using parallelism, between approximately 110 s and 201 s; (iii) the data used by the application to be cleared in the main memory from approximately 201 s. It was possible to analyze these steps by relating CPU and memory consumption (labels CPU and memory), as well as sensor information (power, temperature_cpu1 e temperature_cpu2). During the first stage, the application made little use of the processing cores, where there is little increase in the power consumption and increase in the temperature of only one of the CPUs (temperature_cpu1). However, when performing the decomposition of the matrix, we notice a significant increase in the utilization of the processing cores and power consumption, since all cores worked in this step.

**GPU Execution:** For the same reason as in the CPU experiment, GPU monitoring was started 30 s before the application started executing and ended 30 s after the execution of the application. By performing a brief analysis of the result (Fig. 4), it is possible to notice two distinct steps: (i) the matrix is loaded to the main memory of the CPU, between about 30 s and 110 s; (ii) the kernel that performs the decomposition of the array on the GPU and runs between approximately 110 s and 138 s. In the first step, the execution takes place in an algebraic way in the CPU execution, with idle state GPUs. After the data is loaded into the main memory of the CPU they are copied to the main memory of the GPU and the GPUs are now switched to ready state. These changes of state were observed through the variation of the gpu0_temp and gpu1_temp labels. Once the data has been copied, the kernel is executed only on GPU 0, since it is observed that the utilization of the cores of that GPU (core0_usage) has reached 100% and there has been a significant increase in power consumption.

These results for CPU and GPU experiments were analyzed in easy way by means of the GraphCis by just selecting, among the parameters monitored by SMCis, which one would figure out in the graph.

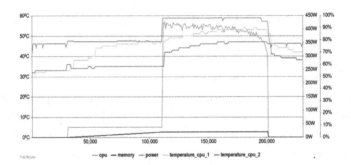

**Fig. 3.** CPU execution graph.

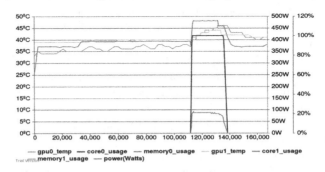

**Fig. 4.** GPU execution graph.

**Overhead:** To measure SMCis *overhead* on resource consumption, experiments were conducted monitoring the own collection module processes. The CPU monitoring module had a CPU consumption of 0.12% and a main memory usage of 0.05%. For the GPU monitoring module, the CPU and memory consumption were, respectively, 0.08% and 0.01%. This low memory consumption is due to the fact that the modules have been developed in a way that saves space in memory by balancing disk-writing operations. Also, the average CPU consumption of the subprocesses that call IPMItool, which had a 0.55% rate, was monitored.

## 5.2   Prediction

These experiments were performed with all the applications of NAS (SP, BT and LU) and LUD. A new set of parameters (performance counters) were collected: Instructions*, Cycles*, CPU Migrations, Branches*, Branch Misses*, Context Switches*, Cache References*, Cache Misses, L1 dcache Stores*, L1 dcache Loads*, L1 dcache LoadMisses, LLC Stores*, LLC Store Misses, LLC Loads, LLC Load Misses, Page Faults, Minor Faults, Runtime*. The parameters with (*) were the ones selected and used for the ML predictive task.

For the train and prediction phase, the output file in .csv are used by *scikit-learn*'s, with **Decision Tree Regressor** algorithm, with the objective to develop a runtime predictive model.

A tree with the max depth of 4 is created and fitted using the train subsets randomly split, which are comprised of 75% of all the original data. Then, a prediction is generated using the test subsets as its target. The training and test were done on a total of 1890 samples, which underwent a 4-fold Cross Validation. The total number of features used were 10, described with (*) in the list.

Initially, we did an experiment using all features available, without limiting the max depth of the tree. While the result, precision-wise, was good (Mean Square Error: 0.00024206418887226167), we should not look solely at precision when analysing the obtained results, but also consider how well the model is able to generalize the data and if overfitting happened. A tree with many leaves with low coverage show that the model was not able to properly generalize the data used for training, creating a large number of rules with very few samples each. It has little to no practical utility and that was the result for this initial experiment.

To improve the generalization capabilities, new experiments were executed using the selected features and limiting the max depth of the tree to 4.

In order to evaluate the accuracy and effectiveness of the DTR a number of test have been done to understand the degree of error in the predicted results. These test results are presented in Table 2.

**Table 2.** Mean Error

| | |
|---|---|
| **Mean Absolute Error** | 0.02255048219039073 |
| **Mean Squared Error** | 0.0011791189649137987 |
| **Root Mean Squared Error** | 0.03433830171854454 |
| **Coefficient of Determination (R2)** | 0.9752297764075215 |

The Mean Absolute Error is the measure of the average difference between continuous variables, while the Mean Squared Error measures the average squared difference between predicted values and what is being predicted and the Root Mean Square Error is the standard deviation of Prediction Errors.

As it can be seen, the model offers a good precision while predicting the results considering all of our data was scaled between 0 and 1. Also, according to the R2, it is apt to predict new values with success. That is, it could successfully predict the runtime for new job executions in an accurate way.

To confirm the validity of these results, we conducted a validation process by using the Decision Tree Regressor model generated during the training and test phase, that is, the runtime prediction model, on data never seen before by the model collected from 210 LUD, runs with the same features and architecture.

As it can be seen in Table 3, the three Error tests are far too high considering all of our data were scaled between 0 and 1 and coefficient of determination is negative, showing that the model is unable to predict new data with success. Some hypotheses were raised about the reason behind these results. The main one is the lack of a feature that represents the workload of each application

Table 3. Mean Error with LUD in validation experiment

| Mean Absolute Error | 0.27762203139153246 |
|---|---|
| Mean Squared Error | 0.15581366404557717 |
| Root Mean Squared Error | 0.3947323954853176 |
| Coefficient of Determination (R2) | −0.30343532487864144 |

in our experimental set, as this is a very relevant parameter that can be used to determine the runtime in a specific architecture. Besides that, a feature that contains architecture-specific information also needs to be added in order to give more significance to the data collected and then allow a better generalization process by the ML algorithm.

## 6    Final Considerations

In this article we present the SMCis, a system that allows the collection of the performance and energy parameters on the execution of an application, with portability for different architectures, high sampling rates and low impact on the consumption of computational resources, to be able to have easy use and to allow to graphically relate all the relevant parameters simultaneously. This environment, developed with a focus on efficiency and effectiveness, has been streamlining the entire process of monitoring the different experimental sets generated by the research. SMCis overcome some of the challenges about monitoring and evaluation by means of directly measuring via internal hardware sensors, which is considered the most accurate source of information. However, when those necessary counters for power and performance profiling may not be available in some settings, the challenge remains. So, there is a need, especially in HPC, for indirect power and performance acquisition methods. Thus, the Modeling module integrates and facilitates the use of ML tools and in future work these predictive runtime and power consumption models will be coupled with the monitoring environment enabling the use of energy saving techniques and the development of a framework for performance and energy optimization.

**Acknowledgments.** This work received financial support from the CNPQ, the EU Program H2020 and the MCTI/RNP-Brazil in the scope of project HPC4e, subsidy contract to No. 689772. Also from FAPERJ process number 26/202.500/2018 and CAPES.

## References

1. High Performance Computing for Energy (HPC4E), August 2017. https://hpc4e. eu
2. Wattsup? pro, September 2017. http://www.wattsupmeters.com
3. Adhianto, L., et al.: HPCTOOLKIT: tools for performance analysis of optimized parallel programs. Concurr. Comput. : Pract. Exper. **22**(6), 685–701 (2010). https://doi.org/10.1002/cpe.v22:6

4. Alvin, K., et al.: On the path to exascale. Int. J. Distrib. Syst. Technol. **1**(2), 1–22 (2010). https://doi.org/10.4018/jdst.2010040101
5. Ashby, S., et al.: The opportunities and challenges of exascale computing. Summary report of the advanced scientific computing advisory committee (ASCAC) subcommittee at the US Department of Energy Office of Science (2010)
6. Balladini, J., Morán, M., Rexachs del Rosario, D., et al.: Metodología para predecir el consumo energético de checkpoints en sistemas de hpc. In: XX Congreso Argentino de Ciencias de la Computación (Buenos Aires 2014) (2014)
7. Bedard, D., Fowler, R., Lim, M.Y., Porterfield, A.: PowerMon 2: fine-grained, integrated power measurement. Technical report TR-09-04, RENCI Technical Report (2009). http://renci.org/technical-reports/tr-09-04/
8. Bergman, K., et al.: Exascale computing study: technology challenges in achieving exascale systems. Defense Advanced Research Projects Agency Information Processing Techniques Office (DARPA IPTO), Technical report 15 (2008)
9. Berral, J.L., Gavalda, R., Torres, J.: Power-aware multi-data center management using machine learning. In: 2013 42nd International Conference on Parallel Processing, pp. 858–867. IEEE (2013)
10. Bhimani, J., Mi, N., Leeser, M., Yang, Z.: FIM: performance prediction for parallel computation in iterative data processing applications. In: 2017 IEEE 10th International Conference on Cloud Computing (CLOUD), pp. 359–366. IEEE (2017)
11. Bridges, R.A., Imam, N., Mintz, T.M.: Understanding GPU power: a survey of profiling, modeling and simulation methods. ACM Comput. Surv. **49**(3), 41:1–41:27 (2016). https://doi.org/10.1145/2962131
12. Che, S., et al.: Rodinia: a benchmark suite for heterogeneous computing. In: IEEE International Symposium on Workload Characterization, IISWC 2009, pp. 44–54. IEEE (2009)
13. Ferro, M., Nicolás, M.F., del Rosario, Q., Saji, G., Mury, A.R., Schulze, B.: Leveraging high performance computing for bioinformatics: a methodology that enables a reliable decision-making. In: 16th IEEE/ACM International Symposium on Cluster, Cloud and Grid Computing, CCGrid 2016, Cartagena, Colômbia, 16–19 May 2016, pp. 684–692. IEEE Computer Society (2016). https://doi.org/10.1109/CCGrid.2016.69
14. Ferro, M., Silva, G.D., Klôh, V.P., Schulze, B.: Challenges in HPC Evaluation: Towards a Methodology for Scientific Applications' Requirements. IOS Press, Amsterdam (2017, accepted to publish)
15. Ge, R., Li, D., Chang, H.C., Cameron, K.W., Feng, X., Song, S.: PowerPack: energy profiling and analysis of high-performance systems and applications. IEEE Trans. Parallel Distrib. Syst. **21**, 658–671 (2009). https://doi.org/doi.ieeecomputersociety.org/10.1109/TPDS.2009.76
16. Guthrie, M.: Instant Nagios Starter. Packt Publishing (2013)
17. Ibeid, H., Meng, S., Dobon, O., Olson, L., Gropp, W.: Learning with analytical models. In: 2019 IEEE International Parallel and Distributed Processing Symposium, IPDPS 2019, pp. 778–786. IEEE Computer Society (2019)
18. Jaiantilal, A., Jiang, Y., Mishra, S.: Modeling CPU energy consumption for energy efficient scheduling. In: Proceedings of the 1st Workshop on Green Computing, pp. 10–15. ACM (2010)
19. Klôh, V.P., Ferro, M., Silva, G.D., Schulze, B.: Performance monitoring using nagios core. Relatórios de Pesquisa e Desenvolvimento do LNCC 03/2016, Laboratório Nacional de Computação Científica, Petropolis - RJ (2016). www.lncc.br

20. Kogge, P., et al.: Exascale computing study: technology challenges in achieving exascale systems. Technical report, DARPA IPTO, Air Force Research Labs, September 2008
21. Labasan, S.: Energy-efficient and power-constrained techniques for exascale computing (2016). Oral Comprehensive Exam. http://www.cs.uoregon.edu/Reports/ORAL-201610-Labasan.pdf. Accessed 18 May 2017
22. Ll Berral, J., Gavaldà, R., Torres, J.: Empowering automatic data-center management with machine learning. In: Proceedings of the 28th Annual ACM Symposium on Applied Computing, pp. 170–172. ACM (2013)
23. Martínez, V., Dupros, F., Castro, M., Navaux, P.: Performance improvement of stencil computations for multi-core architectures based on machine learning. Procedia Comput. Sci. **108**, 305–314 (2017)
24. Messina, P.: The exascale computing project. Comput. Sci. Eng. **19**(3), 63–67 (2017). https://doi.org/10.1109/MCSE.2017.57
25. Nagios Team: Nagios Core Documentation (2016). https://assets.nagios.com/downloads/nagioscore/docs/nagioscore/4/en/
26. NVIDIA: NVML API Reference Manual (2012). http://developer.download.nvidia.com/assets/cuda/files/CUDADownloads/NVML/nvml.pdf
27. Patterson, D.: Orgins and Vision of the UC Berkeley Parallel Computing Laboratory, chap. 1, 1 edn, pp. 11–42. Microsoft Corporation (2013). http://books.google.com.br/books?id=2mJxngEACAAJ
28. Pedregosa, F., et al.: Scikit-learn: machine learning in Python. J. Mach. Learn. Res. **12**, 2825–2830 (2011)
29. Rajovic, N., Carpenter, P.M., Gelado, I., Puzovic, N., Ramirez, A., Valero, M.: Supercomputing with commodity CPUs: are mobile SoCs ready for HPC? In: Proceedings of the International Conference on High Performance Computing, Networking, Storage and Analysis, SC 2013, pp. 40:1–40:12. ACM, New York (2013). https://doi.org/10.1145/2503210.2503281
30. Reed, D.A., Aydt, R.A., Madhyastha, T.M., Noe, R.J., Shields, K.A., Schwartz, B.W.: An overview of the Pablo performance analysis environment. Department of Computer Science, University of Illinois 1304 (1992)
31. Reinders, J.: VTune performance analyzer essentials (2005). http://nacad.ufrj.br/online/intel/vtune/Essentials_Excerpts.pdf
32. Rodola, G.: psutil documentation (2018). https://media.readthedocs.org/pdf/psutil/latest/psutil.pdf
33. Shende, S.S., Malony, A.D.: The TAU parallel performance system. Int. J. High Perform. Comput. Appl. **20**(2), 287–311 (2006). https://doi.org/10.1177/1094342006064482
34. Siegmund, N., Grebhahn, A., Apel, S., Kästner, C.: Performance-influence models for highly configurable systems. In: Proceedings of the 2015 10th Joint Meeting on Foundations of Software Engineering, pp. 284–294. ACM (2015)
35. Wang, Q., Chu, X.: GPGPU power estimation with core and memory frequency scaling. SIGMETRICS Perform. Eval. Rev. **45**(2), 73–78 (2017). https://doi.org/10.1145/3152042.3152066
36. Wu, X., Taylor, V., Cook, J., Mucci, P.J.: Using performance-power modeling to improve energy efficiency of hpc applications. Computer **49**(10), 20–29 (2016)
37. Zomaya, A.Y., Lee, Y.C.: Energy Efficient Distributed Computing Systems, 1st edn. Wiley-IEEE Computer Society Press (2012)

# Video7 Extended Architecture: Project Design and Statistical Analysis

Vanderson S. de O. L. Sampaio[1]([envelope]) [iD], Douglas D. J. de Macedo[1] [iD],
and André Britto[2] [iD]

[1] Federal University of Santa Catarina (UFSC), Florianópolis, SC, Brazil
`vandersons.sampaio@gmail.com`, `douglas.macedo@ufsc.br`
[2] Federal University of Sergipe (UFS), São Cristóvão, SE, Brazil
`andre@dcomp.ufs.br`

**Abstract.** The increasing number of both digital audio and video, brings up the necessity of appropriate tools for the storage and management of those kind of data. As options for the storage, there are non-relational databases (NoSQL). The diversity of existing systems provokes the interest in proposing an architecture for the management of that content, in different types of databases. This work deepens the Video7 architecture for storing and retrieving streaming audio and video files stored in non-relational key-value, tabular, document databases. Based on the architecture and suggested project design, a tool was implemented that makes use of the Apache HBase, Apache Cassandra, Project Voldemort, Redis and MongoDB databases, and is subjected to stressful routines. The purpose of stress routines is to measure insertion and queries times, in addition to their transfer rates in response to requests to a media server. The kruskal-wallis test was used to validated the measurements. Redis database presents better performance in the submitted routines, while Project Voldemort and Apache Cassandra perform poorly than other databases.

**Keywords:** Non-relational database · Performance analysis · Streaming stored media · High performance I/O file systems

## 1 Introduction

At all times, new digital data are generated in Web. This data has several types (e.g., numeric, textual, image) and formats (e.g., MP3, HTML, PDF). Multimedia data (i.e., images, videos, audios) represent a significant part of this scenario. Many platforms collaborate to grow up this data, for instance, YouTube[1] and Vimeo[2] allow users to store, play and share videos [3]. Proliferation of multimedia content requires better methods for data management [2]. Some resources are

---

[1] http://www.youtube.com.
[2] http://www.vimeo.com.

© Springer Nature Switzerland AG 2020
C. Bianchini et al. (Eds.): WSCAD 2018, CCIS 1171, pp. 85–101, 2020.
https://doi.org/10.1007/978-3-030-41050-6_6

required to manage this data, such as: distributed file systems [4]; Non-relational database (NoSQL) [8]; hybrid approach [5].

A conventional approach to storage audio and video is to use file servers [11]. File servers transfer the responsibility of the data storage to the operational system. This way, data management, such as security policies, occurs in the directories or in the files themselves, which is not very positive, depending on the application. The availability of data access is a risk factor. Possible file server failures can generate application failures. Finally, using file servers can be costly, especially due to the lack of tools for direct interoperability with applications (e.g. Web applications).

Databases are an alternative option to store and manage multimedia data. However, there are many models (e.g., SQL, NoSQL, NewSQL) and tools (e.g., PostgreSQL, Redis, MariaDB) of databases that make it difficult to propose a solution. Related works, like [1,9], compare storage performance, query and update of multimedia data in relational (SQL) and non-relational (NoSQL) databases models. These are just two of several studies that approach this problem.

This paper presents Video7 architecture for helping the selection of NoSQL models and databases. The architecture has flexibility for both data types and database models that it wants to use. Finally, it is possible to make comparisons of performance metrics across databases. To validate the architecture, insertion and recovery experiments with the different models of NoSQL databases are performed. The insertion and recovery time metric is used to perform the comparison of the databases (lower time, better performance). For the recovery is also calculated the operation throughput (higher throughput, better performance).

This paper extends our work [10] and our main contributions are: (i) storage architecture of audio and video in varied databases; (ii) experimental analysis of database performance in data insertion and recover process; (iii) comparison of different types of databases for stored audio and video data. In addition to the benefits of managing multimedia data, eventually extensions of standard architecture may allow the extraction of data features.

The remainder of this work is organized as follows. Section 2 discusses related work. Section 3 describes the proposed architecture. The experiments are reported in Sect. 4, and their results presented and discussed in Sect. 5. Finally, Sect. 6 presents conclusions and future work.

## 2   Related Work

In the search for related works, no specific architecture proposal was identified for storing videos in non-relational databases, in this way, there are presented works that own similar approaches.

Li et al. [7] presented the video management analytic system, titled HydVideo. HydVideo uses an expansion pack applied to the relational database. The use of this package allows more efficient analyzes even with the rigidity of the relational model. An alternative to imposed rigidity in the relational data model are NoSQL databases.

Works like in [1,9] make comparisons between relational and NoSQL data models. Rebecca and Shanthi [9] made comparisons between MySQL and MongoDB databases in medical imaging storage. The research concludes that MongoDB database has better insertion and query performances. In [1], image and video data are experienced in the YCSB[3] tool for the MySQL, Redis, Apache Cassandra and MongoDB databases. However, the YCSB tool needed adaptations as it was not designed to process these types of data. It is concluded with these experiments that NoSQL databases have better time measures compared to SQL databases.

Works related identified that approach multimedia audio and video data appear not to worry about managing data storage. The analyzes identified are limited to comparing data insertion and recover times. The analyzes are, often carried out, using tools that do not have such purpose or by techniques that are not sophisticated.

## 3  Proposed Architecture

This section presents the `Video7` architecture. Video7 architecture focuses on Web applications and has a capability to extend the types of files used (e.g., mp4, avi, mjpg) and supported database models. The main goal is to provide a flexible and extensible architecture that enables new multimedia data formats and new databases, which are not yet integrated. The architecture is complementary to the YCSB tool, supporting unstructured audio and video data and simulating busy environments.

The data flow is shown in Fig. 1. The architecture separates new requests according to the user's request. Requests can be of type `Write` or `Read`. Writing requests carry the file for storage, the metadata of this file (e.g., video resolution, audio quality), and the target database to persist the data. This information is sent to the `Selector` that destines the audio/video data and metadata to the server where the database is located. The read/write operation of the file in the database occurs on this server.

The read requests require a `Media Server`. The media server is responsible for controlling the video upload flow to the application. The server communicates with the `Selector` when it needs data from the file. Read requests are composed by the video's resolution to be retrieved and the database to be queried.

Figure 2 shows the proposed architecture. The architecture can be divided into seven layers: `User Types, File Types, Application, Libraries, Multimedia Files, Data Distribution` and `Storage`. User Types layer is an interface where a user can store data of a new video or retrieve of an existing video in some database, through administrator or public access, respectively. `File Types` layer performs the encoding/decoding of the file to be stored/played. The `File Types` layer also allows the inclusion of files with different formats and types, in addition to what has already been presented.

---

[3] https://github.com/brianfrankcooper/YCSB/wiki.

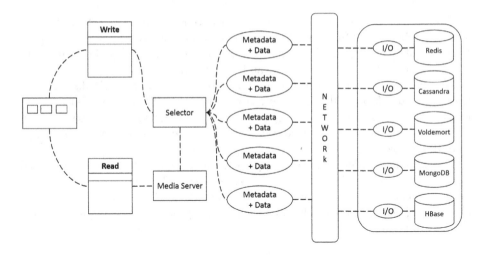

**Fig. 1.** Architecture data flow

The `Application` layer differentiates the desired operation. Requests from the admin interface are processed in the `Write` class, and public interface requests are processed in the `Read` class. The `Libraries` layer provides an API (Application Programming Interface) that allows communication with the database selector or the media server. Read requests are intended for the media server that communicates with the selector. Write requests communicate directly with the selector.

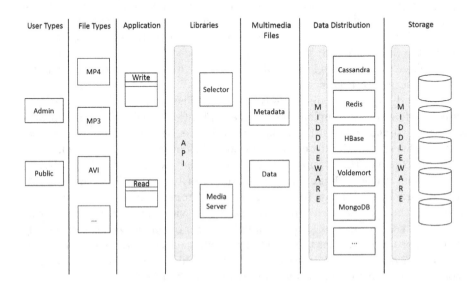

**Fig. 2.** Components of Video7 architecture

The `Multimedia Files` layer contains metadata and data with information such as video resolution, time duration, situation (e.g., started, stopped). Access to this layer occurs through the selector class of the `Libraries` layer, where the selector is responsible for defining whether the data will be stored or queried.

The `Data Distribution` layer adjusts the data according to the model of each database. This layer solves the particularities of each database and information regarding the configurations of the server that contains them. Finally, the `Storage` layer persists, or queries, the data in the database, previously selected. The existence of the `Data Distribution` and `Storage` layers makes the architecture flexible, with expansion of the database models and databases used.

## 3.1 Class Diagram

The media server project class diagram (Fig. 3) consists of nine classes and one interface. Five of these classes are used for data access (pattern Data Access Object - DAO) and two other classes to create video request packets. DAO classes are intended for the databases selected in the experiment (Redis, Apache Cassandra, Apache HBase, Project Voldemort and MongoDB). The classes for creating the video request packets are responsible for the video rendering process for the communication protocols.

The project class diagram also contains the following classes: Server, responsible for listening and answering the requests to the media server, besides defining the type of protocol used in the transport layer, UDP or TCP; RTCPpacket class, whose responsibility is to create the RTCP protocol packets; RTPpacket class, for

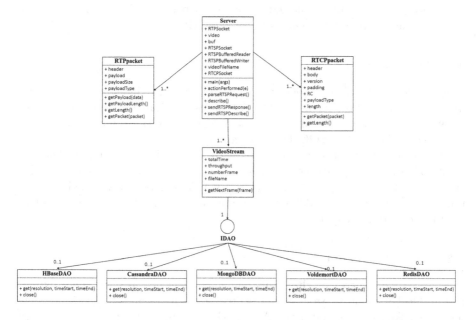

**Fig. 3.** Media server class diagram

the purpose of creating the RTP protocol packets; and the VideoStream class, responsible for communicating with data sources to obtain the desired video stream, as well as identifying and sending the frame expected by the client.

IDAO interface is responsible for generalizing the data access classes. The Interface defines which methods those classes should have. In this way it is possible to add new DAO classes without making any changes in the business classes of the tool. Finally, there are the five data access classes. Each class implements the IDAO interface and is responsible for communicating with a specific data source.

## 4    Experiments

This section describes the experiments applied to validate the proposed architecture. Section 4.1 states the objectives of the experiments. Section 4.2 depicts the test scenarios discussed. Section 4.3 details the experiment settings. Finally, Sect. 3.1 presents a suggestion of classes and design patterns to implement the solution.

### 4.1    Objectives

The experiments aim to measure the performance of NoSQL databases in the storage of audio and video files. The Video7 architecture compares the key-value, tabular, and document categories of NoSQL databases. Databases are submitted to insertion and recovery stress routines. The use of other models databases and distributed storage is not exploited in this paper because of space limitations of the article and will be investigated in future work.

### 4.2    Test Scenario

The experiments evaluate video insertion and recovery times and file transfer rates in the user's browser in NoSQL databases. Preliminary experiments have shown that after recovering an average of 20% of the multimedia file, the transfer rate is constant. Five NoSQL databases are used.

The paper explores three test scenarios, they are: solo, low and high. The solo scenario is a non-compete scenario. The low and high scenarios simulate crowded environments of up to ten and twenty concurrent accesses, respectively. Simultaneous access values were defined according to the computational environment used to perform the experiments.

### 4.3    Experiments Setup

Five NoSQL databases of three different categories are used in these experiments. The key-value category is represented by the Redis and Project Voldemort databases. Apache Cassandra and Apache HBase represent the tabular category of NoSQL database. Finally, MongoDB represents the category of document-oriented databases. These databases are popular and have extensive documentation.

The video file used in the evaluations has different resolution qualities and physical sizes. The resolutions used were: 240$p$, 360$p$, 480$p$, 720$p$, 1080$p$ and 4$k$, and the physical sizes of the files were, in *megabytes*, 13,7, 19,4, 38,4, 65,3, 112 and 671, respectively. The measurements are repeated 25 times for each scenario, database and video resolution. At the end of the repetitions the means and standard deviations of the performance measures are calculated.

The Video7 architecture was coded in the Java programming language in its version 8. The tests were performed in a public Digital Ocean cloud environment. During the process a virtual machine was used with the following configurations: Architecture x86; Intel(R) Xeon(R) Processor CPU E5-2630L 2 GHz with 4 cores; Memory RAM with 8 GB capacity; Secondary memory SSD with 20 GB capacity; Operating System Ubuntu 16.04 x64. The virtual machine has Apache Tomcat 7, a media server, and the databases described in this section.

## 5    Results and Discussion

This section has been divided into three subsections. Section 5.1 presents the results for the insert operation. Section 5.2 discusses the times and transfer rates calculated in the recovery operation. Section 5.3 presents a discussion of the results obtained. The times and throughput are calculated in milliseconds and megabytes per second, respectively.

### 5.1    Insertion

Some databases have restrictions for storing data. Redis database does not allow storing data larger than 512 MB[4] (five hundred and twelve megabytes). To reverse the limitation of the Redis database it was necessary to create a list containing two positions to insert the videos in 4k resolution. MongoDB database also limits the maximum size of stored files to 16 MB (sixteen megabytes). Finally, Project Voldemort presents limitations on simultaneous insertions, forcing the process to be atomic. Therefore, Project Voldemort database does not display values for the Low and High scenarios.

The Kruskal-Wallis statistical test [6] was used to verify the existence of a significant difference between the measured times. The statistical significance was 5%. The result of the statistical test for the insertion times are displayed in Fig. 4. The figure presents the values separated by scenarios and resolutions. In the figure, the colors of the boxes represent the significance: red, there is no significance. gray, 5% significance; light green, 1% significance; and green, significance of 0.1%. Due to the formatting of the article the names of the databases have been replaced by acronyms, in this way: DB1 is Redis, DB2 is Apache Cassandra, DB3 is Apache HBase, DB4 is Project Voldemort and DB5 is MongoDB.

---

[4] https://redis.io/topics/data-types.

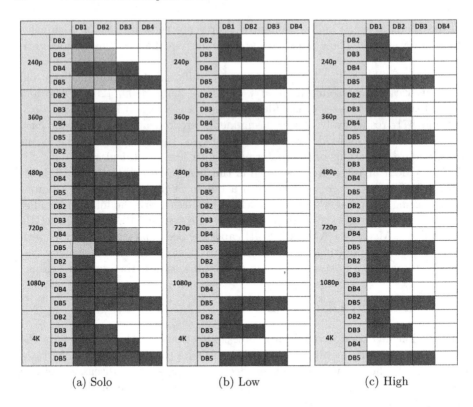

(a) Solo          (b) Low          (c) High

**Fig. 4.** Kruskal-Wallis statistical test - insertion time (Color figure online)

The solo scenario (Fig. 4a) presented a significant difference in 69% of the measurements of the times. The low scenario (Fig. 4b) presented a significant difference in all the measurements. Finally, for the high scenario (Fig. 4c) there is no significant difference in only one case, resolution of 240p and DB3 (HBase) and DB5 (MongoDB).

Table 1 exposes the mean and standard deviation of the times required to complete the insertion in each scenario by resolution and database. For the solo scenario, out of competition, the Redis database presented the best times over Project Voldemort. When performing an analysis according to the category of each database tested, we see a highlight for the Redis database in the key-value category. In the Tabular category, we have the HBase database with better times compared to Cassandra. And as the only representative of the documents category, MongoDB, with the second best times among all the databases tested.

For the low and high scenarios the experiments presented the same order of classification of the databases. The Redis was the best database, and Cassandra had the worst of times. When performing a category analysis of the tested databases, we have Redis as the only representative of the key-value category, since Project Voldemort did not record any time due to its limitation. The

**Table 1.** Measurements - insertion time (seconds)

| Resolutions | | Cassandra | HBase | MongoDB | Redis | Voldemort |
|---|---|---|---|---|---|---|
| Solo | 240p | .84 ± .19 | .19 ± .08 | .17 ± .07 | .02 ± .04 | 1.67 ± .10 |
| | 360p | 1.39 ± .14 | .28 ± .13 | .13 ± .04 | .05 ± .15 | 2.11 ± .12 |
| | 480p | 3.61 ± .50 | .55 ± .23 | .27 ± .10 | .05 ± .09 | 4.25 ± .15 |
| | 720p | 7.74 ± .65 | .76 ± .21 | .54 ± .32 | .08 ± .01 | 6.90 ± .24 |
| | 1080p | 11.32 ± .66 | 1.56 ± .29 | .92 ± .28 | .15 ± .05 | 13.25 ± .22 |
| | 4k | 17.56 ± .42 | 11.67 ± 1.88 | 8.44 ± 1.14 | 1.55 ± .35 | 73.70 ± 2.38 |
| Low | 240p | 3.86 ± 1.97 | 1.75 ± .53 | .61 ± .24 | .13 ± .08 | – |
| | 360p | 3.38 ± 1.29 | 2.26 ± .53 | 1.10 ± .49 | .40 ± .14 | – |
| | 480p | 9.07 ± 1.11 | 6.01 ± 1.31 | 3.04 ± .80 | .77 ± .13 | – |
| | 720p | 12.28 ± .81 | 8.14 ± .61 | 4.74 ± 1.06 | 1.82 ± .28 | – |
| | 1080p | 19.59 ± 1.03 | 14.58 ± .89 | 7.64 ± 1.38 | 3.07 ± .37 | – |
| | 4k | 70.19 ± 1.10 | 30.90 ± 1.15 | 19.03 ± 1.19 | 13.85 ± 1.48 | – |
| High | 240p | 5.77 ± 1.26 | 2.26 ± .84 | 2.07 ± .83 | .43 ± .13 | – |
| | 360p | 8.51 ± 1.63 | 3.93 ± .96 | 2.90 ± .96 | .72 ± .18 | – |
| | 480p | 19.13 ± 1.63 | 6.71 ± 1.56 | 5.53 ± 1.36 | 1.69 ± .29 | – |
| | 720p | 27.42 ± 1.71 | 10.81 ± 1.55 | 9.58 ± 1.58 | 3.44 ± .38 | – |
| | 1080p | 39.95 ± 2.29 | 20.11 ± 2.83 | 16.45 ± 3.19 | 12.06 ± .58 | – |
| | 4k | 93.49 ± 2.82 | 42.04 ± 2.13 | 33.44 ± 3.89 | 19.54 ± .88 | – |

MongoDB database was the only representative of the documents category and recorded the second best times among all the databases tested. Finally, for the tabular category, the HBase presented times inferior to the Cassandra.

The graph of Fig. 5a shows the values of insertion times in the solo scenario. The value measured with Project Voldemort database at 4K resolution is not displayed because the high value made the chart unreadable. The figure shows the growth of database times by changing the resolution of the video. Redis has achieved close to zero times in all video resolutions, except for the 4k resolution. It is possible to identify a linear growth in the HBase and MongoDB databases, with the exception of the video resolution of 4k. Finally, Cassandra and Project

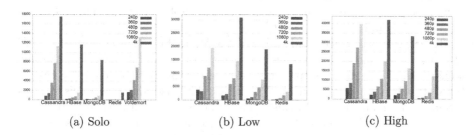

(a) Solo      (b) Low      (c) High

**Fig. 5.** Scenario insertion times (milliseconds)

Voldemort presented the greatest times of the scenario, with a great increase compared to the other databases tested.

The graphs of Figs. 5b and c present the values of the insertion times in the low and high scenarios, respectively. The measured values with the Cassandra database in the 4k resolution are not displayed due to high values rendering the graphs unreadable. The Redis database obtained the shortest times in both scenarios. Note, in Fig. 5b, a linear growth in the Redis and MongoDB databases (except resolution in 4$k$) and decrease in average times between resolutions of 240$p$ and 360$p$ in the database data Cassandra.

Figure 5c shows linear growth between video resolutions at 240$p$ at 720$p$ and new linear growth between resolutions at 720$p$ at 4$k$. The HBase and MongoDB databases showed values close to each other during all video resolutions. Finally, the Cassandra database presented the highest measured times in the scenario, always with a great increase in relation to the other databases.

## 5.2 Recovery

Video recovery metrics are calculated on the media server. The query time is calculated by summing the times of the read requests from the video to the database, until the video is completely downloaded. The throughput is calculated through the ratio of 20% of the physical size of the video to the time it takes to load it.

**Recovery Time.** The Kruskal-Wallis statistical test was used to verify the existence of a significant difference between the measured times. The statistical significance was 5%. The result of the statistical test for the insertion times are displayed in Fig. 4. The figure presents the values separated by scenarios and resolutions. Due to the formatting of the article the names of the databases have been replaced by acronyms, in this way: DB1 is Redis, DB2 is Apache Cassandra, DB3 is Apache HBase, DB4 is Project Voldemort and DB5 is MongoDB.

The solo scenario (Fig. 6a) showed a significant difference in 69% of the time measurements. The low scenario (Fig. 6b) showed a significant difference in 97% of the measurements, only the DB3 (HBase) and DB5 (MongoDB) databases in 480p and 720p resolutions were absent. Already for the high scenario (Fig. 6c) there is no significant difference only in one case, resolution of 480p and databases DB3 (HBase) and DB5 (MongoDB).

Table 2 shows the mean and standard deviation of the times required to complete the video query in each scenario by resolution and database. For the solo scenario the Redis database presented the best recovery times for video resolutions at 240$p$, 360$p$, 480$p$ and 4$k$. The HBase database overcome Redis in resolutions at 720$p$ and 1080$p$. In this same scenario, Cassandra needed more time to perform the video recovery in the resolution at 240$p$. For other resolutions, Project Voldemort database registered the highest times.

The Redis database obtained the lowest recovery times for the low and high scenarios, independent of the resolution. In both scenarios, the Cassandra and

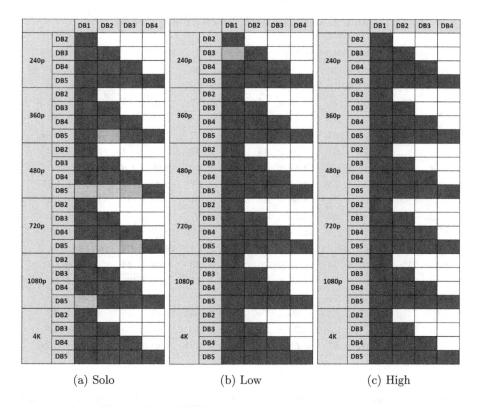

(a) Solo  (b) Low  (c) High

**Fig. 6.** Kruskal-Wallis statistical test - recovery time

Project Voldemort databases recorded the highest times. Cassandra overcome Project Voldemort times in the 240$p$, 360$p$, 480$p$, and 720$p$ resolutions for the low scenario and resolutions and 240$p$ and 360$p$ for the high scenario.

When we analyze the categories of the tested databases, the values do not change. The Redis database prevails in the key-value category. In the tabular category, the HBase database records the best times compared to Cassandra.

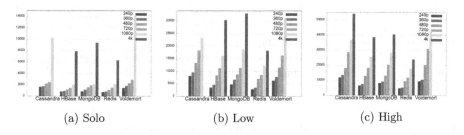

(a) Solo  (b) Low  (c) High

**Fig. 7.** Scenario recovery times (milliseconds)

**Table 2.** Measurements - recovery time (seconds)

| Resolutions | | Cassandra | HBase | MongoDB | Redis | Voldemort |
|---|---|---|---|---|---|---|
| Solo | 240p | 1.63 ± .26 | .80 ± .11 | .83 ± .09 | .70 ± .07 | 1.42 ± .17 |
| | 360p | 1.74 ± .18 | .91 ± .11 | 1.14 ± .18 | .80 ± .05 | 1.81 ± .16 |
| | 480p | 2.20 ± .15 | 1.18 ± .14 | 1.57 ± .22 | 1.10 ± .13 | 2.27 ± .25 |
| | 720p | 2.52 ± .34 | 1.47 ± .12 | 1.91 ± .16 | 1.49 ± .20 | 2.91 ± .16 |
| | 1080p | 10.32 ± .83 | 2.03 ± .20 | 2.12 ± .22 | 2.12 ± .45 | 14.25 ± 1.40 |
| | 4k | 18.24 ± .51 | 7.91 ± .33 | 9.39 ± .47 | 6.32 ± .38 | 22.04 ± .39 |
| Low | 240p | 8.13 ± 1.35 | 3.47 ± .88 | 4.74 ± .60 | 2.80 ± 1.07 | 6.24 ± 1.54 |
| | 360p | 9.56 ± .73 | 4.57 ± 1.05 | 6.63 ± 1.44 | 3.42 ± .46 | 7.74 ± 1.05 |
| | 480p | 13.33 ± .79 | 8.36 ± .82 | 8.79 ± .91 | 7.00 ± .54 | 11.55 ± 1.08 |
| | 720p | 18.32 ± .89 | 11.32 ± 1.12 | 11.36 ± .97 | 8.63 ± .70 | 16.34 ± .95 |
| | 1080p | 23.29 ± 1.65 | 16.14 ± 1.18 | 18.71 ± 1.25 | 12.35 ± 1.37 | 31.03 ± .98 |
| | 4k | 49.52 ± 1.03 | 30.39 ± 1.32 | 32.99 ± 1.11 | 18.22 ± .67 | 69.88 ± .81 |
| High | 240p | 11.91 ± .73 | 6.37 ± .70 | 8.07 ± .70 | 4.59 ± .44 | 9.28 ± .67 |
| | 360p | 13.52 ± .75 | 7.41 ± .73 | 9.12 ± .72 | 5.06 ± .66 | 10.32 ± .69 |
| | 480p | 18.19 ± .74 | 12.84 ± 1.20 | 13.13 ± .80 | 9.23 ± .58 | 20.29 ± .68 |
| | 720p | 28.71 ± .64 | 18.30 ± .78 | 20.39 ± .94 | 11.83 ± .68 | 30.95 ± .72 |
| | 1080p | 36.92 ± 1.01 | 25.70 ± .58 | 28.39 ± .90 | 17.86 ± .70 | 42.677 ± .54 |
| | 4k | 54.04 ± .87 | 38.63 ± .85 | 40.48 ± 1.21 | 23.83 ± .73 | 71.61 ± 1.59 |

MongoDB, the only representative of the documents category, presents the third best times among all the databases tested.

Figure 7 displays recovery time graphs for all scenarios. The measured values for the Cassandra and Project Voldemort databases in the $4k$ resolution are not displayed because of the high values rendering the graphs unreadable. Figure 7a shows the values for the solo scenario. In the image, we notice the growth of recovery times in the databases by changing the resolution of the video. There is great proximity to measured values between the Apache HBase, MongoDB and Redis databases, with a greater distortion in video resolution at $4k$. The Cassandra and Project Voldemort databases also have a close proximity to measured values up to video resolution at $720p$.

The graphs of the Fig. 7b and c present the values for the low and high scenarios, respectively. In the images, we notice the increase in query times by improving the resolutions of the videos. The graph of Fig. 7c presents well-distributed values for each video resolution. Overall, all databases showed linear growth at some point in the measurement in the scenario, for example, Project Voldemort database between video resolutions at $360p$ and $1080p$.

**Throughput.** The Kruskal-Wallis statistical test was used to verify the existence of a significant difference between the measured times. The statistical significance was 5%. The result of the statistical test for the insertion times are displayed in Fig. 8. The figure presents the values separated by scenarios and

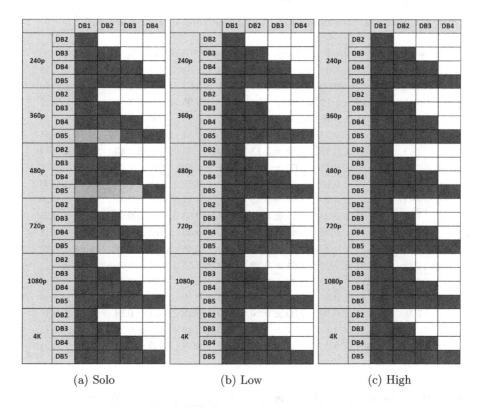

(a) Solo                    (b) Low                    (c) High

**Fig. 8.** Kruskal-Wallis statistical test - throughput

resolutions. Due to the formatting of the article the names of the databases have been replaced by acronyms, in this way: DB1 is Redis, DB2 is Apache Cassandra, DB3 is Apache HBase, DB4 is Project Voldemort and DB5 is MongoDB.

The solo scenario (Fig. 8a) showed a significant difference in 70% of the time measurements. The low scenario (Fig. 8b) showed a significant difference in 95% of the measurements, only the DB3 (HBase) and DB5 (MongoDB) databases in 360p, 480p and 720p resolutions were absent. Already for the high scenario (Fig. 8b) there is no significant difference only in one case, resolution of 480p and databases DB3 (HBase) and DB5 (MongoDB).

Table 3 depicts the mean and standard deviation of the throughput encountered during queries in each scenario by resolution and database. The higher the throughput, the better the database performance. The Redis database presented better throughput, for all resolutions, in the solo scenario. Project Voldemort database presented the worst throughput values.

The Redis database presents the best throughput for the low and high scenarios, regardless of the video resolution. In both scenarios, Project Voldemort and Cassandra databases recorded the worst throughput values. Project Voldemort recorded the worst values compared to Cassandra in video resolutions at

**Table 3.** Measurements - throughput (megabytes per second)

| Resolutions | | Cassandra | HBase | MongoDB | Redis | Voldemort |
|---|---|---|---|---|---|---|
| Solo | 240p | 7.27 ± 1.08 | 14.87 ± 2.35 | 14.23 ± 1.62 | 15.32 ± 2.45 | 8.29 ± 1.03 |
| | 360p | 9.53 ± 0.80 | 18.30 ± 2.17 | 14.81 ± 2.63 | 19.39 ± 2.30 | 9.18 ± 0.96 |
| | 480p | 14.78 ± 1.12 | 27.91 ± 4.04 | 21.19 ± 3.95 | 29.94 ± 3.90 | 14.43 ± 1.77 |
| | 720p | 22.21 ± 2.76 | 37.11 ± 3.33 | 29.05 ± 3.20 | 37.96 ± 7.85 | 18.98 ± 1.34 |
| | 1080p | 9.26 ± 0.83 | 47.21 ± 5.72 | 45.15 ± 4.81 | 47.24 ± 12.54 | 6.73 ± 0.81 |
| | 4k | 15.68 ± 0.88 | 36.16 ± 2.13 | 30.50 ± 2.05 | 45.40 ± 3.85 | 12.97 ± 0.74 |
| Low | 240p | 2.48 ± 0.71 | 3.62 ± 1.30 | 2.48 ± 0.39 | 4.91 ± 2.32 | 1.46 ± 0.27 |
| | 360p | 1.72 ± 0.15 | 3.78 ± 1.00 | 2.60 ± 0.67 | 4.86 ± 0.83 | 2.15 ± 0.33 |
| | 480p | 2.42 ± 0.20 | 3.89 ± 0.45 | 3.70 ± 0.41 | 4.62 ± 0.42 | 2.81 ± 0.29 |
| | 720p | 2.99 ± 0.20 | 4.88 ± 0.61 | 4.85 ± 0.53 | 6.38 ± 0.96 | 3.36 ± 0.26 |
| | 1080p | 4.07 ± 0.36 | 5.87 ± 0.53 | 5.06 ± 0.39 | 7.73 ± 0.96 | 3.04 ± 0.18 |
| | 4k | 5.71 ± 0.30 | 9.31 ± 0.58 | 32.99 ± 0.48 | 15.52 ± 0.89 | 4.04 ± 0.20 |
| High | 240p | 0.97 ± 0.08 | 1.84 ± 0.22 | 1.44 ± 0.15 | 2.54 ± 0.28 | 1.25 ± 0.11 |
| | 360p | 1.21 ± 0.09 | 2.22 ± 0.24 | 1.80 ± 0.16 | 3.29 ± 0.48 | 1.59 ± 0.13 |
| | 480p | 1.77 ± 0.11 | 2.53 ± 0.26 | 2.46 ± 0.19 | 3.50 ± 0.28 | 1.59 ± 0.09 |
| | 720p | 1.91 ± 0.10 | 3.00 ± 0.20 | 2.69 ± 0.18 | 4.64 ± 0.34 | 1.77 ± 0.10 |
| | 1080p | 2.56 ± 0.14 | 3.67 ± 0.20 | 3.33 ± 0.19 | 5.29 ± 0.33 | 2.21 ± 0.11 |
| | 4k | 5.2392 ± 0.26 | 7.33 ± 0.38 | 7.00 ± 0.39 | 11.89 ± 0.71 | 3.96 ± 0.21 |

$240p$, $1080p$ and $4k$ for the low scenario and at $480p$, $720p$, $1080p$, and $4k$ to the high scenario.

The Redis database excels in the key-value category in the different scenarios tested. In the tabular category, the HBase database records the best throughput compared to Cassandra. MongoDB, the only representative of the documents category, presents the third best values among all the databases tested.

Figure 9 displays throughput graphs for all scenarios. In Fig. 9a it is possible to separate the Cassandra and Project Voldemort databases from the Redis, HBase and MongoDB databases for the measured values. The Cassandra and Project Voldemort databases obtained the lowest values in the scenario. The

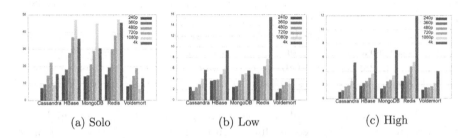

(a) Solo          (b) Low          (c) High

**Fig. 9.** Scenario throughput (megabytes per second)

Redis, HBase and MongoDB databases obtained the highest values in the scenario, especially the resolution of 1080$p$.

In Fig. 9b we notice the constancy of the values assumed by the HBase database in the resolutions in 240$p$, 360$p$ and 480$p$. The values of throughput assumed in the scenario do not show large variations, except for the resolution of 4$k$. The Redis database obtained the highest values in all video resolutions. Finally, the values are similar, Fig. 9c, between video resolutions up to 1080$p$, unsetting only the resolution in 4$k$.

## 5.3    Discussion

Of all the databases used, Redis achieved the shortest insertion times in all the scenarios experienced. The superiority of Redis occurred due to its storage in main memory. Secondary memory storage occurs only at times of low database utilization. The process runs automatically in the background. Project Voldemort database, on the other hand, presented many limitations, among which is the restriction for simultaneous insertions.

Project Voldemort (solo scenario) and Cassandra (low and high scenarios) databases had the worst insertion times. The measured values for the 4$k$ resolution make their use of these databases contraindicated, especially for scenarios with simultaneous access. Finally, the HBase and MongoDB databases presented satisfactory times in all scenarios tested.

We have obtained similar query times between the databases for the different video resolutions. The similarity in recovery times occurs due to the use of main memory for storage, characteristic present in several NoSQL databases. The Redis database was the protagonist in all scenarios analyzed but for certain scenarios and resolution the HBase database presented better times.

Project Voldemort and Cassandra database presented high times, with alternation between them in the last position of the analyzes. Project Voldemort had the worst results for 4K videos, demonstrating that the database does not perform well with large values associated with a key.

The analysis of throughput was not directly related to total recovery times. The shorter query times do not necessarily mean that the database will get a higher throughput. This phenomenon is explained because the experiments took into account the query time of the first 20% of the physical size of the video file. For this analysis, the Redis database obtained the highest rates. The lowest values of throughput were due to Project Voldemort and Cassandra.

Redis database has achieved the best performance by handling multimedia audio and video data. There is no better category of NoSQL database for storing videos. For example, in the key-value category the Project Voldemort database has achieved high insertion and recovery times, in contradiction with Redis. The same discrepancy is verified in the tabular category with the HBase obtaining satisfactory values for the insertions and recovery and the Cassandra obtaining high values for the same operations.

# 6    Conclusion and Future Works

This article proposed the Video7 architecture to store and recover streaming audio and video data in NoSQL databases. Another contribution of this paper is the class diagram for the media server. The validation of the architecture occurred through analyzes of the insertion and recovery operations. For this, the execution time of the operations and the throughput, only for the data recovery, were the measured metrics. This analysis was performed for different video resolution qualities in various NoSQL databases. The Kruskal Wallis statistical test showed a significant difference in 89% of measurements. Finally, the Redis database presented the best values, in comparison to the other databases, both for insertion and for data recovery. Project Voldemort database, on the other hand, presented the worst measured values, in addition to limitations for applying competition in the insertion.

The architecture contributes to analyze different types of input, with the inclusion of unstructured data, but not limited to it. Another advantage is the scalability of the databases under analysis, which allows comparisons between different database models (e.g., relational, newSQL, in memory) or different categories within a same model, as presented in this paper. As future work will be performed comparative analyzes between different database models for different types of unstructured inputs. Another future work will be the addition of more sophisticated metrics (e.g. metrics that exploit horizontal scalability) varying with the type of input selected.

# References

1. Assis, J.O., Souza, V.C.O., Paula, M.M.V., Cunha, J.B.S.: Performance evaluation of NoSQL data store for digital media. In: 12th Iberian Conference on Information Systems and Technologies (CISTI), Lisbon. IEEE (2017)
2. Cheng, X., Dale, C., Liu, J.: Statistics and social network of YouTube videos. In: 16th International Workshop on Quality of Service, Enschede. IEEE (2008)
3. da Costa, J.P.: YouTube vs Vimeo: uma análise comparativa de acessibilidade, usabilidade e desejabilidade para os utilizadores de fluxos videomusicais. In: Revista de Ciências e Tecnologias de Informação e Comunicação (2010)
4. de Macedo, D.D., Capretz, M.A., Prado, T.C., von Wangenheim, A., Dantas, M.: An improvement of a different approach for medical image storage. In: 20th IEEE International Workshops on Enabling Technologies: Infrastructure for Collaborative Enterprises (WETICE), Paris, pp. 140–142. IEEE (2011)
5. de Macedo, D.D., Von Wangenheim, A., Dantas, M.A.: A data storage approach for large-scale distributed medical systems. In: Ninth International Conference on Complex, Intelligent, and Software Intensive Systems (CISIS), Blumenau, pp. 486–490. IEEE (2015)
6. Kruskal, W.H., Wallis, W.A.: Use of ranks in one-criterion variance analysis. J. Am. Stat. Assoc. **47**, 583–621 and errata, ibid. **48**, 907–911 (1952)
7. Li, H., Zhang, X., Wang, S., Du, X.: Towards video management over relational database. In: 12th International Asia-Pacific Web Conference (APWEB) (2010)

8. Li, T., Liu, Y., Tian, Y., Shen, S., Mao, W.: A storage solution for massive IoT data based on NoSQL. In: IEEE International Conference on Green Computing and Communications, Besancon. IEEE (2012)
9. Rebecca, D., Shanthi, I.: A NoSQL solution to efficient storage and retrievel of Medical Images. Int. J. Sci. Eng. Res. **7**, 545–549 (2016)
10. Sampaio, V., Macedo, D., Britto, A.: Video7: Uma Arquitetura para Armazenamento e Recuperação de Arquivos de Áudio e Vídeo. In: Anais do XVIII Simpósio em Sistemas Computacionais de Alto Desempenho (2018)
11. Suchomski, M., Militzer, M., Meyer-Wegener, K.: RETAVIC: using meta-data for real-time video encoding in multimedia servers. In: Proceedings of the International Workshop on Network and Operating Systems Support for Digital Audio and Video, NOSSDAV 2005 (2005)

# Parallel Stream Processing with MPI for Video Analytics and Data Visualization

Adriano Vogel[1]([✉])(iD), Cassiano Rista[1], Gabriel Justo[1], Endrius Ewald[1], Dalvan Griebler[1,3](iD), Gabriele Mencagli[2], and Luiz Gustavo Fernandes[1](iD)

[1] School of Technology, Pontifical Catholic University of Rio Grande do Sul, Porto Alegre, Brazil
{adriano.vogel,cassiano.rista,gabriel.justo,
endrius.ewald,dalvan.griebler,luiz.fernandes}@edu.pucrs.br
[2] Department of Computer Science, University of Pisa, Pisa, Italy
[3] Laboratory of Advanced Research on Cloud Computing (LARCC),
Três de Maio Faculty (SETREM), Três de Maio, Brazil

**Abstract.** The amount of data generated is increasing exponentially. However, processing data and producing fast results is a technological challenge. Parallel stream processing can be implemented for handling high frequency and big data flows. The MPI parallel programming model offers low-level and flexible mechanisms for dealing with distributed architectures such as clusters. This paper aims to use it to accelerate video analytics and data visualization applications so that insight can be obtained as soon as the data arrives. Experiments were conducted with a Domain-Specific Language for Geospatial Data Visualization and a Person Recognizer video application. We applied the same stream parallelism strategy and two task distribution strategies. The dynamic task distribution achieved better performance than the static distribution in the HPC cluster. The data visualization achieved lower throughput with respect to the video analytics due to the I/O intensive operations. Also, the MPI programming model shows promising performance outcomes for stream processing applications.

**Keywords:** Parallel programming · Stream parallelism · Distributed processing · Cluster

## 1 Introduction

Nowadays, we are assisting to an explosion of devices producing data in the form of unbounded data streams that must be collected, stored, and processed in real-time [12]. To achieve high-throughput and low-latency processing, parallel processing techniques and efficient in-memory data structures are of fundamental importance to enable fast data access and results delivery [4,16]. Such features and problems characterize a very active research domain called *Data Stream Processing* [2] in the recent literature.

© Springer Nature Switzerland AG 2020
C. Bianchini et al. (Eds.): WSCAD 2018, CCIS 1171, pp. 102–116, 2020.
https://doi.org/10.1007/978-3-030-41050-6_7

The demand of efficient on-the-fly processing techniques presents several research challenges. One of the most compelling ones is related to how to exploit at best the underlying parallel hardware, both in the form of *scale-up servers* (i.e. single powerful servers equipped with NUMA configurations of multi-core CPUs and co-processors like GPUs and FPGAs) as well as *scale-out platforms* (i.e. based on multiple machines interconnected by fast networking technologies).

In scale-out scenarios, several streaming frameworks have been developed over the years such as Apache Flink [7] and Apache Storm [13]. Both of them are based on the Java Virtual Machine to ease the portability and the distribution of application jobs onto different interconnected machines. However, the penalty of executing partially interpreted code is widely recognized in the literature [8]. In the field of High Performance Computing, MPI [22] (Message Passing Interface) is the most popular approach to develop distributed parallel applications, and it is the *de-facto* standard programming model for C/C++ distributed processing. The programming model is based on the MPMD paradigm (Multiple Program Multiple Data), where a set of processes is created during program initialization, with each process running a different program. The MPI run-time system provides a set of low-level distributed communication mechanisms, point-to-point communications and complex collective ones (e.g., scatter, gather and reduce).

Following this idea, in previous work [5] we presented a MPI-based distributed support for a data stream preprocessing and visualization DSL. In this paper, we extend this prior work by delivering the following scientific contributions:

- Distributed stream parallelism support to real-time data visualization. This is made possible by the distributed preprocessing implementations using the MPI programming model (Sect. 4.1).
- Distributed stream parallelism support for video analytics with a real-world application using the MPI programming model (Sect. 4.2).
- Experiments and evaluation of the applications with two task distribution strategies running in a cluster environment.

The remainder of this paper is organized as follows. Section 2 introduces the problem tackled in this work. Section 3 presents the solution that supports distributed processing in a streaming like manner. In Sect. 4, we present the case studies used to experimentally evaluate our solution. Then, the related works are discussed in Sect. 5. Finally, in Sect. 6 we draw the conclusion and discuss some possible future directions.

## 2    Problem

Currently, the majority of real-world stream processing applications are facing challenges for increasing their performance. On one hand, the applications are demanding more processing power for speeding up their executions. On the other hand, we are viewing lately the end of Moore's law [27], which is limiting the performance provided by a single processor. The solution is to introduce stream parallelism in such a way that multi-core/multi-computer architectures are exploited.

However, parallel software developing is not a trivial task for application programmers that are experts in sequential coding. To tackle this problem, several high-level parallel programming frameworks where introduced, aiming at facilitating parallel programming for non-experts in computer architecture targeting single machines (multi-cores). It is worth mentioning as high-level frameworks Intel TBB [23] and FastFlow [1,6]. We also have DSLs suitable for expressing high-level parallelism, such as StreamIt [28] and SPar [9]. SPar[1] was specifically designed to simplify the stream parallelism exploitation in C++ programs for multi-core systems [9]. It offers a standard C++11 annotation language to avoid sequential source code rewriting. SPar also has a compiler that generates parallel code using source-to-source transformation technique.

Offering higher-level abstractions, GMaVis is a DSL for simplifying the data visualization generation [15]. The parallelism is completely transparent for the users. GMaVis expressiveness allows users to filter, format and specify the target data visualization. Among the steps performed by a GMaVis execution, Data Preprocessing is the most computational intensive one. Preprocessing is important to abstract from users to avoid the need to manually handling huge data sets. This step already runs in parallel compatible with SPar backend in a single machine.

A representative experimental result when running the data preprocessing in parallel is shown by [15], where the parallel execution ran on a single multi-core machine with several number of replicas (degree of parallelism) achieved limited performance gains. There, even using up to 12 replicas, the performance presented a limited scalability. Such a limited performance is caused by the single machine (number of processors available) and I/O bottleneck.

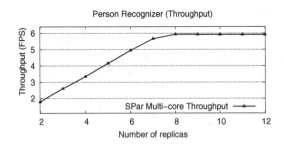

**Fig. 1.** Person recognizer throughput on multi-core.

Another relevant example of the limited multi-core performance is shown in Fig. 1 with the Person Recognizer [10] application. This application is used to

---

[1] SPar's home page: https://gmap.pucrs.br/spar.

identify faces in video feeds, which is described in more details in Sect. 4.2. In Fig. 1 it is possible to note that the performance does not increase when using more than 8 threads, which is also caused by the limited processing capability of a single machine. Moreover, considering that stream processing applications are required to produce results in as soon as data arrive under low latencies, there is a need for new programming models for increasing the performance of stream processing applications.

## 3  Stream Parallelism Strategy with MPI

In Sect. 2, we have seen two examples of real-world applications achieving a limited performance when running on a single machine. Considering the inherent performance limitations achieved when running an stream processing application on a multi-core machine, in this work we propose and implement the support for running stream processing applications on distributed clustered architectures. When referring to distributed processing and High-Performance Computing (HPC), MPI (Message Passing Interface) [22] is the *de facto* standard programming model. Consequently, MPI is exploited for implementing real-world applications running on architectures with distributed memory.

The solution is proposed using a task decomposition strategy accordingly to the parallel stream processing context. A Farm pattern [17] was used for building the distributed application workflow. The first part is the Emitter (E) that schedules and distributes task to the Worker (W) entities. The computations performed by the worker are usually the most intensive ones. Consequently, this part is replicated, in such a way that additional parallelism is achieved for dividing the tasks and processing them concurrently. The last part of the Farm is the Collector (C), which gathers the results given by the Workers. The Collector can also perform the ordering when needed [11].

The MPI distributed computing support for the two stream processing applications is designed with two task distribution strategies: the Static and Dynamic. The Static is similar to the a Round-Robin, where the Emitter distributes one task for each worker and continuously performs this step until all tasks are distributed to Worker replicas. In the Dynamic distribution, the Emitter sends one task for each worker, then the Workers request ondemand new tasks to the Emitter. In general, the Static scheduling tends to reduce the communication overhead by sending fewer messages, while the Dynamic one tends to improve the performance due to the sensitive load balancing.

We used MPI functions to communicate among the Farm entities as well as for sending tasks. They are the *MPI_Send* and *MPI_Recv*. For instance, the Emitter sends a task to a given Worker replica with a *MPI_Send* and the Worker replica receives the task with the *MPI_Recv* function. The same logic is used for communication between the Worker replicas and the Collector.

## 4    Evaluation

In this section, we present the implementations considering the aforementioned research problem (Sect. 2) as well as the proposed solution (Sect. 3) for HPC clusters. Subsection 4.1 presents the parallel stream processing for data visualization. Additionally, Subsect. 4.2 shows the parallel stream processing for video analytics.

### 4.1    Parallel Stream Processing for Data Visualization

GMaVis is a DSL that provides a high-level description language and aims to simplify the creation of visualizations for large-scale geospatial data. GMaVis enables users to express filter, classification, data format, and visualization specifications. In addition, GMaVis has limited expressiveness to reduce complexity and automatize decisions and operations such as data pre-processing, visualization zoom, and starting point location.

The data preprocessing module is responsible for transforming the input data through filtering and classification operations. This module enables GMaVis to abstract the first phase of the pipeline to create the view [19], preventing users from having to manually handle large datasets. The module works by receiving the input data, processing and saving in an output file. The data preprocessing operations are showed in Table 1.

**Table 1.** Data preprocessing operations [15].

| Definition | Description |
|---|---|
| $F = \{\alpha_1, \alpha_2, \alpha_3, ..., \alpha_n\}$ | $F$ is a set of input files to be processed and $\alpha$ represents a single file from a partitioned data set |
| $Split(\alpha)$ | It splits a data set file of $F$ into $N$ chunks |
| $D = \{d_1, d_2, d_3, ..., d_n\}$ | $D$ is a set of chunks of a single file. We can say that $D$ is the result of a $Split(\alpha)$ function |
| $Process(D)$ | It processes a single file $D$ of $F$ |
| $Read(d)$ | It opens and reads a data chunk $d$ of a $\alpha$ in $F$ |
| $Filter(d)$ | It filters a given data chunk $d$ in $D$, producing a set of registries to create the visualization |
| $Classify(...)$ | It classifies the results of $Filter(...)$ |
| $Write(...)$ | It saves the results of $\sum_{i=1}^{n} Process(F)$, where $F$ represents a set of files $(\alpha)$ in an output file to be used in the visualization generation |

GMaVis compiler uses source code details to generate the data preprocessing using the C++ programming language [15]. C++ enables the use of a wide range of parallel programming APIs (Application Programming Interfaces) as well as low-level improvements for memory management and disk reading. Thus, the compiler generates a file named *data_preprocessor.cpp*. All code is generated and executed sequentially or with SPar annotations that target single multi-core machines by default. In addition, the relevant GMaVis source code information is transformed and written to that file.

Thus, to support for distributed parallel stream processing in this application, we implemented the stream parallelism using the Farm pattern [10] with MPI, as described in Sect. 3. Figure 2(a) shows the preprocessing functions decomposition accordingly to a Farm pattern with MPI for distributed processing. In this case, the Emitter corresponds to the first stage that distributed the Input Data to the next stage, where the worker replicas generate the Data Preprocessing Operations, as showed in Table 1. The results of the data preprocessing operations are given to the last stage, which is the Collector that orders and save an Output File with structured and formatted data. Moreover, Fig. 2(b) illustrates the visualization generating a Heatmap of traffic collision in the city of Porto Alegre, Brazil.

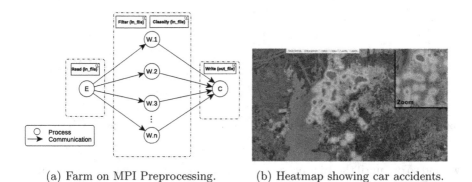

(a) Farm on MPI Preprocessing.          (b) Heatmap showing car accidents.

**Fig. 2.** Data preprocessing and visualization.

Performance tests were executed on a homogeneous HPC cluster using six machines. Each machine is equipped with a dual socket Intel(R) Xeon(R) CPU 2.40 GHz (12 cores with Hyperthreading disabled) and 32 GB - 2133 MHz memory configurations. The machines were interconnected by a Gigabit Ethernet network. The operating system used was Ubuntu Server, G++ v. 5.4.0 with the -O3 compilation flag.

In Figs. 3(a) and (b) we show the performance of distributed implementations for data preprocessing stage with a large 40 GB sized file, and data items with 1 MB and 8MB respectively. The data amount in megabytes per second (MBPS) processed is used as throughput metric. The processes distribution occurs in rounds enforcing that each process is placed on each physical machine and the next process goes to the subsequent machine. For instance, if we have 4 machines and 16 processes, the first process goes to machine one, the second to machine

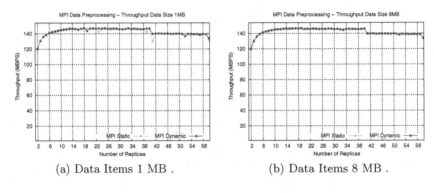

**Fig. 3.** Data preprocessing with large 40 GB sized file.

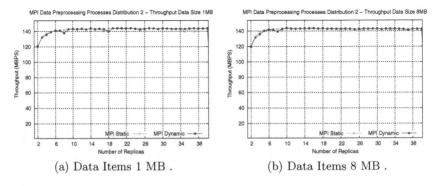

**Fig. 4.** Custom processes distribution - Data preprocessing with large 40 GB sized file.

two and so on, until the 16 processes are running on the 4 machines. This strategy called Process Distribution 1 aims at overcoming the single node I/O limits by distributing the processes among all machines.

The results from Fig. 3 emphasize a poor performance. Although using two data sizes and up to 60 replicas, the performance did not scale up very well. Consequently, we tested a new processes distribution called Processes Distribution 2 that first used all physical cores of a given machine, then places the next processes to additional machines. In short, each node is fully allocated and only then a new node is considered if necessary. Similarly, it is possible to view in Figs. 4(a) and (b) a custom distribution of tasks with the same input parameters, called of Process Distribution 2. In general, it is possible to view a limited performance scalability both with Process Distribution 1 and Distribution 2. In this test with a huge input file of 40 GB, the static and dynamic scheduling did not have significant performance differences. The best throughput over 140 MBPS with six replicas demonstrated the limited performance even with more replicas available. This behavior led us to assume that the cluster data storage system could be limiting the tests performance.

In order to minimize the data storage overhead, the file size was reduced to 4GB. Using smaller file size reduced the IO utilization. Consequently, as shown in Figs. 5(a) and (b), the performance improved dramatically. In this case, it is possible to view that the performance significantly improved with the MPI support, which is a relevant outcome considering the hypothesis of data storage system I/O being the bottleneck. The strategy with a Dynamic behavior using Distribution 1 reached a throughput of 1200 MBPS with data items of 1MB, and a throughput of 1000 MBPS with data items 8MB. In general, both strategies (Static and Dynamic) using Processes Distribution 2 presented a lower performance compared to Distribution 1.

Different relevant aspects can be viewed in the best performatic results shown in Fig. 5(a). The strategy with a Dynamic processes distribution achieved the highest throughput rates due to its optimized load balancing. Regarding the Static strategy, a significant drop in performance with Processes Distribution 1 can be viewed when using more that 6 replicas, which occurs when more than 1 process is running on each machine, causing concurrency for network and storage access. This increases the performance variability that unbalances the load and causes performance overhead with the Static tasks distribution. It is also relevant to note that the scalability limitation is achieved around 18 replicas. In this case, the potential bottleneck was the network and storage saturation. The next results show additional insights corroborating this finding.

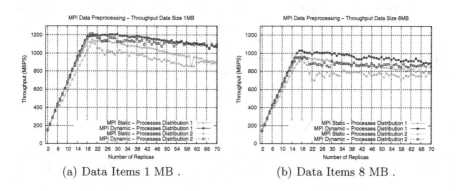

(a) Data Items 1 MB .                    (b) Data Items 8 MB .

**Fig. 5.** Data preprocessing with large 4 GB sized file.

In Fig. 6, the file size was increased to 8GB in order to comprehensively evaluate our implementation. The intention was to verify if the previously used workload (4GB) was providing enough load for the distributed executions. The results emphasize significant performance gains, similar to tests performed with large 4GB sized file, as showed in Fig. 5. Consequently, the workload with file sizes of 4GB and 8GB was presumably enough for our distributed implementations. With these results it is possible to assume that the performance bottleneck was generated by data storage and network system.

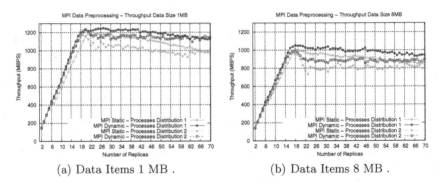

(a) Data Items 1 MB .                    (b) Data Items 8 MB .

**Fig. 6.** Data preprocessing with large 8 GB sized file.

An overview of the MPI distributed implementations shows significant performance gains. For instance, the peak multi-core performance viewed in [15] was 140 MBPS. Here, the distributed implementation achieved a throughput higher that 1200, which is a speedup of almost 10 over an already parallel version. Comparing the data sizes used, 1 MB achieved a best performance than 8 MB. Although a smaller data size tends to increase the number of messages exchanged, this fine granularity gains in performance by reducing I/O demands and improving the load balancing.

Supporting visualization in real-time tends to be a challenge due to the preprocessing bottleneck. For instance, the registers used for generating each visualization line often are not computed fast enough for presenting timely results. A significant outcome of our distributed stream processing is the fact that with the peak performance 1178 registers were processed per second, such a high number enables a visualization to be generated quickly enough to provide insights.

### 4.2   Parallel Stream Processing for Video Analytics

This video analytics application is used to recognize people in video streams. It starts by receiving a video feed and detecting the faces. The faces that are detected are then marked with a red circle, and then compared with the training set of faces. When the face comparison matches, the face is marked with a green circle. A relevant example of using Person Recognition is on security surveillance systems.

The parallel version of this application is composed by a three staged Farm [10]. The Emitter corresponds to the first stage that sends the Frames to the next stage, where the worker replicas detect and mark the faces. The results of the faces are given to the last stage, which is the Collector that orders the frames and produces the output video.

Person Recognition workflow was implemented using the stream parallelism strategy with MPI proposed in Sect. 3. The distributed Farm implementation is illustrated in Fig. 7, where a video input is processed by the application's functions and the output is produced with marks in the faces detected. The Emitter

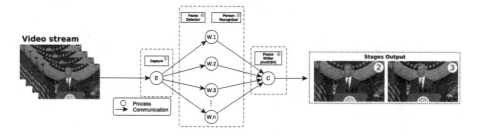

**Fig. 7.** Farm on person recognizer.

sends a frame for each Worker replicas using the *MPI_Send* function, the same function is used by replicas when sending the processed frames to the Collector. It is important to note that the Static and Dynamic tasks distribution strategies, presented in Sect. 3, were implemented in this application. These strategies are compared for evaluating which one is more suitable for the distributed video processing with MPI.

Performance tests were executed on a HPC cluster where each node is equipped by 2 Sockets Intel(R) Xeon(R) CPU 2.40 GHz (8 cores-16 threads) with Hyperthreading intentionally disable. Each node had available 16 GB of RAM memory - DDR3 1066 MHz. The hosts were interconnected by a Gigabit (10/1000) network. The Worker replicas run on 5 nodes with up to 40 processes (at most 8 per machine - one process per hardware core). The Emitter and Collector were executed on dedicated machines for reducing the variability and managing I/O bottlenecks. Moreover, the input simulating a representative load used a file with 1.4 MB, which has a duration of 15 s and 450 frames. The intensive computations performed in the input is can be view due to the fact that the sequential execution takes around 450 s to process the 15 s video. Consequently, our distributed implementations are expected to accelerate the video processing.

In Fig. 8 it is shown the performance of distributed implementations of Person Recognition using the throughput metric of frames processed per second. In general, it is possible to view that the performance significantly improved with the MPI support, which is a relevant outcome considering the limited performance seen in a multi-core machine in Fig. 1.

Noteworthy, in Fig. 8, the performance increased linearly with the Dynamic tasks distribution strategy. The strategy with a Static behavior presented a lower throughput, but still achieved significant performance gains. The Dynamic strategy outperformed the static version because of its improved load balancing, which is justified by the fact that Person Recognition presents a irregular and unbalanced execution in terms of the time taken to process each video frame. In some cases, for example, with 30 and 38 replicas, the Static strategy achieved a performance similar to the Dynamic. In such cases, the number of frames (load) was divided evenly by the number of worker replicas. Consequently, a higher throughput was achievable as all Worker replicas finished their tasks in a similar time.

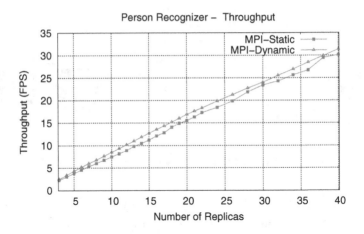

**Fig. 8.** Person recognizer throughput.

## 5    Related Work

In this section we present different approaches for parallel and distributed processing and DSLs for visualization and preprocessing of large amounts of data for geovisualization applications. We also consider as related work those approaches that address distributed video stream processing.

In the work of Seo et al. [24], an implementation of MPI nonblocking collective I/O is described. The implementation in MPICH was based on ROMIO's collective I/O algorithm, replacing all blocking operations used in ROMIO's collective I/O algorithm with nonblocking counterparts. The results indicate a better performance (if compared to blocking collective I/O) in terms of I/O bandwidth and is capable of overlapping I/O and other operations. Latham et al. [14] proposes an extension for MPI-3, enabling to determine which nodes of a system share common features. The extension provided a portable approach for investigating the topology of a compute system, making it possible to determine which nodes share faster local devices. The results obtained with benchmark tests demonstrated the efficiency of the approach to investigate the topology of a system. Mendez et al. [18] presents a methodology to evaluate the performance of parallel applications based on the I/O characteristics, requirements and severity degree. The implementation defined the use of five severity degrees considering the I/O requirement of parallel applications and parameters of the HPC system. Results showed that the methodology allows to identify if a parallel application is limited by the I/O subsystem and to identify possible causes of the problem.

Ayachit [3] describes the design and features of ParaView, which is a multi-platform open source tool that allows visualization and analysis of data. In ParaView data manipulation can be done interactively in 3D or through batch processing. The tool was designed to analyze large data sets using distributed memory computing capabilities. Wylie and Baumes [30] present an expansion project for the open source tool Visualization Toolkit (VTK). The project was named Titan, and supports the insertion, processing, and visualization of data. In addition, the data distribution, parallel processing, and client/server feature of the VTK tool provides a scalable platform.

Steed et al. [25] describes a visual analysis system, called Exploratory Data Analysis Environment (EDEN) with specific application for the analysis of large datasets inherent to climate science. EDEN was developed as an interactive visual analysis tool allowing to transform data into insights. Thus, improving the critical understanding of terrestrial system processes. Results were obtained based on real-world studies using point sets and global simulations of the terrestrial model (CLM4). Perrot et al. [21] presents an architecture for Big Data applications that allows the interactive visualization of large-scale heat maps. The implementation performed in Hadoop, HBase, Spark, and WebGL includes a distributed algorithm for computing a canopy clustering. The results show the efficiency of the approach in terms of horizontal scalability and quality of the visualization produced.

The study presented by Zhang et al. [31] explores the use of geovisual analytics and parallel computing technologies for geospatial optimization problems. Development has resulted in a set of interactive geovisual tools to dynamically steer the optimization search in an interactive way. The experiments show that visual analytics and the search through the use of parallel trees are promising approaches in solving multi-objective land use allocation problems.

The work of Pereira *et al.* [20] addressed the need for stream processing systems that are able to process large data volumes. Particularly, in video processing a new distributed processing architecture was proposed using split and merges operations according to a MapReduce system. The solution was validated with a real-world application from the video compressing scenario running on dedicated cluster and on cloud environments. The results emphasize significant performance gains with the proposed distributed architecture. Tan and Chen [26] in its turn, propose an approach for parallel video processing on MapReduce-based clusters. To illustrate details of implementing a video processing algorithm, were used three algorithms: face detection, motion detection, and tracking algorithm. Performance tests with Apache Hadoop show that the system is able to reduce the running time to below 25% of that of a single computer.

Comparing the related approaches, it is notable that [14,24] focused on performance improvement of I/O applications, while others [18] allow to identify if the application is limited by the I/O subsystem. Some approaches [3,30] were concerned with the visualization and analysis of data sets and others in allowing the interactive visualization of Big Data applications [21,25]. The approach of [31] demonstrates the use of geovisual analysis technologies through parallel trees and finally [20] and [26] are focused in parallel video processing on MapReduce-based clusters.

It is possible to note that the literature does not present studies with focus on distributed programming models for video and data preprocessing taking into account a distributed environment. In contrast to this observed behavior, we focused essentially on stream parallelism and MPI programming model for video and data preprocessing. Also, different applications and file sizes are tested in this paper.

# 6  Conclusion

In the previous work [5], a moderated scalability was achieved with MPI distributed data preprocessing. In this study, we presented a solution for processing in a stream manner producing results as soon as the data arrives. Moreover, the distributed stream processing support enabled the applications to overcome a single machine performance bottleneck. Two MPI strategies were proposed, one for reducing communication overhead and other for optimizing load balancing. Then, the strategies were evaluated for data visualization and video analytics scenarios.

The MPI strategy with a Dynamic tasks distribution outperformed the Static one in both scenarios. The dynamic mode achieved a better load balancing among the running processes. Load balance is so important for stream processing because such executions are usually characterized with irregular and fluctuating workloads.

In the data visualization application, we noticed a significant impact of the file sizes in the performance, too large files cause the I/O saturation resulting in performance losses. Although the scalability was suboptimal in the data preprocessing because of the I/O subsystem, our implemented solution showed promising performance outcomes. The performance in the video analytics has proven to be effective and efficient, performing with QoS for end users.

It is important to note that our work is limited in some aspects. For instance, the performance trend can be different in other applications or environments. Although both applications were reading the input from a file (I/O operations), the applications could be easily adapted for reading from a more realistic external source (e.g., network). Moreover, the strategy with dynamic tasks distribution is expected to be efficient in heterogeneous environments, but our results are limited to homogeneous clusters with dedicated resources for the running applications.

We plan to extend this work for other real-world stream processing application scenarios. The long term goal is to identify patterns in parallelizing stream processing applications and exploit this findings for developing a library. This library can be generic enough for application programmers easily parallelize stream processing applications. In the future, modern stream processing features such as self-adaptivity [16,29] are aimed to the encompassed in our solution. Moreover, low-level optimizations could be provided by I/O experts for tuning the performance of the storage system for data visualization applications.

**Acknowledgements.** This study was financed in part by the Coordenação de Aperfeiçoamento de Pessoal de Nível Superior - Brasil (CAPES) - Finance Code 001, by the FAPERGS 01/2017-ARD project ParaElastic (No. 17/2551-0000871-5), and by the Universal MCTIC/CNPq N° 28/2018 project called SParCloud (No. 437693/2018-0).

# References

1. Aldinucci, M., Danelutto, M., Kilpatrick, P., Torquati, M.: Fastflow: High-level and Efficient Streaming on Multicore, Chap. 13, pp. 261–280. Wiley-Blackwell, Hoboken (2014)
2. Andrade, H., Gedik, B., Turaga, D.: Fundamentals of Stream Processing: Application Design, Systems, and Analytics. Cambridge University Press, Cambridge (2014)
3. Ayachit, U.: The ParaView Guide: A Parallel Visualization Application. Kitware Inc., New York (2015)
4. De Matteis, T., Mencagli, G.: Proactive elasticity and energy awareness in data stream processing. J. Syst. Softw. **127**(C), 302–319 (2017). https://doi.org/10.1016/j.jss.2016.08.037
5. Ewald, E., Vogel, A., Rista, C., Griebler, D., Manssour, I., Gustavo, L.: Parallel and distributed processing support for a geospatial data visualization DSL. In: Symposium on High Performance Computing Systems (WSCAD), pp. 221–228. IEEE (2018)
6. FastFlow: FastFlow (FF) Website (2019). http://mc-fastflow.sourceforge.net/. Accessed Feb 2019
7. Friedman, E., Tzoumas, K.: Introduction to Apache Flink: Stream Processing for Real Time and Beyond, 1st edn. O'Reilly Media Inc., Sebastopol (2016)
8. Georges, A., Buytaert, D., Eeckhout, L.: Statistically rigorous java performance evaluation. SIGPLAN Not. **42**(10), 57–76 (2007). https://doi.org/10.1145/1297105.1297033
9. Griebler, D., Danelutto, M., Torquati, M., Fernandes, L.G.: SPar: a DSL for high-level and productive stream parallelism. Parallel Process. Lett. **27**(01), 1740005 (2017). https://doi.org/10.1142/S0129626417400059
10. Griebler, D., Hoffmann, R.B., Danelutto, M., Fernandes, L.G.: Higher-level parallelism abstractions for video applications with SPar. In: Parallel Computing is Everywhere, Proceedings of the International Conference on Parallel Computing, ParCo 2017, pp. 698–707. IOS Press, Bologna (2017). https://doi.org/10.3233/978-1-61499-843-3-698
11. Griebler, D., Hoffmann, R.B., Danelutto, M., Fernandes, L.G.: Stream Parallelism with ordered data constraints on multi-core systems. J. Supercomput. **75**, 1–20 (2018). https://doi.org/10.1007/s11227-018-2482-7
12. Hirzel, M., Soulé, R., Schneider, S., Gedik, B., Grimm, R.: A catalog of stream processing optimizations. ACM Comput. Surv. **46**(4), 46:1–46:34 (2014)
13. Jain, A.: Mastering Apache Storm: Real-time Big Data Streaming Using Kafka, Hbase and Redis. Packt Publishing, Birmingham (2017)
14. Latham, R., Bautista-Gomez, L., Balaji, P.: Portable topology-aware MPI-I/O. In: IEEE International Conference on Parallel and Distributed Systems (ICPADS), pp. 710–719, December 2017. https://doi.org/10.1109/ICPADS.2017.00096
15. Ledur, C., Griebler, D., Manssour, I., Fernandes, L.G.: A high-level DSL for geospatial visualizations with multi-core parallelism support. In: 41th IEEE Computer Society Signature Conference on Computers, Software and Applications, COMPSAC 2017, pp. 298–304. IEEE, Torino (2017)
16. Matteis, T.D., Mencagli, G.: Keep calm and react with foresight: strategies for low-latency and energy-efficient elastic data stream processing. In: Proceedings of the ACM Symposium on Principles and Practice of Parallel Programming, pp. 13:1–13:12 (2016)

17. McCool, M., Robison, A.D., Reinders, J.: Structured Parallel Programming: Patterns for Efficient Computation. Morgan Kaufmann, Burlington (2012)
18. Mendez, S., Rexachs, D., Luque, E.: Analyzing the parallel I/O severity of MPI applications. In: IEEE/ACM International Symposium on Cluster, Cloud and Grid Computing, pp. 953–962 (2017). https://doi.org/10.1109/CCGRID.2017.45
19. Moreland, K.: A survey of visualization pipelines. IEEE Trans. Visual Comput. Graph. **19**(3), 367–378 (2013)
20. Pereira, R., Azambuja, M., Breitman, K., Endler, M.: An architecture for distributed high performance video processing in the cloud. In: international Conference on Cloud Computing, pp. 482–489. IEEE (2010)
21. Perrot, A., Bourqui, R., Hanusse, N., Lalanne, F., Auber, D.: Large interactive visualization of density functions on big data infrastructure. In: IEEE Symposium on Large Data Analysis and Visualization (LDAV), pp. 99–106, October 2015. https://doi.org/10.1109/LDAV.2015.7348077
22. Quinn, M.J.: Parallel Programming in C with MPI and OpenMP. McGraw-Hill, New York (2003)
23. Reinders, J.: Intel Threading Building Blocks: Outfitting C++ for Multi-core Processor Parallelism. O'Reilly Media, Sebastopol (2007)
24. Seo, S., Latham, R., Zhang, J., Balaji, P.: Implementation and evaluation of MPI nonblocking collective I/O. In: IEEE/ACM International Symposium on Cluster, Cloud and Grid Computing, pp. 1084–1091, May 2015. https://doi.org/10.1109/CCGrid.2015.81
25. Steed, C.A., et al.: Big data visual analytics for exploratory earth system simulation analysis. Comput. Geosci. **61**, 71–82 (2013). https://doi.org/10.1016/j.cageo.2013.07.025
26. Tan, H., Chen, L.: An approach for fast and parallel video processing on apache Hadoop clusters. In: 2014 IEEE International Conference on Multimedia and Expo (ICME), pp. 1–6, July 2014. https://doi.org/10.1109/ICME.2014.6890135
27. Theis, T.N., Wong, H.S.P.: The end of Moore's law: a new beginning for information technology. Comput. Sci. Eng. **19**(2), 41 (2017)
28. Thies, W., Karczmarek, M., Amarasinghe, S.: StreamIt: a language for streaming applications. In: Horspool, R.N. (ed.) CC 2002. LNCS, vol. 2304, pp. 179–196. Springer, Heidelberg (2002). https://doi.org/10.1007/3-540-45937-5_14
29. Vogel, A., Griebler, D., De Sensi, D., Danelutto, M., Fernandes, L.G.: Autonomic and latency-aware degree of parallelism management in SPar. In: Mencagli, G., et al. (eds.) Euro-Par 2018. LNCS, vol. 11339, pp. 28–39. Springer, Cham (2019). https://doi.org/10.1007/978-3-030-10549-5_3
30. Wylie, B.N., Baumes, J.: A unified toolkit for information and scientific visualization. In: VDA, p. 72430 (2009)
31. Zhang, T., Hua, G., Ligmann-Zielinska, A.: Visually-driven parallel solving of multi-objective land-use allocation problems: a case study in Chelan, Washington. Earth Sci. Inf. **8**, 809–825 (2015)

# Tangible Assets to Improve Research Quality: A Meta Analysis Case Study

Alessander Osorio$^{(\boxtimes)}$ (ID), Marina Dias (ID), and Gerson Geraldo H. Cavalheiro (ID)

Federal University of Pelotas, Pelotas, RS, Brazil
{alessander.osorio,mldias,gerson.cavalheiro}@inf.ufpel.edu.br
http://www.ufpel.edu.br

**Abstract.** This paper presents a meta-analysis of the publications from all 18 previous editions of WSCAD in order to understand how performance results are validated and reported. This meta-analysis extract from these papers terms (keywords) belonging to three categories: statistics, metrics and tests. From all 426 papers analyzed, 93% referred at least one of the terms considered, indicating that there is a concern that results should be reported in order to the paper be considered relevant for this conference. Nevertheless, this analysis shows that only 3% of the papers applies reliable statistical tests to validate them. This paper depicts the meta-analysis achieved and proposes a direction to promote the adoption of a guideline to improve the results reporting in this conference and other with related subjects.

**Keywords:** Performance results analysis · Research evaluation · Statistical analysis · Research methodology

## 1 Introduction

The proposition of a new technique or algorithm is usually followed by a performance analysis. It must take care to ensure that the performance study is performed so that the gain, if any, can be attested. It is usual, in experimental research, to dedicate a large amount of time to perform the experiments as well as a large amount of space on papers to present them, but performing a statistical study that validates the performance data comes second.

The *statistical study* considered in this paper is the one that results from the consistency and coherence analysis of the performance data obtained. Such study must precede the inference of behaviors, interpretations about the results collected and obtained conclusions. Therefore, the effective accomplishment of the statistical study allows associate reliability to the results presented in any scientific report.

In this work, a qualitative meta-analysis of a conference through an automated process of data mining was made. From the papers of the conference was

This paper was realized with support of the National Program of Academic Cooperation from CAPES/Brasil.

extract the synthesis on the statistical and metric methods used. The objective of this work is present a landscape of how those papers statistically demonstrate their results, in order to provide indicators to qualify their submissions in the up coming years.

The case study is the Symposium of High Performance Computing Systems (WSCAD), a yearly Brazilian conference, starting in 2000, presented mostly in Portuguese. Where analyzed all 426 papers, wrote in Portuguese, from all firsts 18 editions (2000 to 2017). In addition, the present work also aims contribute to characterize, briefly, relevant statistical methods and techniques applicable for performance evaluation in high performance processing.

This work extends [17] bringing to the discussion ways of qualitatively improving scientific publications, specially in the domain of the statistical methods and techniques applicable for performance evaluation in high performance processing. Topics in statistics are explained to introduce basic concepts of data analysis and prove of measurements. Guidelines for the design, execution and reporting of research and its importance in the modern research scenario are also discussed.

The remaining of this paper is divided into 7 sections. The Sect. 2 characterize related works to the study presented in this paper. The quantitative analysis criteria are presented in Sect. 3 and the discussion about the methodology used is presented in Sect. 4. The results of the data obtained are discussed in Sect. 5. Section 6 are presented improvements of quality followed by Sect. 7 that have the conclusions of the paper.

## 2     Related Works

In this section we present some works developed in the context of the identification of methodologies of validation of results in scientific papers of the great area of Computation.

[18] evaluated 190 papers published on *Neural Networks Journal*, in the years 1993 and 1994 and showed that only 1/3 of the works had no quantitative comparison with previously known techniques. [22] analyzed 400 papers, published in ACM (Association for Computing Machinery), to determine whether computer scientists support their results with experimental evaluation. This study found that 40% of the papers did not have any type of evaluation. [23] reproduces the [22] research analyzing 147 papers published by ACM in the year 2005 concluding that 33% of papers are in the same situation. The work of [21] reinforces this evidence and cites the community's lack of experience in the correct analysis of the data in order to produce statistical evidence to prove the results as a cause.

Recently, the work of [1] study 183 papers from IPIN (International Conference on Indoor Positioning and Indoor Navigation) and concluded that although in many publications there was some concern in the evaluation of results, the quality of the description of the analysis methods was poor. Only 35% clearly report not only the methodology of the experiment itself, but what the results actually statistically represents.

Based on the results of the works above mentioned, the objective is to evaluate the publications of the Symposium of High Performance Computing Systems (WSCAD) focusing in how the statistical analysis of performance are described in their papers so that the gain can be attested, if there is.

## 3   Quantitative Analysis Criteria

Computer Science research, in most cases involves the development of a new application, algorithm or new computational system model [24]. Within this process, the research object is compared to similar techniques for effective performance evaluation of the proposed solution. This evaluation should be done by the quantitative analysis of the summarized results obtained by the use of synthetic data and statistical techniques of comparison of sets of measures.

Synthetic data, obtained by workloads, benchmarks, simulations and competitions, are classified into three categories. The first is used to evaluate the response time of a solution, the second to evaluate whether a solution can achieve the result (effectiveness) and the third to evaluate the quality of the response of the solution (efficiency) [24].

The performed experiments on a solution need to have effective statistical significance, according to the type of measurement performed and the appropriate statistical test to analyze this measurement. The types of measurement are categorical or nominal, ordinal, interval and reason [24]. Statistical tests are procedures used to test the null hypothesis, as the assumption is that there is no difference or relationship between the groups of data or tested events in the research object and that differences are due to random events, as well as the alternative hypothesis, the assumption is that there are statistically significant differences between measurements.

Calculating the probability of the null hypothesis being true or not, by the appropriate test according to the type of measurement performed, we found a number called p-value. When the level of significance represented by this value is lower than an indicator, with 0.05 (5%) being the most used value, the null hypothesis is rejected and the alternative hypothesis is accepted, that there is a difference and this one was not found randomly [3, 24]. Although the hypothesis test is useful, when comparing values obtained in different experiments the hypothesis test is not enough. It is necessary to know how much these values effectively differ, using the so-called confidence interval. In [12], this confidence interval is set to at least 95%, which represents the largest and the smallest values assuming a p-value of 0.05 [24]. The confidence interval does not overlap, or invalidate, the standard deviation measure. The latter corresponds to the indication of how much the experiment data may vary from the mean and is used as a parameter in some tests.

The indicated, and therefore most commonly used, tests for comparing up to two sets of measurements and obtaining the p-value are: T-Test, Paired T-Test, U-test Mann-Whitney or Wilcoxon Rank-sum Test, Wilcoxon Signed-rank Test, Chi-square, and Fisher's Exact Test. For multiple comparisons, with more than two sets of values, they are: ANOVA Test and Kruskal-Wallis [24].

Knowing that the statistical study should be applied to a collection of $n$ performance samples collected, the remaining problem is how to define the value of $n$ for a given experiment. The Central Limit Theorem (CLT) is the most important result in statistics, in which many commonly used statistical methods are based [14] to have validity. This theorem says that if a sufficiently large sample is drawn the behavior of the averages tends to be a normal distribution [2,14] or Gaussian [15]. The normal (or Gaussian) distribution is the statistical model that best represents the natural behavior of an experiment, where a random variable can assume any value within a defined range [15].

Sample here refers to the measurements of the research objects, number of replicates or iterations performed in the tests or experiments. Depending on the type of the research object, there are specific calculations for the sample size, however the CLT suggests that for most cases a sample size of 30 or greater is large enough for the normal approximation to be adequate [14].

There are applicable measurements criteria for each research object. According to [5] performance measurement can be classified as System or User-oriented measures. System-oriented measurements typically travel around the throughput and utilization. Transfer rate is defined as an average per time interval, be it tasks, processes or data. Usage is the measure of the time interval in which a particular computational resource is occupied. User-oriented measurements comprise response time and turnaround time.

Within this concept, it is possible to identify specialized metrics such as Reaction Time, Strech Factor, MIPS (Millions of Instructions Per Second), PPS (Packets Per Second), MFLOPS (Millions of Floating-Point Operations Per Second), BPS (Bits Per Second), TPS (Transactions Per Second), Nominal Capacity, Bandwidth, Usability Capacity, Efficiency, Idle Time, Reliability, Availability, Downtime, Uptime, MTTF, Cost/Performance Ratio [2,5] are inserted within these two generalizations.

The metrics terminology is quite extensive and diverse. It can also change according to the personal opinion of researchers or according to the country region. However, [2] and [5] illustrate both the definition and the use of each metric mentioned above.

## 4   Methodology

For data collect, all published works from 2000 to 2017 were saved locally, numbered and separated by folder according to the year of publication. Works in abstract format and those written in a foreign language were not part of the sample of the 426 analyzed publications. This is due to the fact that, given the nature of the abstract format, certain details of the data analysis of the studied object could be suppressed which could generate a bias. As well as works in foreign language would greatly increase the number of search terms if your diversity.

Following, through an automated software process (NVivo[1]), we searched for citations of terms, used in statistical analysis as well as metrics and tests used for gauging results, thus categorized in this article. These categories refer to good practices in data collection and analysis of results in scientific research, according to Tables 1, 2 and 3.

**Table 1.** Statistical terms selected for data collection

| Description | Research key |
|---|---|
| Sample (AM) | amostra |
| Standard Deviation (DP) | "desvio padrão" |
| Normal Distribution (DN) | "distribuição normal" |
| Frequency (FR) | "frequência" OR "frequência" |
| Gaussiana (GA) | gaussiana |
| Confidence Interval (IC) | "intervalo de confiança" |
| Mean (ME) | "média" |
| Num. Execution (NE) | "número de execuções" |
| Num. Iteration (NI) | "numero de iterações" |
| Test/Experiment (TE) | teste OR experimento OR simulação |
| Variance (VR) | variância |

After organization, the data were summarized by year according to the category of the term. Tables 4, 5 and 6 show the results obtained in the search of statistical terms, metrics and tests respectively. Note that only terms that obtained results are summarized, those where there's no occurrences were suppressed. Still in Table 4, the results of the term frequency were suppressed due to the bias the results obtained. Frequency is quoted as the unit of measure of the processor clock. The results of the terms normal and Gaussian distribution were summarized together because they were the same object.

Table 7 summarizes the results from Tables 4, 5 and 6, as well as the distribution of citations by category of the term and year. In which is showed the total number of papers in the year, the number of papers containing at least one occurrence of the term. It also identifies the number of occurrences within papers separated by term category.

## 5   Discussion

The objective is not invalidate the results obtained in the experiments performed on papers that were analysed, but verify the care in publishing these results as well as the evolution of scientific research since they are almost 20 years of WSCAD. It is assumed that all possible errors and issues to avoid them have

---

[1] http://www.software.com.br/p/qsr-nvivo.

**Table 2.** Metrics selected for data collection

| Description | Research key |
|---|---|
| Bandwidth (BW) | "bandwidth" OR "largura de banda" |
| BPS (BP) | "bits por segundo" OR bps |
| Nominal Capacity (CN) | "capacidade nominal" |
| Usable Capacity (CU) | "capacidade utilizável" |
| Confidentiality (CO) | Confiabilidade |
| Performance (CP) | "performance" |
| Availability (DI) | disponibilidade |
| Downtime/Uptime (DU) | downtime or uptime |
| Efficiency/Accuracy (EA) | eficiência OR eficácia |
| Stretch Factor(FE) | "fator de estiramento" |
| Idle Time (TO) | "tempo ocioso" |
| MFLOPS (MF) | MFLOPS |
| MIPS (MI) | MIPS |
| MTTF (MT) | MTTF |
| PPS (PP) | PPS |
| Speed up (SU) | "speedup OR speed-up" OR "speed up" |
| Reaction time (TR) | "tempo de reação" |
| TPS (TP) | TPS |

already been taken into account [2]. In this analysis, the proportion of papers with occurrence was used instead of the total of papers in the year and not the number of papers to allow the comparison between the years, since the number of papers per year is not the same having great variability Fig. 1(a). Of the 426 papers analyzed, 79% cited statistical terms, 67% metric and only 2% statistical tests.

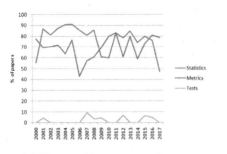

(a) Papers with occurrence by year

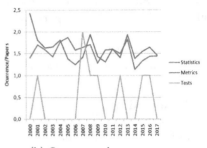

(b) Occurrence by paper year

**Fig. 1.** Results graphs

**Table 3.** Statistical tests selected for data collection

| Description | Research key |
|---|---|
| P-Value (PV) | "p-valor OR p-value" OR "valor p" |
| ANOVA (AN) | anova |
| Chi-square (CH) | chi-quadrado OR qui-quadrado |
| Wilcoxon (TC) | "wilcoxon signed-rank" |
| Fisher (FI) | "teste exato de fisher" or "fisher" |
| Kruskal-Wallis (KR) | kruskal-wallis |
| T (TT) | "teste t" OR "teste-t" OR "teste de student" OR "Student" |
| U (TU) | "teste U" OR "mann-whitney" OR "wilcoxon rank-sum" |

The ratio was obtained by means of the data Table 7, dividing the number of papers with citations by the number of citations. The average citation of the three categories was 1.46 citations per article. Individually it is observed that for statistical terms (1,57) and metric (1,59) the values were above the general average in almost every year.

From the tests analysed, only T-Test or Student's test resulted in 9 occurrences, and two occurrences of the level of statistical significance (p-value), none of them were papers with the occurrence of Test T.

Due to the low occurrence of statistical tests in the results, around 2%, it was decided to investigate this data more closely. For this, a second sample from the total 426 papers was calculated, disregarding the 9 studies where the occurrences of these terms were already found, with a 95% confidence interval and a sampling error of 5%, reaching a total of 30 randomly selected papers.

The second sample was sent to two reviewers, who read and analyzed the methodology and analysis of the results of these papers according to some criteria. Experimentation, whether carried out or not; Sample method referring to the method used to find the sample size, by the use of benchmarks, estimation or calculation; Size of the sample represented by the number of experiments performed, repetitions, instructions, jobs and the like; If the size of the sample is evident and if its size is adequate; Use of metrics; If there was a comparison with another technique and this technique was adequately demonstrated in some way.

From the papers analyzed in the second sample, none showed equality or deficiency in their results, the worst case only points to "evidence of performance improvement". From this sample, 24 of them performed experimentation, 6 are theoretical models or descriptive memorials of implementations of computational systems or solutions, without numerical analysis of results. Of those who carried out experimentation 10 they used benchmarks, 13 estimated the sample size and 1 did not quote numbers.

Sample sizes were considered adequate for all those who used benchmarks since they are large collections of records and it is implied that for each input

**Table 4.** Citation number of statistical terms by year

| Year | n | AM | DP | DN | IC | ME | NE | NI | TE | VR |
|------|----|----|----|----|----|----|----|----|----|----|
| 2000 | 7 | – | – | – | – | 2 | – | 1 | 4 | – |
| 2001 | 34 | 4 | 1 | – | – | 10 | 1 | 1 | 16 | 1 |
| 2002 | 35 | 1 | 2 | – | – | 9 | 1 | 2 | 20 | – |
| 2003 | 40 | 2 | 3 | – | – | 11 | 1 | 2 | 21 | – |
| 2004 | 53 | – | 4 | – | – | 19 | 1 | 4 | 24 | 1 |
| 2005 | 58 | 3 | 6 | – | 1 | 17 | – | 2 | 28 | 1 |
| 2006 | 38 | – | 2 | 1 | – | 7 | 1 | 3 | 24 | – |
| 2007 | 28 | – | 1 | – | – | 7 | 1 | 1 | 17 | 1 |
| 2008 | 41 | 1 | 3 | 1 | 1 | 12 | – | 1 | 22 | – |
| 2009 | 18 | – | – | – | – | 4 | – | – | 14 | – |
| 2010 | 19 | 2 | – | 1 | – | 5 | – | – | 11 | – |
| 2011 | 8 | – | – | – | – | 3 | – | – | 5 | – |
| 2012 | 33 | – | 1 | 1 | 1 | 7 | 1 | – | 21 | 1 |
| 2013 | 31 | 2 | 2 | 2 | – | 11 | – | – | 14 | – |
| 2014 | 33 | – | – | – | – | 3 | – | 2 | 27 | 1 |
| 2015 | 16 | – | 1 | 1 | 1 | 1 | – | 1 | 11 | – |
| 2016 | 23 | 1 | – | 1 | 1 | 2 | – | 1 | 16 | 1 |
| 2017 | 13 | 2 | 1 | – | – | 2 | – | – | 8 | – |

record there is an output measurement and recording, also because they are a method widely accepted in the scientific community [24]. From those studies where the sample was estimated (13) in 11 of them the sample size was considered adequate, given the sample size and in 2 it was considered inadequate because they were below the minimum stipulated by CLT [14]. It is necessary to be aware, since a benchmark can represent the input load to which an experiment

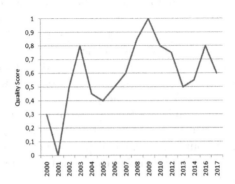

**Fig. 2.** Quality score per year

**Table 5.** Citation number of metrics terms by year

| Year | n | Disp. | BW | BP | CP | DU | EA | ID | MF | MI | PP | CO | SU |
|------|----|----|----|----|----|----|----|----|----|----|----|----|----|
| 2000 | 17 | 5 | 1 | – | – | – | 6 | 1 | – | 1 | – | 1 | 2 |
| 2001 | 29 | 7 | 3 | – | – | – | 9 | – | – | 1 | – | 2 | 7 |
| 2002 | 31 | 5 | 1 | – | – | – | 12 | – | – | 3 | – | 4 | 6 |
| 2003 | 38 | 11 | 2 | – | – | – | 8 | – | 3 | 2 | – | 5 | 7 |
| 2004 | 38 | 10 | – | – | – | – | 14 | – | – | 1 | – | 6 | 7 |
| 2005 | 36 | 10 | 1 | – | – | – | 9 | 1 | – | 1 | – | 4 | 10 |
| 2006 | 15 | 3 | 2 | – | – | – | 4 | – | – | 1 | – | – | 5 |
| 2007 | 17 | 3 | 1 | – | – | – | 3 | 1 | – | 2 | – | – | 7 |
| 2008 | 33 | 6 | 5 | – | – | – | 7 | – | 1 | 3 | – | 3 | 8 |
| 2009 | 23 | 6 | 1 | 1 | – | – | 4 | 1 | 1 | 1 | – | 1 | 7 |
| 2010 | 21 | 5 | – | – | – | 1 | 2 | 1 | – | 5 | – | 2 | 5 |
| 2011 | 8 | 3 | – | – | – | – | 1 | – | – | 1 | – | – | 3 |
| 2012 | 24 | 9 | 2 | 1 | – | – | 4 | – | – | 4 | – | – | 4 |
| 2013 | 31 | 5 | – | 1 | – | 3 | 5 | 1 | – | 3 | – | 2 | 11 |
| 2014 | 32 | 6 | – | – | – | – | 5 | 1 | – | 3 | – | 1 | 16 |
| 2015 | 17 | 1 | – | – | – | – | 3 | 1 | 1 | 2 | 1 | – | 8 |
| 2016 | 28 | 6 | 3 | – | 1 | – | 1 | 4 | 1 | 1 | – | 1 | 10 |
| 2017 | 22 | 5 | 1 | – | – | 1 | – | 2 | – | 1 | – | 1 | 11 |

**Table 6.** Citation number of tests by year

| Year | n | PV | TT |
|------|---|----|----|
| 2001 | 1 | 1 | – |
| 2007 | 4 | 1 | 3 |
| 2008 | 1 | – | 1 |
| 2009 | 1 | – | 1 |
| 2012 | 2 | – | 2 |
| 2015 | 1 | – | 1 |
| 2016 | 1 | – | 1 |

is submitted and not the amount of data collected, looking at this aspect only 8 papers had adequate samples with statistical analysis power specified in the text.

In all papers where there were experiments (24) were metrics, from this total 15 compared their results to other techniques and 9 did not. Confirming the results for using metrics from the first sample at 70%.

The second sample show only in 3 papers were the results are based on scientific criteria (statistical methods and mathematical models), but only 1

**Table 7.** Distribution of citations by type of term and year

| Ano | n | Statistic | | Metric | | Test | |
|---|---|---|---|---|---|---|---|
| | | Art. | Cit. | Art. | Cit. | Art. | Cit. |
| 2000 | 9 | 5 | 7 | 7 | 17 | – | – |
| 2001 | 23 | 20 | 34 | 16 | 29 | 1 | 1 |
| 2002 | 27 | 22 | 35 | 19 | 31 | – | – |
| 2003 | 32 | 28 | 40 | 23 | 38 | – | – |
| 2004 | 33 | 30 | 53 | 21 | 38 | – | – |
| 2005 | 34 | 31 | 58 | 26 | 36 | – | – |
| 2006 | 28 | 24 | 38 | 12 | 15 | – | – |
| 2007 | 21 | 17 | 28 | 12 | 17 | 2 | 4 |
| 2008 | 28 | 24 | 41 | 17 | 33 | 1 | 1 |
| 2009 | 23 | 14 | 18 | 16 | 23 | 1 | 1 |
| 2010 | 20 | 12 | 19 | 16 | 21 | – | – |
| 2011 | 6 | 5 | 8 | 5 | 8 | – | – |
| 2012 | 28 | 22 | 33 | 17 | 24 | 2 | 2 |
| 2013 | 20 | 17 | 31 | 16 | 31 | – | – |
| 2014 | 39 | 29 | 33 | 23 | 32 | – | – |
| 2015 | 15 | 12 | 16 | 11 | 17 | 1 | 1 |
| 2016 | 21 | 16 | 23 | 17 | 28 | 1 | 1 |
| 2017 | 19 | 9 | 13 | 15 | 22 | – | – |

article minimally used statistical methods (p-value and DP) to confirm their results. The values for the first and second sample evaluation criteria are similarly 2% and 3% respectively.

To calculate the evolution of the WSCAD in terms of quality of publication, each positive result of the categories analyzed in the second sample was assigned weight 1, and zero for negative or nonexistent results. The sums of each year and averages were calculated in a score which comprises values between 0 and 1. Figure 2 shows the evolutionary line of the score of quality of the publications, evidencing the maturation of the event over time. Although there are alternations in the line, the trend of the curve is upward with most years above average.

## 6  Improving the Quality

As presented in Sect. 5, statistical tests are not so cited as terms and metrics. The assumption, is that this may happen for two reasons. First the statistical test was not effectively applied to obtain the results, and second, due the fact that it not described in the paper methodology or discussion sections. To improve the results quality is necessary avoid both issues, applying the adequate test to calculate the results, and reporting how it was done. Next in this section, is discussed some statistical subjects and report strategies to try mitigate these issues.

## 6.1   Subjects in Statistics

The absence of the statistical analysis in the results verification could be an indicator that it was not performed. Second [21] one of the reasons for this, is the lack of knowledge of the authors for the execution of this stage of the research. In an attempt to mitigate this situation, the basic concepts in statistics are described below.

*Normal Distribution or Gaussian* (DN) - [7] describes the normal distribution, how the most commonly used distribution in data analysis. [12] enrols DN as a central role of data analysis. As already described in Sect. 2, DN is the model that best represents the natural behaviour of an experiment. Graphically the DN is represented by a symmetric bell curve, in which the bigger part of the sample values is around the center of the curve (mean) with some variability. It's important know about DN, because many of the statistical procedures like correlation, regression, t-tests, and analysis of variance needs that the data follows a DN [7].

*Central Limit Theorem* (CLT) - says that if a sample is large enough the behavior of the values tends to be a normal distribution [2,7,14]. The CLT suggests that samples with 30 or more observations are sufficient to have a normal distribution of the data. The CLT allows that a non-normal distribution population be sampled to a DN by a representative sample of this population, in this way statistical procedures that needs a DN of data can be executed.

*Sample* (AM) - is a part of a population. Population is a complete universe of all individuals that will be studied [7]. The statistics objective is make inferences of a population by using samples of this one [12]. For this reason is important distinguish sample from population. In most of cases it's impossible, or expensive, study the whole population. So a representative sample is needed, keeping in mind the CLT statements not only for sampling, but with the number of executions (NE) or iterations (NI).

*Hypothesis Test* (HT) - most of experiments are trying to proof something. For example: "there are improvements between technique A in relation to B?". This sentence is the hypothesis statement. The *null hypothesis* (*H0*) is equality hypothesis, and the *alternative hypothesis(H1)* are the opposite. In this case the *H0* is that there are no improvements from technique A to B, and the *H1* is that A have improvements over B. The HT works rejecting or accepting one or other hypothesis by calculating the *p-value* using an appropriate statistical test and a significance level (1% or 5% generally used). If the *p-value* is smaller than the significance level used in to calculate, *H0* is rejected and *H1* accepted (there are significant improvements), otherwise, *H0* is accepted and *H1* rejected (there are no significant improvements).

*Confidence interval* (IC) - adding the concepts for confidence interval listed on Sect. 2, the IC is commonly used to indicate reliability from research results. Note that the more critics need to be the search results the greater the confidence interval. The pharmaceutical industry, for example, adopts a 99% IC in drug tests (p=0.01). In some cases not of non-critical result studies, more relaxed values of IC are acceptable, however the scientific community adopts the value of 95% (p = 0.05) as standard.

*Mean* (ME) - is one measure of summarization of the sample. Is obtained by the quotient of summarizing the data by sample size. It's important distinguish mean from other two summarization measures: median and mode. Median is the central point of a sample data, that separates the sample in two halves. Mode is the value of a sample with major occurrence. These measures in a DN tend to be the same.

*Standard Deviation* (DP) - is one dispersion measure and your values have the same unit of the data. Your results represents how far (big DP values) or close (smaller DP values) to the ME of the data. Represents the variability of the sample and is used for many other calculations in statistics, for example IC.

*Variance* (VR) - is another dispersion measure, similar to the standard deviation. His unit is expressed in the square of the unit of the sample measurement. For this reason it is not commonly used, being its square root, the standard deviation, most used to represent the variability of the data. Variance is more used to compare when performing variance analysis of more than one set of values (ANOVA).

*P-Value* (PV) - is the probability that the test statistic will take on a value that is at least as extreme as the observed value of the statistic when the null hypothesis H0 is true [12] in other words represents the lowest level of significance which null hypothesis is rejected. PV is the result of most of statistical tests. His value helps to improve the power of research results.

With the advance of many statistical software packages in the market nowadays, knowing how exactly a test is calculated is not (sometimes) necessary the software does the heavy job by typing a single command. What is most important is know the hard concepts and where to find the answers, and which test to be used in a certain situation or not. Table 8 briefly summarizes the most common tests and his usages.

**Table 8.** Statistical tests and his usage [9]

| Test name | Usage |
| --- | --- |
| ANOVA (AN) | Tests to detect the mean difference of 3 or more independent groups |
| Chi-Square (CH) | Tests the differences of the association between two categorical variables |
| Wilcoxon (TC) | Tests for the difference between two independent variables, takes into account magnitude and direction of difference |
| Fisher (FT) | Tests two nominal variables when is wanted to see whether the proportions of one variable are different depending on the value of the other variable. Use it when the sample size is small |
| Kruskal-Wallis (KR) | Tests the medians of two or more samples to determine if the samples come from different populations |
| Mann–Whitney (MW) Or U-Test (TU) | Test to compare two sample means that come from the same population, and used to test whether two sample means are equal or not |
| T-Test (TT) | Tests for the difference between two related variables |

## 6.2   Follow a Guideline

Although a good statistical analysis was done, as demonstrated, it is not described in most of the papers. This can occur for several reasons. Due to the fact that the researcher judge not necessary, due the small limit of pages of the conferences where these papers are submitted and the statistical analysis is deferred in favor of the demonstration of the technique itself. Regardless the reason, the statistical analysis, as well as other stages of the research, must, even briefly, be described to demonstrate the robustness of the results and consequently of the technique developed.

In [13] is suggested that 85% of biomedical research effort is waste due to issues of low quality of results. Would be this the case of Computer Science too? It should be noted, on related works, that exist evidences, since 1993, that the results present in scientific works in Computer Science are weakly based from the statistical point of view. According to [21], the cause of this weak foundation is the little intimacy of the area with statistical methods (another reason to complement what was already described). However, these same works do not effectively present, or suggests, a verification method or guide to be followed before publication submission, and, similarly to the reviewers of these papers to establish selection criteria for publication in their journals.

In other areas of knowledge, such as the Medical for example, there are several protocols and guidelines to different types of studies developed in this area. These not only help during the development of the research, but also in the design phase as well as in the presentation of results including statistical analysis. In these documents are described, methodologically speaking, all sections of a scientific work and all particularities that need to be contained in each of them, according to the type of study performed.

According to [13], there are about 300 different types of medical research guides[2]. Initiatives such as **PRISMA**[3] [11], **STROBE**[4] [4,8], **CONSORT**[5] [10] and **TOP**[6] [16], are widely adopted by journals and periodicals as authors and reviewers guidelines. Individually, these initiatives do not meet the specifics of computing area, but could be a starting point to research guide and reporting, till a specifics computer science guidelines are not complete formulated.

In this way, initiatives of guidelines to fill this gap in computer science are still sparse. Most of them are restricted to the software engineering or simulation. When considered the verification of execution performance indexes, these initiatives do not address all possible types of studies or specificities such as the use of benchmarks and workloads as sample space [19]. This miss orientation, could contribute to impossibility do understand and reproduce most of studies reported in papers.

---

[2] http://www.equator-network.org/library/.
[3] Preferred Reporting Items for Systematic Reviews and Meta-Analyzes.
[4] Strengthening the Reporting of Observational Studies in Epidemiology.
[5] Consolidated Standards of Reporting Trials.
[6] Transparency and Openness Promotion.

A literature review of this theme was done to investigate guidelines to research and reporting in Computer Science. The word "protocol" was discharged due to a bias related to network protocols. The research was limited to **papers** in **English** or **Portuguese**, published on the **last 10 years** (2009 to 2019). The terms "computer science", "reporting standards", "reporting evaluation", "reporting guidelines", "reporting statements", "reporting checklist", "research standards", "research evaluation", "research guidelines", "research statements", "research checklist" were submitted to Springer Link[7], IEEE Digital Library[8], ACM Digital Library[9] and Science@Direct[10] obtaining a total of 1528 searched results. Where after paper title reading (62 selected), abstract reading (24 selected) and full paper reading, results in 10 papers with related information, but only four with complete relationship with the theme, the rest of them have some interest relation.

The highlight came from [6] showing as the most relevant reference of the 15 obtained. The related works cited by this publication in specific, was published before 2009. Thus the conclusion is that nothing new was published in the last decade in this sense, except the paper itself. If take into account the results of a literature review described above.

The concerns of [6] and [13] touched on the same situations raised here, reinforcing the argument. The lack of certain information in the publications may lead to the impossibility of understanding, replicating, auditing and evaluating the quality of the results obtained. In this respect [13] argues that the use of guidelines improves the orientation of researchers in both design and description of results.

Although it seem only bureaucratic processes, by the scientific community, guidelines is a robust way to improve the research as well as the reporting of it. [13] points that with the rapid adoption of guidelines in areas of knowledge, like Biomedical and Social Science, the problems related to the quality of the results of the researches are being overcome. Not only for individual researches, but for journals and periodicals. Publications that not adopted guidelines show poorer reporting quality compared with that have adopted [20].

## 7    Conclusion

In this paper we present a research and analysis about the occurrence of statistical terms, metrics and statistical tests used to prove the results in scientific research. Publications of all WSCAD editions till 2017 were analyzed in a total sample of 426 papers.

From the analyzed sample, 398 publications referred to at least one of the searched terms, corresponding to 93% of the total. This shows that there is concern in research conducting and reporting, even inadequate or incomplete given

---

[7] http://link.springer.com.

[8] http://ieeexplore.ieee.org.

[9] http://portal.acm.org.

[10] http://www.sciencedirect.com.

the occurrence of only 3% of statistical tests confirmed by a second independent sample of 30 papers. It is necessary not only to focus on the design and development of the research object itself, but also on the measurements and reporting of the results.

Almost all of the papers only present the measurements of the implemented technique, and the questioning is inevitable: is just a simple measurement of the metric sufficient to compare similar techniques, disregarding error factors and considering that they were performed within the same standards? Are those results reproducible?

The research described here should be a warning to the scientific community. There is clearly a need for attention in the points highlighted. The findings of this work should promote reflection on undergraduate and postgraduate courses about the need to include methodology of statistical analysis of data applied to computing in basic formation classes. The adoption of research and reporting guidelines is a highly recommended alternative to mitigate issues, both with regard to study design, experimentation, collection of data of the experiment in adequate quantity and quality, in the application of statistical tests in a way that results have the effective power to show what is proposed.

The contribution with the WSCAD is to indicate in the call for papers the need for the papers to show their performance analysis accompanied by the methodological and statistical validation of their results, asking the reviewers of those papers to observe if such study was duly presented, by using specific and appropriate guide for the conference, which of course, needs to be formulated with the community of this event.

# References

1. Adler, S., Schmitt, S., Wolter, K., Kyas, M.: A survey of experimental evaluation in indoor localization research. In: 2015 International Conference on Indoor Positioning and Indoor Navigation (IPIN), pp. 1–10. IEEE (2015)
2. Bukh, P.N.D.: The Art of Computer Systems Performance Analysis, Techniques for Experimental Design, Measurement, Simulation and Modeling (1992)
3. Dean, A., Voss, D., Draguljić, D., et al.: Design and Analysis of Experiments, vol. 1. Springer, New York (1999). https://doi.org/10.1007/b97673
4. Ebrahim, S., Clarke, M.: STROBE: new standards for reporting observational epidemiology, a chance to improve (2007)
5. Fortier, P., Michel, H.: Computer Systems Performance Evaluation and Prediction. Elsevier, Amsterdam (2003)
6. de França, B.B.N., Travassos, G.H.: Experimentation with dynamic simulation models in software engineering: planning and reporting guidelines. Empir. Softw. Eng. **21**(3), 1302–1345 (2016)
7. Jain, R.: The Art of Computer Systems Performance Analysis: Techniques for Experimental Design, Measurement, Simulation, and Modeling. Wiley, Hoboken (1990)
8. Malta, M., Cardoso, L.O., Bastos, F.I., Magnanini, M.M.F., da Silva, C.M.F.P.: Iniciativa strobe: subsídios para a comunicação de estudos observacionais. Revista de Saúde Pública **44**, 559–565 (2010)

9. University of Minnesota: Types of statistical testes (2019). https://cyfar.org/types-statistical-tests. Accessed 23 May 2019
10. Moher, D., et al.: Consort 2010 explanation and elaboration: updated guidelines for reporting parallel group randomised trials. Int. J. Surg. 10(1), 28–55 (2012)
11. Moher, D., Liberati, A., Tetzlaff, J., Altman, D.G.: Preferred reporting items for systematic reviews and meta-analyses: the prisma statement. Ann. Intern. Med. 151(4), 264–269 (2009)
12. Montgomery, D.C.: Design and Analysis of Experiments. Wiley, Hoboken (2017)
13. Munafò, M.R., et al.: A manifesto for reproducible science. Nat. Hum. Behav. 1(1), 0021 (2017)
14. Navidi, W.: Probabilidade e estatística para ciências exatas. AMGH (2012)
15. Neto, B.B., Scarminio, I.S., Bruns, R.E.: Como Fazer Experimentos-: Pesquisa eDesenvolvimento na Ciência e na Indústria. Bookman (2010)
16. Nosek, B.A., et al.: Promoting an open research culture. Science 348(6242), 1422–1425 (2015)
17. Osorio, A., Dias, M., Cavalheiro, G.G.H.: WSCAD: uma meta-analise. In: WSCAD 2018, October 2018. http://wscad.sbc.org.br/2018/anais/anais-wscad-2018.pdf
18. Prechelt, L.: A quantitative study of experimental evaluations of neural network learning algorithms: current research practice. IEEE Trans. Neural Netw. 6, 457–462 (1994)
19. Runeson, P., Höst, M.: Guidelines for conducting and reporting case study research in software engineering. Empir. Softw. Eng. 14(2), 131 (2009)
20. Stevens, A., et al.: Relation of completeness of reporting of health research to journals' endorsement of reporting guidelines: systematic review. BMJ 348, g3804 (2014)
21. Tedre, M., Moisseinen, N.: Experiments in computing: a survey. Sci. World J. 2014 (2014)
22. Tichy, W.F., Lukowicz, P., Prechelt, L., Heinz, E.A.: Experimental evaluation in computer science: a quantitative study. J. Syst. Softw. 28(1), 9–18 (1995)
23. Wainer, J., Barsottini, C.G.N., Lacerda, D., de Marco, L.R.M.: Empirical evaluation in computer science research published by ACM. Inf. Softw. Technol. 51(6), 1081–1085 (2009)
24. Wainer, J., et al.: Métodos de pesquisa quantitativa e qualitativa para a ciência da computação. Atualização em informática 1, 221–262 (2007)

# Processors and Memory Architectures

# High-Performance RISC-V Emulation

Leandro Lupori$^{(\boxtimes)}$, Vanderson Martins do Rosario$^{(\boxtimes)}$, and Edson Borin$^{(\boxtimes)}$

Institute of Computing, UNICAMP, Campinas, SP, Brazil
leandro.lupori@gmail.com, {vanderson.rosario,edson}@ic.unicamp.br

**Abstract.** RISC-V is an open ISA that has been calling the attention worldwide by its fast growth and adoption. It is already supported by GCC, Clang and the Linux Kernel. However, none of the currently available RISC-V emulators are capable of providing good, near-native, emulation performance. Thus, in this work, we investigate if faster emulators for RISC-V could be created. Since Dynamic Binary Translation (DBT) is the most common, and fastest, technique to implement emulators, we focus our investigation on the quality of the translated code, arguably the most important source of overhead when emulating code with DBT. To this end, we implemented and evaluated a LLVM-based Static Binary Translation (SBT) engine to investigate whether or not it is possible to produce high-quality translations from RISC-V to x86 and ARM. We explored different translation techniques and managed to design an SBT engine that produces translated code that is only 1.2x/1.3x slower than native x86/ARM code, which supports the claim that it is possible to build near-native RISC-V emulators for x86 and ARM hosts. We also analyze the main sources of overheads, compare the code produced by our SBT against the code produced by a popular DBT and provide insights on the potential performance impact of the proposed techniques on DBTs.

**Keywords:** RISC-V · Binary translation · LLVM · Emulation

## 1 Introduction

RISC-V is a new, open and free Instruction Set Architecture (ISA), initially developed at the University of California [28] and now maintained by the RISC-V foundation [10], with a handful of companies supporting its development. It is a small RISC-based architecture divided into multiple modules that support integer computation, floating-point, atomic operations, and compressed instructions [28]. RISC-V is calling attention worldwide by its fast growth and adoption. By now, it is supported by the Linux Kernel, GCC, Clang, not to mention several RISC-V simulators [17,26] and emulators [9,11]. However, RISC-V CPU chips are still hard to find and until then emulation plays a crucial role, because it enables the use of a new ISA while there are no (or few) physical CPUs available for it.

C. Bianchini et al. (Eds.): WSCAD 2018, CCIS 1171, pp. 135–151, 2020.
https://doi.org/10.1007/978-3-030-41050-6_9

The main job of an ISA emulator is to emulate guest instructions using host instructions, with the goal of making the host perform an equivalent computation to what would be achieved by the guest instructions being executed on the guest platform. However, not only mimicking the behavior is important, but normally performance also plays a crucial role. Our research indicates that, at the current time, RISC-V still lacks an emulator that can achieve near-native performance—which in this work is considered to be up to 1.2x slower than native (s.t.n.)—as the best RISC-V emulators performances are more than 2 times s.t.n. This limits the scope of RISC-V emulators, by excluding them from use cases where performance plays a major role.

One approach to implement a high-performance emulator is by using Dynamic Binary Translation (DBT) [20], a technique that selects and translates regions of code dynamically during the emulation. As we shall see in Sect. 2, there are two DBT design choices which affect most of the quality of translation: (1) the DBT's Region Formation Technique (RFT) which defines the shape of the translation units [24] and (2) the characteristics of the guest and host ISA which can hinder or facilitate the translation [1]. While RFT design choice is well explored in the literature, the translation quality of each pair of guest and host ISA needs to be researched and retested for every new ISA.

We investigate the quality and difficulty of code translation for a pair of ISAs is by implementing a Static Binary Translation (SBT) engine [1]. SBTs are limited in the sense that they are not capable of emulating self-modifying code and may have difficulty differentiating between data and code, but its design and implementation are usually much simpler than those of a DBT. Since the translation mechanisms in a DBT and an SBT are very similar, if one is able to create an SBT engine which can emit high-quality code for a pair of architectures, it implies that the same can be done for a DBT engine.

In a recent work [19], we implemented and evaluated a LLVM-based SBT to investigate whether or not it was possible to produce high-quality translations from RISC-V to x86 and ARM. Our SBT was capable of producing high-quality translations, that execute almost as fast as native code, with around 1.2x/1.3x slowdown in x86/ARM. In this way, the main contributions of that work were the following:

- A novel Open Source RISC-V Static Binary Translator based on LLVM.[1]
- We showed with our RISC-V SBT that it is possible to perform a high-quality translation of RISC-V binaries to x86 and ARM.
- We compared the performance of our SBT engine with that of state-of-the-art RISC-V emulators and argued that there was room for improvement.

In this paper, we extend our previous work by pursuing further improvements for our SBT of RISC-V. We implemented a new register mapping technique that achieves better results, together with other implementation refinements. We also added a larger benchmark and performed a deeper analysis of the overheads

---

[1] https://github.com/OpenISA/riscv-sbt

of each benchmark evaluated by us, which revealed new insights of code constructions and optimizations that can hinder high-quality translations, such as aggressive loop unrolling. Furthermore, we performed a more complete comparison between our SBT engine and other DBT engines, taking into account the differences between SBT and DBT and how they impact performance and comparing the code produced by our SBT two popular RISC-V DBT engines. Our new contributions are as follows.

- An improved Open Source RISC-V Static Binary Translator based on LLVM.[2]
- A deeper performance comparison of our SBT engine with that of state-of-the-art RISC-V emulators, showing that current RISC-V DBT engines have other sources of overhead besides those inherent to the DBT approach.
- We show that it is not trivial to make LLVM vectorize code when translating optimized code from an ISA that does not support vectorization.
- We show that aggressive loop unrolling on guest code can impact performance significantly when translated to an ISA with less registers.

These additional results allow the reader to understand the sources of overhead and reason about the potential performance impact of the proposed techniques on DBTs. Besides, the results continue to indicate that our SBT engine is able to produce high-quality translations, with overheads around 1.2x/1.3x—and even lower when considering the new register mapping mode—when compared to native x86/ARM execution, evidencing the opportunity towards RISC-V emulators with higher performance than current ones and showing that RISC-V is indeed an easy to emulate ISA.

The rest of this paper is organized as follows. Section 2 further describes ISA emulation techniques and related work. Then, in Sect. 3 we discuss our SBT engine for RISC-V, in Sect. 4 we describe our experimental setup, and in Sect. 5 we discuss the results we have obtained with our RISC-V SBT engine. Lastly, Sect. 6 presents our future work and conclusions.

## 2   ISA Emulation and Related Work

Interpretation and DBT are well-known methods used to implement ISA emulators. In this section, we examine them in more details, along with SBT and works that achieved good performance results with each method.

### 2.1   Interpretation

Interpretation is a technique that relies on a fetch-decode-execute loop that mimics the behavior of a simple CPU, a straightforward approach. Nonetheless, it usually requires the execution of tens (or hundreds) of native instructions to emulate each guest instruction. For instance, Bochs [18] is a well-known and mature x86 interpreted emulator, able to emulate the entire system and boot

---

[2] https://github.com/OpenISA/riscv-sbt.

operating systems. But, by emulating x86 over x86, its performance varies from 31 to 95 host cycles per instruction emulated (or about 31 to 95x slower than native) on average, measured using the SPEC CPU2006(int) benchmark [7]. Therefore, we conclude that even high-performance interpreted emulators such as Bochs are not good enough when compared to native execution performance.

**RISC-V Interpreters:** The gem5 simulator [21,27] is a modular platform for computer-system architecture research, supporting multiple distinct CPU architectures, such as x86, ARM, SPARC, and now also RISC-V (gem5 for RISC-V is a.k.a. RISC5). While a strong point of this simulator is its ability to perform accurate CPU simulation and capture microarchitectural details, this ends up resulting in a much slower emulation speed—around 175 KIPS (Thousand Instructions per Second) when emulating RISC-Vcode [27]. Even though it performs well above other in-depth simulators, such as the Chisel C++ RTL simulator, it is much slower than other RISC-V emulators that do not try to capture microarchitectural details, such as Spike and QEMU.

TinyEMU [3] is a system emulator for RISC-V and x86 architectures. Its purpose is to be small and simple while being complete. It even supports the 128-bit RISC-V variant and quadruple-precision floating-point (Q extension). While we found no performance data available for it yet, it should be similar to that of purely interpreted emulators. On x86 it makes use of KVM, which in general achieves a performance well above that of interpretation due to hardware acceleration, but that does not help on improving RISC-V performance.

ANGEL [12] is a Javascript RISC-V ISA (RV64) Simulator that runs RISC-V Linux with BusyBox. Our simple run achieved ≈10 MIPS in Chrome, on an Intel Core i7-2630QM CPU running at 2.0 GHz, or about 200 times slower than native.

Spike [13], a RISC-V ISA simulator, is considered by the RISC-V Foundation to be their "golden standard" in terms of emulation correctness. As expected from an interpretation-based simulator, its performance is not very high, although quite higher than other emulators in some cases, varying from 15 to 75 times slower than native on SPECINT2006 benchmarks [17]. This performance is due to several DBT-like optimizations, such as instruction cache, software TLB, and unrolled PC-indexed interpreter loop to improve host branch prediction.

## 2.2  Dynamic Binary Translation (DBT)

Dynamic Binary Translators translate (map) pieces of guest code into host code and usually obtain greater performance with the cost of being more complex and harder to implement. Because of this, translation is commonly used on high-performance emulators, such as QEMU [4]. A DBT engine uses two mechanisms to emulate the execution of a binary, one with a fast-start but slow-execution and another with a fast-execution but a slow start. The former is used to emulate cold (seldom executed) parts of the binary, normally implemented using an interpreter. The latter is used to emulate hot (frequently executed) parts of the code by translating the region of code and executing it natively. A translated region of code normally executes more than 10x faster than an interpreter [5]. It is important to notice that the costs associated with the translation process impact directly on the final emulation time. As a consequence, DBTs usually employ region formation techniques (RFTs) that try to form and translate only regions of code so that the execution speedup (compared to interpretation) pays off the translation time cost.

In most programs, the majority of their execution is spent in small portions of code [24]. Thus, when emulating these programs, DBT engines also spend most of their time executing small portions of translated code. This implies that the translation quality of these portions of code is crucial to the final performance of a DBT engine. In fact, this is evidenced by the low overhead of same-ISA DBT engines [6], also known as binary optimizers, as they always execute code with the same or better quality than the native binary (this happens because same-ISA do not actually impose translations, but only optimizations). Designing and implementing high-performance cross-ISA DBT engines, on the other hand, is more challenging as the quality of the translated code depends heavily on the characteristics of the guest (source) and the host (target) ISA. For instance, ARM has a conditional execution mechanism that enables instructions to be conditionally executed depending on the state of the status register, however, since x86 does not have this feature and it may require several instructions to mimic this behavior on x86 [22]. Experience has shown that when emulating a guest-ISA which is simpler than the target-ISA it is normally easier to obtain high quality translation [1]. Next, we examine some well-known DBT engines with high-performance emulation.

Hong et al. created HQEMU [16] in an effort to enhance QEMU [4] with LLVM and try to achieve near-native performance. It uses QEMU standard Tiny Code Generator (TCG) for fast translation of cold regions, while LLVM runs on another core to aggressively optimize traces of hot regions. The geometric mean of the overhead compared to native execution is 2.5x for x86 emulation on x86-64 (almost same-ISA emulation) and 3.4x for ARM emulation on x86-64 (cross-ISA setup), with an i7 3.3 GHz as the host machine. This same work also evaluates the performance of QEMU as a baseline, reporting 5.9x on the same-ISA emulation setup and 8.2x on the cross-ISA setup.

In a more recent work, Zhang et al. [29] proposed HERMES, a cross-ISA binary translation that drop the architecture of QEMU in favor of a host-specific data dependency graph, which allows exploring optimizations at a representation that is closer to the host instead of the generic IR of QEMU. HERMES achieves the performance of, on average, 2.66x slower than native for SPEC CPU2000 programs, which is very competitive for a cross-ISA translation.

One of the best performances we see in the literature is achieved by IA32-EL, introduced by Baraz et al. [2], an ISA translator that runs x86 guest programs on the discontinued Itanium architecture. They built a specialized DBT engine that runs x86 programs, on average, 1.35x slower than native Itanium programs, albeit their DBT is focused on only a specific guest and host machine pair.

For same-ISA emulation, the best performance we found so far is that of StarDBT by Borin and Wu [6]: 1.1x slower than native (x86) emulation.

These works show that it is possible to achieve near-native performance by means of DBT techniques, even with cross-ISA emulation, as shown by IA32-EL. In the cross-ISA scenario, however, the performance of the DBT is highly dependant on guest and host ISA characteristics, as we mentioned earlier.

**RISC-V Dynamic Binary Translators:** Ilbeyi et al. [17] showed that the Pydgin Instruction Set Simulator can achieve better performance than Spike by means of more sophisticated techniques, mainly, DBT. Pydgin with DBT is able to perform between 4x to 33x slower than native. While achieving a better result than Spike, Pydgin is still slower than the newer QEMU for RISC-V.

QEMU [4], a famous DBT with multiple sources and targets, also gained support for RISC-V. Clark and Hoult [9] reported that QEMU is, on average, 4.57x slower than native execution and that one of its main performance disadvantages comes from floating-point emulation, as its Intermediate Representation (IR) does not have any instruction of that kind and it needs to simulate them by calling auxiliary functions.

The OVP Simulator [26] implements the full functionality of RISC-V User and Privileged specifications. It is developed and maintained by Imperas Software [25], being fully compliant to the OVP open standard APIs. As we show in Sect. 5, it is on average 4.92x s.t.n., a result close to that of QEMU.

Clark and Hoult [9] presented the RV8 emulator, a high-performance RISC-V DBT for x86. Using optimizations such as macro-op fusion and trace formation and merge, RV8 is able to achieve a performance 2.62x slower than native, on average, overcoming QEMU and being the fastest known RISC-V DBT engine. Note, however, that RV8 is currently more limited than QEMU, as it does not support running as many program types as QEMU and it can run only on x86. Besides, although 2.62x s.t.n. is a good performance result, it is still far from near-native performance.

### 2.3 Static Binary Translation (SBT)

Having a high-performance DBT for a pair of ISAs would prove that, for these ISAs, it is possible to achieve good translation quality. However, implementing a DBT is a complex project and a challenge by itself. Another possibility is to implement an SBT engine to translate the binary. An SBT engine translates statically the whole binary at once. SBT engines are not usually used to emulate binaries in industry, despite being easier to implement than a DBT engine, because they cannot execute all kinds of applications. Self-modifying code, code discovery problems and indirect branches are some of the emulation problems that may not be handled statically [8]. However, for the purpose of testing the difficulty of translating code with high-quality, an SBT is enough.

A remarkable SBT engine we see in literature is LLBT [23], a static binary translator based on LLVM that emulates ARM code on Intel Atom based processors ans is only 1.40x slower than native for the EEMBC benchmark.

Going further, according to Auler and Borin [1], it is possible to achieve near-native performance in cross-ISA emulation if the guest architecture is easy to be emulated. They showed this to be possible with OpenISA, an ISA based on MIPS but modified with emulation performance in mind. Using SBT to emulate OpenISA on x86 and ARM, they were able to achieve an overhead of less than 1.10x for the majority of programs. In fact, among the main motivations for this work was the near-native performance that Auler and Borin were able to achieve with their OpenISA emulator, and the similarities between OpenISA and RISC-V, which suggested that RISC-V could also be emulated very efficiently. OpenISA's work [1] discusses several characteristics that may ease or difficult an ISA emulation. RISC-V has most of the characteristics pointed by the authors to be easy to emulate: it is simple, it hardly uses status registers and it has a small number of instructions—RISC-V has 107 and OpenISA 139, with 66% of them being equivalent—all indicating that RISC-V is also an easy to emulate ISA. This is the reason why we use the same approach as that used by Auler and Borin to test OpenISA emulation performance and this is the methodology that we use to test if RISC-V translation can achieve good performance.

# 3   A Static Binary Translator for RISC-V

Static translation of RISC-V binaries into native form for other architectures, such as ARM and x86, involves several steps. Our Static Binary Translator starts by reading a RISC-V object file and disassembling each instruction in it, with the help of LLVM libraries. Then, for each RISC-V instruction, our translator emits equivalent, target independent, LLVM Intermediate Representation (IR) instructions (a.k.a. bitcode). The remaining steps are performed with existing software. LLVM tools are used to optimize the IR and to generate assembly code for x86 or ARM. After that, a standard assembler and linker for the target platform, such as GNU *as* and *ld*, can be used to produce the native binary for the host architecture. All these steps for SBT are summarized in the diagram from Fig. 1. The code generation flows used in our experiments are further detailed in Sect. 4.

## 3.1   RISC-V to LLVM Code Emission

In general, most RISC-V instructions have a direct, one-to-one, or close enough, LLVM IR instruction that eases the task of implementing a binary translator for it. However, some classes of instructions are difficult to translate by nature, such as branches and jumps. Next, we first go through some general implementation decisions of how we translate branches and jumps from RISC-V code to LLVM IR.

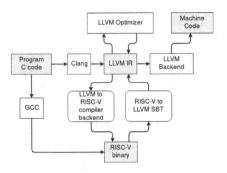

**Fig. 1.** Our RISC-V SBT engine architecture.

**Arithmetic Logic Operations:** For the arithmetic and logic instructions, in the vast majority of cases the translation is trivial—not considering the register mapping code—as there is a direct correspondent instruction in LLVM IR. Examples are *add*, *sub*, and *xor*. Some instruction forms were optimized, such as *xor a, b, −1*, that is used in RISC-V to perform a logical *not*, that does not have a distinct instruction for it, but is present in other ISAs, that usually execute it faster than a *xor*. In such cases the translator emits the optimal LLVM IR instruction, that would be a *not* in this case. In a few cases, however, there is no direct equivalence in LLVM IR, such as in the *mulh* instruction, that returns the upper 32 bits of a multiplication. In this case, this instruction is translated to a 64-bit multiplication, an arithmetic shift right of 32 bits and a truncate instruction. Here it would be possible to optimize the case where both *mul* and *mulh* instructions were performed with the same inputs, but we left this optimization out, as we did not detect this to have a significant impact in our benchmarks.

**Shadow Image:** Before translating the code present in the `.text` section, all other sections are processed and a *Shadow Image* of the binary is built, that is, a copy of the sections of the original binary. This copy is then modified, by translating most of the guest addresses, during the relocation process, adding helper data.

**Handling Relocations:** We handle all memory accesses to data by using the guest address as an offset that is relative to the base address of the binary *Shadow Image*. In the case of relocations that point to the `.text` section, however, we need to defer the relocation, until the corresponding code location is translated and its host address or label is known. This way, for addresses that point to instructions inside a function that are potential indirect branch targets, pending relocations are created and resolved during code translation.

**Direct Branches and Jumps:** All branch and jump instructions are translated in the same way. First, the correct condition test is emitted, if the instruction is a branch. Next, a conditional or an unconditional jump is emitted. To compute the target guest address, the displacement operand of the branch or jump instruction is added to the current guest address, that in our case is equal to the address of the instruction being translated. If the resulting address is greater than the current one, a new basic block is created at the target address and added to the basic blocks' map. Otherwise, a lookup by address is performed at the function's basic blocks, to check if there is already one starting at the target guest address. If not, the basic block that contains the instruction at the target address is located and split in two at that point. The branch to the correct basic block can then be emitted.

**Indirect Jumps:** The translation of indirect jumps is performed in three steps: (1) pending relocations are created for addresses that can be target of indirect jumps; (2) when the instructions at these addresses are translated the pending relocation is updated with the right addresses; and (3) after all function instructions have been translated, we update all addresses discovered in the pending relocations into all jump tables, so the indirect jump can occur naturally. But note that our translation of indirect jumps handles only common cases: indirect jumps emitted by compilers, with a limited number of targets, loaded from jump tables. For the general case, it should be handled efficiently by others known DBT techniques [14] that we did not implemented. However, indirect jumps were very uncommon in our benchmarks, and thus it had little impact on their performance.

### 3.2   Unlinked Objects as Input

Instead of translating final linked binaries, we chose to translate relocatable object files to avoid dealing with some issues inherent to SBT, such as differentiating code from data. It also enables us to translate only the benchmark code, leaving the C runtime out, which simplifies the implementation and debugging of the SBT engine, saving a considerable amount of work that would otherwise be required. With this approach, however, the translator must be able to identify C library calls in guest code and forward these to the corresponding ones on native code. This was done by listing all C functions needed by the benchmarks we used, together with their types and arguments and then, at the call site, copying RISC-V registers corresponding to arguments to the appropriate host arguments' locations, as defined by their ABIs. It is worth mentioning that, although most benchmarks spent most time in the main binary, some of them spent considerable time in non-translated *libc* code, that must not be considered when calculating the slowdown of the translated binaries. To handle this and improve the accuracy of the results, we also measure and factor out the time that the binaries spend in *libc*, as shall be explained in more details in Sect. 4. With this measure, the results obtained by our SBT engine are not benefited by the non-translated native *libc* code that is executed.

### 3.3   Register Mapping

Regarding register mapping between architectures during the translation, our SBT engine implements 3 techniques:

**Globals** – RISC-V registers are translated to global variables. In this technique, the translator emits load/store instructions to read/write from/to these global variables whenever registers are used/modified by guest instructions. The main advantages of this approach are that it is simple and it does not need any kind of inter-function synchronization. The main disadvantage of it, however, is that the compiler is unable to optimize most accesses to global variables.

**Locals** – RISC-V registers are translated to function's local variables. In this technique, the translator emits load/store instructions to read/write from/to these local variables whenever registers are used/modified by guest instructions. The main advantage of this approach is that the compiler is able to perform aggressive optimizations on those. The main disadvantage is that the values of these local variables need to be synchronized with those of other functions at function calls and returns, what can impact performance significantly on hot spots. We implement the synchronization by copying local register variables from/to global variables, when entering and leaving functions.

**ABI** – this technique is very similar to Locals, with the main difference being that only registers that are specified as non-volatile in RISC-V ABI are preserved through function calls. This reduces the synchronization overhead considerably, but limits the translatable programs to those that conform to RISC-V ABI.

## 4    Experimental Setup and Infrastructure

In order to quantify the performance overhead introduced by the SBT, we compared the performance of benchmarks emulated with SBT against the performance of their native execution. For the benchmarks, we have used MiBench [15], which provides a reasonable set of programs with sufficient variation to cover most CPU emulation aspects. The experiments were performed on two host ISAs: x86 and ARM. The x86 machine used was an Intel Core i7-6700K running at 4.0 GHz, with 32 GiB of RAM, running on Debian 9. As for the ARM machine, we used a Raspberry Pi 3 Model B, that had a Quad Core CPU running at 1.2 GHz, with 1 GiB of RAM, running Raspbian 9.

The RISC-V binaries used as input for our SBT engine, as well as the native ones, were built with GCC 6.3(native)/7.3(RISC-V) toolchains, while our SBT engine makes use of LLVM 7.0 infrastructure to produce assembly code for x86 and ARM, and then GCC 6.3 toolchain is used to assemble and link the program, as LLVM's assembler and linker did not support RISC-V binaries during the time of our experiments. GCC 7.3.0 was used for RISC-V because there was practically no support for it in GCC 6.3.0. This however leads to some uncertainty about different compiler versions affecting the performance results. To rule this out, we have compiled and translated all benchmarks for x86 and ARM using GCC 7.3.0 and compared it with the results obtained with GCC 6.3.0. The differences in performance were minimal (2%). To minimize performance differences, we have used the same compilers and optimization flags (-O3 was used in all cases) for the experiments.

We chose to use the RISC-V 32-bit IMFD variant, composed by the instruction sets of the integer base I (mandatory), standard extensions M (integer multiplication and division), F and D (floating-point operations with single and double precision). These extensions compose the general-purpose RISC-V instructions. The only general extension we left out was A (atomic instructions) as we only used single-threaded benchmarks, making no use for these instructions. Moreover, we chose 32-bit to make it easier to compare our RISC-V experiments with OpenISA, which is also 32-bits.

To compile the benchmarks, our initial plan was to use Clang for every target: ARM, RISC-V and x86. However, during the experiments, we found out that Clang's support for RISC-V was still incomplete and considerably behind GCC's, as our initial measurements confirmed. The major inefficiency we have noticed was that LLVM did not support RISC-V hard-float ABI. Although it was able to generate code that made use of floating-point instructions, function arguments were always passed through integer registers and stack, instead of using floating-point registers whenever possible. Because of this, we chose to perform our experiments using GCC to compile the code, in order to have a higher quality RISC-V input code, especially on benchmarks that make heavy use of floating-point operations.

### 4.1 Measurement Methodology

To perform the experiments, after compiling and translating all needed binaries, each one was run 10 times. Their execution times were collected using Linux *perf* and summarized by their arithmetic mean and standard deviation (SD). The execution times showed to follow a normal distribution with a small SD.

Moreover, we also decided to factor out from the results the time spent on *libc* functions. We followed the same methodology aforementioned, executing the benchmarks 10 times and calculating the arithmetic mean of the percentage of execution time spent in the main binary, thus excluding the time spent in shared libraries, such as *libc*. The final run time of each benchmark was then multiplied by this percentage.

## 5 Experimental Results

In this section we present the performance of our RISC-V SBT engine in terms of slowdown when compared to native execution (GCC based RISC-V binaries translated by our SBT engine compared to GCC based native binaries). Hence, the higher the value the worse the emulation performance. A slowdown equal to 1 means that the translated binary is as fast as the native. In all cases, the guest binaries were translated using the Globals, Locals and ABI translation schemes.

In Fig. 2 we can see the slowdowns obtained by translating MiBench benchmarks from RISC-V code to x86 and ARM. When translating RISC-V to x86, we

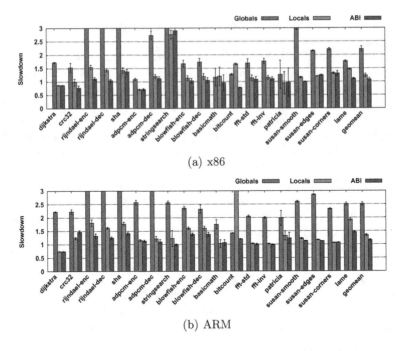

(a) x86

(b) ARM

**Fig. 2.** MiBench slowdown of RISC-V translated binaries.

obtained an average slowdown of 2.21x, 1.23x, and 1.08x, for Globals, Locals, and ABI, respectively. On ARM, the average slowdowns were 2.51x, 1.34x, and 1.16x. Moreover, Locals and ABI performance outstands the Globals performance in almost 2-fold, showing the importance of the register mapping approach. In the following paragraphs we analyze the results of each benchmark.

ADPCM-Decode, FFT-Standard, and FFT-Inverse show near-native performance, both on x86 as on ARM, in Locals and ABI modes. On ARM, ADPCM-Encode also shows near-native performance. ADPCM-Encode on x86 and Dijkstra had better performance than native. Our analysis indicates that this is due to a better optimization from the LLVM infrastructure used by our translator when compared to GCC, for these specific benchmarks. Susan-Smooth and Susan-Edges show good performance on both x86 and ARM.

StringSearch and Susan-Corners have a good result on ARM, but perform badly on x86, especially in StringSearch case. As we shall see further, this is caused by missed vectorization optimizations by the compiler.

Rijndael-Encode, Rijndael-Decode, and SHA show a high slowdown on both x86 and ARM. The SHA case is investigated in a later subsection. Blowfish-Encode and Blowfish-Decode present a good result on x86 but high overheads on ARM, mainly due to the compiler taking advantage of special ARM-only instructions to manipulate bits in native compilation. In BitCount we can see that Locals overhead is very high, even worse than Globals mode. By comparing it with ABI mode however, it becomes clear that register synchronization represents a large portion of its execution time.

Overall, BasicMath and Patricia benchmarks show good performance results, but their high error range calls the attention. The problem is that the percentage of time these benchmarks spend in the main binary is very low: oscillating from 2% to 4%. Instead, most of the time is spent in *libc* calls. As our slowdown calculation takes into account only time spent in the main binary, small variations in this low percentage result in large variations in the execution time considered. Note, however, that BasicMath and Patricia are the two benchmarks who spend the most time in *libc*, which is not the case for most benchmarks.

**Translated Code not Vectorized:** The analysis of generated code in benchmarks such as StringSearch revealed that several loops were not being vectorized from the IR produced by our SBT engine, while they were when compiling the program from source. Further investigation is needed to fully understand the causes of this issue, but by comparing native IR with translated IR, it seems that LLVM is only capable of vectorizing IR at a given format it supports/expects. In order to evaluate the performance impact of code not being vectorized, we have performed a native run of MiBench with vectorization disabled and compared it to our previous results. This confirmed that, in StringSearch case, practically all overhead was caused by this missed vectorization opportunity. We also noted significant differences in Rijndael-Encode, SHA, Susan-Smooth, Susan-Edges, and Susan-Corners, while for the remaining benchmarks the performance stayed almost the same.

**The SHA Case:** On both x86 and ARM, SHA's main source of overhead is somewhat similar to that of Rijndael: too many spills when a large number of registers is used. In SHA's case, this is seen at the *byte_reverse()* function, whose main loop is completly unrolled on RISC-V, resulting in a series of loads followed by stores, using most of the 32 RISC-V registers. When the code is translated to x86 or ARM, however, that have a much smaller register set, there is a huge number of spills and reloads. Native x86/ARM code performs better because code generation limits more the loop unrolling, to make better usage of the host registers available. To confirm this hypothesis, we have performed an experiment that consists in adding *pragmas* around *byte_reverse()* function, to disable loop unrolling only in it. This change greatly improved performance results: on x86, with vectorization disabled, Locals slowdown went from 1.61x to 1.19x while on ARM ABI slowdown went from 1.48x to 1.18x.

**RISC-V vs OpenISA:** When comparing the performance of our SBT engine with that obtained by OpenISA's [1], when translating RISC-V/OpenISA to x86 and ARM, we verified that the results obtained by both are similar, as we expected, given the same approach taken by both. When considering the geometric means of the results, on x86, the result of our SBT engine is practically the same as that of OpenISA, while on ARM the results are a little worse than OpenISA's, but still close. However, when comparing each benchmark individually, considerable differences are noted in some cases, such as in StringSearch, where the older LLVM version used on OpenISA's experiments was unable to vectorize native code, and thus obtained a much better result than ours.

### 5.1   Our SBT Engine vs DBT Engines Available

Finally, we compared our results with the most known DBT engines for RISC-V available: QEMU, RV8 and Imperas OVP Simulator for RISC-V. For RV8 and OVP, however, we were not able to run any benchmark that makes use of floating-point instructions, as they either crash, hang or produce wrong results. Also, it was not viable for us to use the same measurement approach as that of RISC-V SBT engine and OpenISA SBT engine, where we could easily factor out time spent at *libc*, and thus, in the following chart, the slowdowns were all measured considering only the execution time. That is why its slowdowns are a little different than that of previous graphs.

In Fig. 3, we can clearly see that our RISC-V SBT engine was the one with the best performance for all tested programs. It achieved, on average, a 1.11x slowdown in Locals mode, while QEMU, RV8 and OVP achieved 6.13x, 2.85x and 4.92x, respectively.

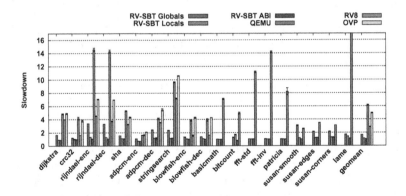

**Fig. 3.** Slowdown comparison between our SBT, QEMU, RV8 and OVP, on x86.

**SBT vs DBT Code Quality:** Comparing only the execution times of binaries translated with SBT against those translated by DBT is not very fair, as DBT engines have many other overhead sources that are absent in SBT engines, as we discussed previously. As this work's main concern is code quality, in this subsection we take a brief look at code generated by QEMU, RV8 and our SBT engine, when translating RISC-V code to x86, using the Dijkstra benchmark as example.

Analyzing the generated code, we noticed that QEMU and RV8 end up fragmenting the translated function in several regions. This fragmentation has two issues: (1) it hinders the application of optimizations, that do not see the whole functions; and, (2) Prologue and epilogue code added into regions by DBT engines cause extra overheads on region transition. Besides that, by taking a closer look at the code generated by each engine we noticed some performance issues with QEMU and RV8.

QEMU seems to map RISC-V registers to memory locations only, making its prologue and epilogue code considerably shorter than that of RV8, which is analogous to our RISC-V SBT Globals mode, but as discussed before, this approach results in slowdowns that are about twice bigger than Locals mode. We also observed that, while QEMU is able to detect and avoid unnecessary register reloads, it skips some important optimizations, such as performing the address calculation and load in the same instruction. Therefore, we conclude that QEMU's code quality can still be greatly improved.

RV8 statically maps the most used RISC-V registers to x86 registers, but then it needs to save/restore those—in its epilogues/prologues—when switching from/to the translator's code, which is analogous to our RISC-V SBT Locals mode. However, we noticed that RV8 synchronize all x86 registers used for direct mapping of RISC-V registers, instead of only those used in the translated region, as our SBT engine does. Otherwise, the RV8 code that we analyzed presented a very high-quality. Note, however, that this is not always the case, as the other, not so often used RISC-V registers, are mapped to memory locations on x86, resulting in extra memory accesses. Besides, RV8 takes advantage of x86-64 extra registers, even when emulating RISC-V 32-bit code, that is not the case for our SBT, that uses only those registers available in IA-32.

## 6    Conclusions

In this work, we demonstrated that RISC-V is an architecture that enables its code to be translated into high-quality x86 and ARM code. A strong evidence that DBT engines with high-performance can be built for RISC-V. We did this by building a RISC-V static binary translator that is able to translate RISC-V to x86 and ARM with an average execution overhead of 1.23x in the former and 1.34x in the latter, being the fastest RISC-V emulator presented so far in the literature. During our experiments, we have seen that the major obstacles that prevented us from achieving near-native performance in some benchmarks were vectorized code in native binaries and aggressive loop unrolling in optimized RISC-V code.

In future works, we intend to experiment with the 64-bit variant of RISC-V, to check if it can also be translated to high-quality code. We also intend to investigate further the causes of missed vectorizations by LLVM and propose ways to handle it. Finally, in a future work we plan to build a RISC-V DBT engine that makes use of the translation techniques discussed in this work.

**Acknowledgments.** We would like to thank CNPq (Grant #: 313012/2017-2), CAPES (PROCAD 2966/2014), and the São Paulo Research Foundation, FAPESP (Grant #: 2013/08293-7) for supporting this research.

# References

1. Auler, R., Borin, E.: The case for flexible ISAs: unleashing hardware and software. In: SBAC-PAD 2017 (2017)
2. Baraz, L., et al.: IA-32 execution layer: a two-phase dynamic translator designed to support IA-32 applications on Itanium®-based systems. In: 36th MICRO (2003)
3. Bellard, F.: TinyEMU. https://bellard.org/tinyemu. Accessed 27 Oct 2018
4. Bellard, F.: QEMU, a fast and portable dynamic translator. In: USENIX, FREENIX Track (2005)
5. Böhm, I., von Koch, T.J.E., Kyle, S.C., Franke, B., Topham, N.: Generalized just-in-time trace compilation using a parallel task farm in a dynamic binary translator. ACM SIGPLAN Not. **46**(6), 74–85 (2011)
6. Borin, E., Wu, Y.: Characterization of DBT overhead. In: 2009 IEEE International Symposium on Workload Characterization (2009)
7. Cesar, D., Auler, R., Dalibera, R., Rigo, S., Borin, E., Araujo, G.: Modeling virtual machines misprediction overhead. In: 2013 IISWC (2013)
8. Cifuentes, C., Malhotra, V.M.: Binary translation: static, dynamic, retargetable? In: ICSM (1996)
9. Clark, M., Hoult, B.: rv8: a high performance RISC-V to x86 binary translator. In: 1st CARRV (2017)
10. RISC-V Foundation. http://riscv.org/risc-v-foundation. Accessed 21 Oct 2018
11. RISC-V Foundation: RISC-V QEMU. https://github.com/riscv/riscv-qemu. Accessed 21 Oct 2018
12. RISC-V Foundation: RISCV-angel. https://github.com/riscv/riscv-angel. Accessed 24 Oct 2019
13. RISC-V Foundation: Spike RISC-V ISA simulator. https://github.com/riscv/riscv-isa-sim. Accessed 24 Jan 2019
14. Gomes, G.F.T., Borin, E.: Indirect branch emulation techniques in virtual machines. Dissertation, University of Campinas (2014)
15. Guthaus, M.R., Ringenberg, J.S., Ernst, D., Austin, T.M., Mudge, T., Brown, R.B.: Mibench: a free, commercially representative embedded benchmark suite. In: WWC-4 (2001)
16. Hong, D.Y., et al.: HQEMU: a multi-threaded and retargetable dynamic binary translator on multicores. In: CGO 2012 (2012)
17. Ilbeyi, B., Lockhart, D., Batten, C.: Pydgin for RISC-V: a fast and productive instruction-set simulator. In: 3rd CARRV (2016)
18. Lawton, K.P.: Bochs: a portable PC emulator for Unix/x. Linux J. **1996**(29es), 7 (1996)
19. Lupori, L., do Rosario, V.M., Borin, E.: Towards a high-performance RISC-V emulator. In: WSCAD 2018 (2018)
20. Probst, M.: Dynamic binary translation. In: UKUUG (2002)
21. Roelke, A., Stan, M.R.: RISC5: implementing the RISC-V ISA in Gem5. In: 1st CARRV (2017)
22. Salgado, F., Gomes, T., Pinto, S., Cabral, J., Tavares, A.: Condition codes evaluation on dynamic binary translation for embedded platforms. IEEE Embed. Syst. Lett. **9**(3), 89–92 (2017)
23. Shen, B.Y., Chen, J.Y., Hsu, W.C., Yang, W.: LLBT: an LLVM-based static binary translator. In: CASES 2012 (2012)
24. Smith, J., Nair, R.: Virtual Machines: Versatile Platforms for Systems and Processes. Elsevier, Amsterdam (2005)

25. Imperas Software: Imperas RISC-V solutions. https://www.imperas.com/imperas-riscv-solutions. Accessed 02 Dec 2018
26. Imperas Software: OVP simulator for RISC-V. https://github.com/riscv/riscv-ovpsim. Accessed 02 Dec 2018
27. Ta, T., Cheng, L., Batten, C.: Simulating multi-core RISC-V systems in Gem5. In: 1st CARRV (2018)
28. Waterman, A., Lee, Y., Patterson, D.A., Asanovi, K.: The RISC-V instruction set manual. Volume 1: user-level ISA, version 2.0. Technical report, EECS Department, University of California, Berkeley (2014)
29. Zhang, X., Guo, Q., Chen, Y., Chen, T., Hu, W.: HERMES: a fast cross-ISA binary translator with post-optimization. In: CG0 2015 (2015)

# Evaluation and Mitigation of Timing Side-Channel Leakages on Multiple-Target Dynamic Binary Translators

Otávio Oliveira Napoli[1][(✉)], Vanderson Martins do Rosario[1],
Diego Freitas Aranha[1,2], and Edson Borin[1]

[1] Institute of Computing, University of Campinas (Unicamp), Campinas, Brazil
{otavio.napoli,vanderson.rosario,edson}@ic.unicamp.br
[2] Department of Engineering, Aarhus University, Aarhus, Denmark
dfaranha@eng.au.dk

**Abstract.** Timing side-channel attacks are an important issue for cryptographic algorithms. If the execution time of an implementation depends on secret information, an adversary may recover the latter through measuring the former. Different approaches have emerged to exploit information leakage on cryptographic implementations and to protect them against these attacks, and recent works extend the concerns to dynamic execution systems [3,15,24]. However, little has been said about Cross-ISA emulation and its impact on timing leakages. In this paper, we investigate the impact of dynamic binary translators in the constant-time property of known cryptographic implementations, using different Region Formation Techniques (RFTs). We show that the emulation may have a significant impact by inserting non constant-time constructions during the translation, leading to significant timing leakages in QEMU and HQEMU emulators. These leakages are then verified using a statistical approach. In order to guarantee the constant-time property, we have implemented a solution in the QEMU dynamic binary translator, mitigating the inserted timing side-channels.

**Keywords:** Timing side-channels · Dynamic binary translation · Virtual Machines · Just-in-time compilation · Leakage detection

## 1 Introduction

Cryptographic algorithms are designed to be secure against attacks targeting their underlying hardness assumptions, but valuable information can still be extracted by peculiarities in their implementation and execution. This undesired leakage of information (like variations in execution time or system power consumption) is statistically exploited by side-channel attacks aiming to infer secret information used by the algorithms. Among the different types of side-channel attacks, timing attacks are a class of side-channel attacks that try to

© Springer Nature Switzerland AG 2020
C. Bianchini et al. (Eds.): WSCAD 2018, CCIS 1171, pp. 152–167, 2020.
https://doi.org/10.1007/978-3-030-41050-6_10

infer secrets based on the execution time behavior of the algorithm. Roughly speaking, if this behavior depends on a secret value, secret information can be leaked. These attacks were demonstrated feasible even when including network noise in remote attacks, becoming more relevant to various applications in different scenarios. To mitigate the problem, techniques to achieve constant-time execution were proposed [16,24]. The rules for constant-time implementation are very conservative and consist of avoiding: branching based on secret data, variable-latency instructions, and table look-ups with secret indexes, among others. Thus, the binary code must be carefully generated and inspected to guarantee constant-time execution, which can be difficult for larger cryptographic libraries.

Dynamic execution systems such as emulators may also have an impact on cryptographic implementations, either by adding noise or by applying optimizations or code transformations that could create leakages. In brief, an emulator is a piece of software that enables the execution of a binary compiled to one ISA (guest) into another (host) [22]. One of the fastest and most common ways to emulate code is through dynamic compilation (a.k.a. Dynamic Binary Translation, DBT or JIT Compilation), a technique which usually selects frequently executed pieces of code (regions) with a heuristic (Region Formation Techniques, RFTs) and compiles/translates to the host ISA for faster (native) execution. In this context, works handling constant-time execution and exploitation in dynamic execution scenarios also emerged recently [3,15,24]. However, little has been studied about timing leakage on dynamic Cross-ISA translators that also addresses other challenges such as: emulating complex instruction sets, instruction discovery during indirect jumps, among others.

In a previous work [18], we investigated the impact of multiple-target Cross-ISA emulation in constant-time property using a Cross-ISA DBT named OI-DBT, which emulates OpenISA code, an architecture designed for emulation. In this paper, we extended our previous work by investigating the feasibility of timing leakages when emulating real instruction sets (x86 and ARM ISAs) on two popular DBT engines, namely: QEMU and HQEMU, which use different mechanisms to emulate binaries. We observed the introduction of non constant-time constructions on the dynamically generated code in both DBTs, which caused a timing side-channel leakage. More precisely, a branch controlled by secret data is generated and which can be verified by using a timing leakage detection model based on the **dudect** Tool, presented by Reparaz et al. [20]. Finally, we also discussed and implemented a solution for generating code with QEMU Just-In-Time compiler mitigating the introduced timing leakage. Thus, the main results and contributions of this paper are:

- We show that an emulator can interfere with the constant-time property of some implementations and verified the occurrence of known timing leakages on some cryptographic implementations using a statistical method.
- We demonstrate that timing side-channels can be introduced by QEMU and HQEMU JIT compilers when translating code from ARM32 and x86 architectures, due to emulation of conditional codes. We implemented and

experimentally validated a solution to mitigate the timing side-channels generated.
- We tested 12 known cryptographic routines on 2 different emulators, some of them using 3 different region formation techniques. We show that the Region Formation Techniques may have a minimal impact on the leakages presented in the translated codes.
- To the best of our knowledge, this was the first work performing an analysis on timing leakages in Cross-ISA Dynamic Binary Translator using a statistical method.

This article is organized as follow: Sect. 2 presents a background in DBT (Sect. 2.1), the QEMU and HQEMU infrastructure, timing side-channel information (Sect. 2.2) and the used timing leakage model (Sect. 2.3); Sect. 3 describes relevant related works; Sects. 4 and 5 present the methodology and our results; Sect. 6 describes the counter-measures and, finally; Sect. 7 presents our conclusion.

## 2   Background

This section introduces some key concepts about DBT, information leakage through execution time and the timing leakage detection model.

### 2.1   Emulation and Dynamic Binary Translation

Emulators allow the execution of binaries compiled to one ISA on another, and they have been useful in a handful of applications such as Virtual Machines (VMs), support of legacy code, simulators and others [22]. The two main ways of implementing an emulator are by interpretation or by translation. The former is the slowest technique, but the most portable. The latter, on the other hand, is the one that results in higher performance, but it is less portable and far more complicated to implement. The translation of an ISA can be done either statically, by translating the whole binary beforehand (Static Binary Translation, SBT), or dynamically, by translating pieces of code (regions) from the binary while executing. These regions can be simple basic blocks (on demand, as it is being executed) or DBT engines may also collect some execution frequency information (e.g. branch targets) which are used by heuristics (Region Formation Techniques, RFTs) to detect regions of code that form a cycle or have a high probability of being executed many times in the future. Once selected, these regions of code are sent to a compiler to produce native code (in the target ISA) mimicking the behavior of the guest ISA region. These translated regions are put in a cache, known as Translated Code Cache (TCC), and every time the emulator needs to execute one instruction that is the start address of one of the TCC regions, the emulator simply jumps to the native code in the TCC, executing the translated code. Translation (or compilation) in a DBT happens together with binary emulation (or during the interpretation, in hybrid schemes) and so, its execution time impacts directly to the final emulation time. However, as the execution of translated code is faster than interpretation, if a region is executed enough times, the translation cost is paid off by the speedup from using the translated code instead of interpretation.

A DBT engine needs to decide which regions of code it is going to translate and optimize. This is a responsibility of the RFT which determines when to start recording a region, what to record and when to stop and send it to be translated or compiled. Different techniques have been proposed in the literature to address this challenge. **NET** [9] creates super-blocks composed of instructions that are executed in sequence. It considers that every target of backward branches or super-blocks exit is a candidate for starting a region. A region starts to be recorded when the execution of one these points passes an established execution threshold. When recording, every instruction emulated is added to the new region and it only stops when a backward branch is executed or another region entrance is found. **NET-R** does not end recording a region when a backward branch is found; instead, it ends when a cycle is found (repeated instruction address), creating larger regions. **NETPlus** [8] first runs NET and then instead of just finishing the super-block formation, it also runs a forward search looking for paths which could extend the region. The search looks for paths which exits the NET region and which returns to its entrance with less than a given number of steps (branches). **NETPlus-e-r** [13] is an extended and relaxed version of NETPlus. It uses NET-R to form regions and when expanding, and it does not only include paths which return to the entrance of the region, but all paths which return to any part of the region.

For multi-target DBT, reducing the number of transitions between regions is essential to achieve good performance, thus techniques such as NETPlus-e-r and NET-R have demonstrated to have the least amount of transitions and the best performance with this kind of DBT engines [13]. Following, we present the mechanisms of two DBTs: QEMU and HQEMU.

**QEMU.** QEMU [2] is a widely known retargetable dynamic binary translation system that allows full-system and process-level emulation from several CPUs (x86, PowerPC, ARM and Sparc) on several hosts (x86, PowerPC, ARM, Sparc, Alpha and MIPS). To perform the emulation, QEMU consists in a main loop that executes a single basic block at time. If the block was already translated, QEMU simply jumps to it, passing through epilogue and prologue codes, when entering and exiting the block, respectively, to maintain internal state coherence. Otherwise, QEMU fetches the basic block from the guest code (translation block), disassembles it and then maps it to a small set of intermediate representation operations (TCG Operations) provided by the Tiny Code Generator (TCG), the core of QEMU DBT Engine, to later be translated to the host architecture. The TCG intermediate instruction set is RISC-like, thus there are only few straightforward instructions supported directly. Lastly, the intermediate code is translated to the native code, for the host ISA and inserted in the TCC to be further executed.

**HQEMU.** Hybrid QEMU [13] is a cross-ISA, retargetable and multi-threaded dynamic binary translator that integrates the LLVM compiler into QEMU. The authors proposed a hybrid scheme using QEMU TCG as a fast emulator and once hot regions are detected (using NETPlus-E-R), they are compiled and optimized by the LLVM toolchain on another thread. To achieve this goal, it uses QEMU and translates a single guest binary basic block at time, emitting translated codes to the TCC (block code cache). A profile is executed and when the emulation module detects that some code region has become hot it converts the TCG IR instructions from the selected region to the respective LLVM IR instructions and using the LLVM back-end to emit a highly optimized host code to the trace cache. Then, every time the guest PC matches the start address of the region, the code from the trace cache is executed, otherwise the code from the block cache is executed.

## 2.2 Timing Leakage

Timing leakage happens when the execution time of a program or the emulation of a program depends on secret information. In practice, if there is a data dependence between a secret and the execution time, an attacker executing a program, even remotely, with different inputs and measuring its execution time, can infer secret information from the program using statistical methods. The three most common implementation/architecture characteristics which end up creating a dependence between data and time are: (1) having control flow depending on secret information, which will lead to different executions paths with a different number of instructions or memory pattern access when using different secrets; (2) changing the memory access pattern depending on the secret information, as it could lead to different cache performance, for instance, indexing a array access with secret data; (3) manipulating secret information with processor instructions that vary their execution time depending on the processed data [7,24].

## 2.3 Timing Leakage Detection Model

Our leakage detection model was based on the `dudect` tool from Reparaz et al. [20]. The tool uses a Test Vector Leakage Assessment (TVLA) methodology which is commonly used to assess the security of a system against side-channel attacks. This methodology consists in maintaining two vectors with executions times from two different classes of inputs and then comparing the two vectors using some statistical hypothesis test to evaluate if they represent the same measurement of time. If not, both vectors have a different execution time for two different classes of input and, therefore, the implementation is not considered constant time.

In summary, for each test a cryptography key is chosen and $N$ inputs are randomly generated with a uniform distribution for two classes of inputs: $C_1$ (consists in only one defined plain text which is the same among all $C_1$ inputs) and $C_2$ (consists of different random plain texts, one for each input of its class). In other words, $N$ inputs are generated with near to half of them fixed ($C_1$) and another half of them varying. Then, the time to execute each one of these inputs is measured and inserted each measurement into its respective vector depending on its class. Finally, a Welch's $t$-test is performed to infer if both vectors are measuring the same execution time. The Welch's $t$-test statistical test outputs a $t$-value that is the magnitude of the difference between the execution time of the two classes. As statistical tests such as Welch's $t$-test can have their results accumulated, we can run this test (of $N$ inputs) several times (which we call executions) and each time cleaning the two time vectors, generating new $N$ inputs and running the $t$-test to accumulate knowledge about the algorithm being constant or not. This fixed-vs-random kind of test is very popular in the literature and is considered one of the most powerful schemes for detecting timing leakages [23].

Moreover, after every execution and before running the $t$-test, a post processing is applied in the two vectors, removing some time outliers. The samples distribution may have a long right tail, as most executions take little time and some of them take a lot (due to other activities, interrupts, and others). So, we discarded samples with large cycle count, removing execution times which exceeds the average by 100% (speeding up the test).

## 3  Related Work

Although not being a recent problem, side-channel analysis is still relevant and, because of new attacks appearing from time to time, it is frequently in the spotlight. To quantify and mitigate timing leakages, several methodologies were proposed in the literature coming from diverse areas. Becker et al. [1], uses statistical tests with different vector assignments. Gianvecchio and Wang [10] showed an entropy-based model using a Kolmogorov-Smirnov test to detect covert timing channels based on estimation. Chen and Venkataramani [5] presents an algorithm to detect the existence of a covert timing channel tracking contention patterns on shared processors and memory. Nevertheless, to our experiments, we used the dudect approach [20], mainly because of its simplicity to reproduce.

Once detected the leakages, there are approaches to remove or mitigate them. Van Cleemput et al. [24], discussed about side-channel when generating JIT code with invariable latency paths and proposes a profile-based JIT protection by applying compiler transformations to regions with leakages. Wu et al. [25] studies static analysis and transformation-based methods for eliminating cache-timing side channels, which operates in LLVM IR. Several static analyses are performed to identify the sensitive variables and timing leaks associated to the same. Renner et al. [15] discussed the timing side-channels in JavaScript runtime systems and pointed that runtime components such as garbage collectors and JIT compilers can trivially introduce timing leaks in constant-time implementations and proposed changes to the WebAssembly language. Brennan et al. [3] observed that JIT compiler mechanisms can be induced to generate timing side-channels if the input distribution to a program is non-uniform. Other works and countermeasures were also proposed aiming to analyse and maintain the constant-time execution property [6, 7].

However, none of these works studied and analyzed the potential for multiple-target Cross-ISA DBT to change the leakage from a program, adding or removing it, during emulation of a binary. They just perform the analysis over High Level Languages Virtual Machines (HLL-VM). HLL-VMs are built into a virtual-ISA (bytecode) which is designed to support virtualization and portability. It usually includes metadata information to allows type-safe code verification, interoperability, and performance, giving more advantages to optimize code at runtime. Conventional ISAs are not designed for being emulated and their emulators may addresses several issues, such as: maintaining precise exceptions; instruction set features (different register banks, conditional codes); instruction discovery during indirect jumps and; self-modifying and self-referencing code [2, 19].

## 4    Experimental Setup

The experiments were executed in two different systems. The first one contains a GNU/Linux Ubuntu 16.04.4 LTS (kernel 4.13.0) O.S. and a 4-core 64-bit processor Intel(R) Core(TM) i7-7700 CPU running at 3.60 GHz with 32 GB of RAM. The second one contains a GNU Debian 8.10 (kernel 4.4.23) O.S. and a 4-core 64-bit processor ARM Cortex-A53 CPU, up to 1.2 GHz per core and 1 GB of RAM. Experiments with x86 and x86-64 ISAs were compiled using gcc (v7.1) and ARM32 and AArch64 architectures were cross-compiled using arm-linux-gnueabi-gcc (v5.4), all of them using the O3 optimization set. The emulators employed were QEMU (v2.12.1) and HQEMU (v2.5.2).

We executed 12 algorithms that are used on cryptographic code, between constant-time and non constant-time implementations. Non constant-time implementations include timing leakage through common timing channels, while the other performs counter-measures to achieve constant-time execution. The source code of the experiments was implemented in C language and then compiled to four instruction sets: x86, x86-64, ARM32 and AArch64. These implementations are all divided into four main parts: (1) a routine which generates all random inputs and allocates the time vectors, (2) a loop which iterates over each of the inputs calling the cryptographic routine, (3) the cryptographic routine and (4) the data-processing routine. We only measured the execution time of the third part (cryptographic routine) and after all the steps we apply the statistical test in a cumulative online fashion. The steps can be repeated indefinitely and, after each test performed, the statistical test updates its assumptions about the algorithm. In the results, we used the $t$-value in a categorical form and algorithms with output values higher than 4.0 are classified as not executing in constant-time [11]. To measure the time, we added a special instruction to get the execution cycle before and after the routine execution. In x86 we used the rdtsc instruction[1] and in ARM, we use the standard library clock_gettime function. All these steps are compiled to one whole binary allowing us to factor out the time for starting the emulator and the time to construct all random inputs. In multi-threaded DBT engines, the execution time for simple measurements

---

[1] Read timestamp counter (rdtsc).

**Table 1.** List of tested algorithm implementations and their respective timing leakages.

| Algorithm | Description | Implementation | Timing leakage |
|---|---|---|---|
| Memory Comparison | A very common algorithm for checking message authentication codes. It compares two 256-bit strings | Non-constant time memory comparison (Glibc `memcmp` function) | Aborts on pair of different bytes, thus control-flow behavior depends on secret data |
| | | Constant-time memory comparison | None |
| Conditional Selection | Selects between the two inputs values depending on the value of a third input parameter | Constant-time Implementation | None |
| | | Constant-time Implementation[a] | None |
| Get Zeros Padding | Computes the number of elements before the all 0x00 suffix (padding) | Non constant-time ARM's mbedTLS `get_zeros_padding` function | Control-flow behavior depends on secret data |
| | | Constant-time ARM's mbedTLS `get_zeros_padding` function[b] | None |
| Big Digits Compare | Compares two given big integer numbers, checking for their relation | Non-constant time BigDigits [14] routine `mpCompare` implementation | Control-flow behavior depends on secret data |
| | | Constant-time BigDigits [14] `mpCompare_ct` routine | None |
| AES | A popular block cipher, based on Substitution-Permutation Network (SPN) model. It encrypts blocks of 128-bit of data | T-Table Implementation [21] | Table look-ups access indexed with secret data |
| | | Constant-time Bitsliced version [16] | None |
| Curve25519 | An elliptic curve algorithm for key agreement protocols (ECDHE). It uses a Montgomery curve defined over prime a field defined by $2^{255} - 19$ | Non-Constant time curve25519-donna[c] | Variable-latency multiplication routine |
| | | Constant-time Curve25519-donna[d] | None |

[a] In this particular case, two equivalent constant-time implementations were used, but with different Assembly code. One performs the selection using conditional codes and the another uses only logical and arithmetical instructions
[b] Extracted from actual ARM mbedTLS [12] repository.
[c] Implementation following the prescriptions of informational RFC 7748 [17] with a variable-latency long integer multiplication routine.
[d] https://code.google.com/archive/p/curve25519-donna/.

could also be somehow affect by the JIT Compiler. To mitigate this problem, we perform a warm-up phase on the DBT engines, aiming to generate all needed JIT code, before we start to take measurements. It is important to note that a presence of leakage is a necessary, but not a sufficient condition for a timing side-channel attack to work.

### 4.1 Cryptographic Algorithms Implementations

In order to perform the desired experiments in a valid manner, we select 12 routines that are widely used in cryptographic constructions showed in Table 1.

## 5 Experimental Results

Tables 2a to b exhibit the output values of the leakage detection test on the presented emulators and architectures. The tables highlights the entries in which the behaviour was not expected. Concerning with the emulation, in HQEMU we performed the experiments using Basic Block RFT (which performs a directly block translation from QEMU TCG to LLVM IR, from every QEMU translation block, without any heuristic), NET RFT and NETPlus-E-R RFT ("Netp.ER", in the Tables). The "Cond. Select CC" implementation in Tables refers to the Conditional Selection algorithm, using conditional codes. We also executed natively the algorithms compiled to 32-bit architectures in both host systems, but these executions were omitted in the tables, because they offer the same results as 64-bit native executions.

**Table 2.** a (up), b (down): Results for executing the leakage detection test on the Intel and ARM host systems, respectively.

| Emulators | Native | | QEMU | | | | HQEMU B. Block | | | | HQEMU NET | | | | HQEMU Netp.ER | | | |
|---|---|---|---|---|---|---|---|---|---|---|---|---|---|---|---|---|---|---|
| Guest Arch. | x64 | arm 64 | x86 | x64 | arm 32 | arm 64 | x86 | x64 | arm 32 | arm 64 | x86 | x64 | arm 32 | arm 64 | x86 | x64 | arm 32 | arm 64 |
| Memcmp | NC | NC | NC | NC | NC | NC | NC | NC | NC | NC | NC | NC | NC | NC | NC | NC | NC | NC |
| Const. Str Comp. | CT | CT | CT | CT | CT | CT | CT | CT | CT | CT | CT | CT | CT | CT | CT | CT | CT | CT |
| Conditional Select | CT | CT | CT | CT | CT | CT | CT | CT | CT | CT | CT | CT | CT | CT | CT | CT | CT | CT |
| Cond. Select (CC) | CT | CT | CT | CT | **NC** | CT | **NC** | CT | CT | CT | **NC** | CT | CT | CT | **NC** | CT | CT | CT |
| GetZerosPadding | NC | NC | NC | NC | NC | NC | NC | NC | NC | NC | NC | NC | NC | NC | NC | NC | NC | NC |
| GetZeroPad.(const) | CT | CT | CT | CT | **NC** | CT | CT | CT | CT | CT | CT | CT | CT | CT | CT | CT | CT | CT |
| BD Comp. | NC | NC | NC | NC | NC | NC | NC | NC | NC | NC | NC | NC | NC | NC | NC | NC | NC | NC |
| BD Comp.(const) | CT | CT | CT | CT | **NC** | CT | CT | CT | CT | CT | CT | CT | CT | CT | CT | CT | CT | CT |
| AES32 | NC | NC | NC | NC | NC | NC | NC | NC | NC | NC | NC | NC | NC | NC | NC | NC | NC | NC |
| AES32 Bitsliced | CT | CT | CT | CT | CT | CT | CT | CT | CT | CT | CT | CT | CT | CT | CT | CT | CT | CT |
| Curve25519 | NC | NC | NC | NC | NC | NC | NC | NC | NC | NC | NC | NC | NC | NC | NC | NC | NC | NC |
| Curve25519 (const) | CT | CT | CT | CT | CT | CT | CT | CT | CT | CT | CT | CT | CT | CT | CT | CT | CT | CT |

| Emulators | Native | | QEMU | | | | HQEMU B. Block | | | | HQEMU NET | | | | HQEMU Netp.ER | | | |
|---|---|---|---|---|---|---|---|---|---|---|---|---|---|---|---|---|---|---|
| Guest Arch. | x64 | arm 64 | x86 | x64 | arm 32 | arm 64 | x86 | x64 | arm 32 | arm 64 | x86 | x64 | arm 32 | arm 64 | x86 | x64 | arm 32 | arm 64 |
| Memcmp | NC | NC | NC | NC | NC | NC | NC | NC | NC | NC | NC | NC | NC | NC | NC | NC | NC | NC |
| Const. Str Comp. | CT | CT | CT | CT | CT | CT | CT | CT | CT | CT | CT | CT | CT | CT | CT | CT | CT | CT |
| Conditional Select | CT | CT | CT | CT | CT | CT | CT | CT | CT | CT | CT | CT | CT | CT | CT | CT | CT | CT |
| Cond. Select (CC) | CT | CT | CT | CT | **NC** | CT | **NC** | CT | CT | CT | **NC** | CT | CT | CT | **NC** | CT | CT | CT |
| GetZerosPadding | NC | NC | NC | NC | NC | NC | NC | NC | NC | NC | NC | NC | NC | NC | NC | NC | NC | NC |
| GetZeroPad.(const) | CT | CT | CT | CT | **NC** | CT | CT | CT | CT | CT | CT | CT | CT | CT | CT | CT | CT | CT |
| BD Comp. | NC | NC | NC | NC | NC | NC | NC | NC | NC | NC | NC | NC | NC | NC | NC | NC | NC | NC |
| BD Comp. (const) | CT | CT | CT | CT | **NC** | CT | CT | CT | CT | CT | CT | CT | CT | CT | CT | CT | CT | CT |
| AES32 | NC | NC | NC | NC | NC | NC | NC | NC | NC | NC | NC | NC | NC | NC | NC | NC | NC | NC |
| AES32 Bitsliced | CT | CT | CT | CT | CT | CT | CT | CT | CT | CT | CT | CT | CT | CT | CT | CT | CT | CT |
| Curve25519 | NC | NC | NC | NC | NC | NC | NC | NC | NC | NC | NC | NC | NC | NC | NC | NC | NC | NC |
| Curve25519 (const) | CT | CT | CT | CT | CT | CT | CT | CT | CT | CT | CT | CT | CT | CT | CT | CT | CT | CT |

The native executions showed a well-defined behaviour regarding to the leakage detection. The constant-time algorithm implementations don't reject the null-hypothesis (having the $t$-value below 4.0) while non constant-time implementations do the opposite, exhibiting a significant timing difference and validating the correctness of the used model during a emulation. This is showed in the tables, on the "native" columns. Concerning the leakage during emulation, we verified that the emulator performs a high-quality translation preserving the major algorithm characteristics (regarding of timing channels) for most part of the algorithms, behaving as expected for the most part of the algorithms. The results show that some implementations behave differently (the yellow ones in the Tables) than the native execution when they are being emulated, as the case of the emulating ARM32 "Conditional Selection (CC)" in QEMU, listed in Tables of both systems. In fact, some DBTs emulation mechanisms can compromise constant-time implementations exposing significant vulnerabilities on translated code and they are discussed next.

## 5.1    Conditional Selection (CC) Case

**QEMU DBT.** The emulation of the algorithm in QEMU presents a significant time variation when emulating code compiled for the ARM32 architecture, due to emulating conditional codes, as showed in Tables 2a and b. The ARM32 architecture takes a great advantage of conditional codes, as the resource is present in almost all instructions. To ensure a simple and portable translator, QEMU transforms conditional instructions (from guest code) into forward jumps to the next instruction (in its intermediate representation), to be performed after evaluating the corresponding flags for the condition code. The translation for this algorithm is illustrated on Fig. 1. The native ARM32 binary uses a move on equal instruction (moveq) to select between the two incoming parameter values from r0 and r1 registers depending on the value of r2. This original branchless version results in a straightforward Control-Flow Graph, showed as a single basic block in leftmost part of the Figure. Then, the QEMU front-end disassembles the block and maps each instruction to a corresponding set of TCG Operations, as showed in the middle block of the figure. The conditional movement instruction, moveq, is translated to a set of instructions, including a branch instruction (brcond_i32 TCG opcode) used to skip the computation if the condition code is evaluated to false. Finally, the QEMU back-end performs code generation to the host architecture, simply mapping each of the TCG Opcode to a corresponding set guest instructions directly. The brcond_i32 and its condition code is directly mapped to a conditional jump instruction in both x86-64 and AArch64 back-ends implementations and translation results in the CFGs illustrated in rightmost blocks of the Fig. 1, for x86-64 host (above) and AArch64 (below). The shaded blocks (and arrows) represent the basic blocks inserted in the host generated code to handle the condition part.

Figures 2a and b show the $t$-value difference of the execution time of the two classes of inputs, for Intel and AArch64 systems, respectively. The executions presented in the x axis show the number of individual measurements performed

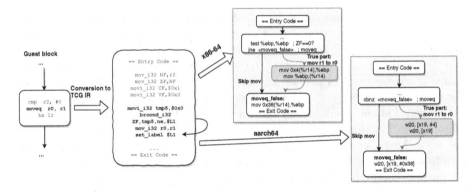

**Fig. 1.** Boolean conditional select code generation in QEMU DBT.

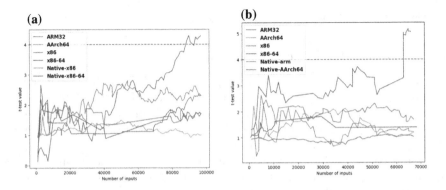

**Fig. 2.** a: Conditional selection leakage test from different guest architectures using QEMU on the Intel System as host. b: Conditional selection leakage test from different guest architectures using QEMU on the AArch64 System as host.

in the algorithm for each batch of plain texts (inputs). The higher the $t$-value, the more evident is the inconstancy in the execution time of the implementations or emulation. Due to the instruction's conditional codes, both translations from ARM32 (to x86-64 and to AArch64) end up with a different CFG from the original, compromising its constant-time property. The inserted branches cause a timing leakage on the implementation which is quickly verified by the detection model.

**HQEMU DBT.** When converting the QEMU Translation Block code to LLVM IR, the branch introduced in QEMU with the `brcond_i32` from the condition flags is also converted to a branch instruction in LLVM IR. However, after LLVM optimization passes, the forward branch is simplified to a predicated LLVM `select` instruction, which is used to choose one value based on a condition, without branching, since the instruction may have several advantages, such as:

being easier to vectorize.[2] The ARM32 conditional instructions for this implementation are also translated to a predicated instruction for the host system and no timing leakages were found, as shown in Tables 2a and b.

Similarly to QEMU, HQEMU also leads to a timing leakage as shown in Table 2a, however, the leakage occurs when translating from the x86 ISA architecture, as illustrated in Fig. 3. The x86 `cmovnel` conditional instruction in the guest block (showed in the leftmost part of the Fig. 3) is disassembled and mapped to a conditional TCG Opcode (`movcond_i32`) that is posteriorly mapped to the LLVM `select` instruction. The translation from architectures with different bit widths (e.g. 32-bit to 64-bit) usually requires an address space translation for memory accesses from Guest Address (that is address used in the guest binary) to its Host Physical Address (HPA). For LLVM to perform the address calculation and a memory access to store the desired result may be costly using predicated instruction. Thus, it selects a different set of instructions and a forward branch is inserted, as showed in the rightmost part of the Fig. 3 for x86-64 (above) and AArch64 (below). Thus, alike QEMU, HQEMU also compromises the CFG by inserting a significant timing leakage through branches. This leakage can be quickly verified by the detection model.

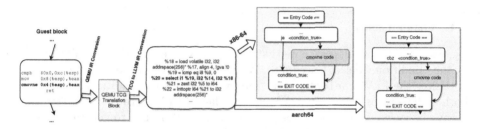

**Fig. 3.** Boolean conditional select code generation in HQEMU DBT (NETPlus-E-R).

## 5.2 The mbedTLS `get_zeros_padding` Case

The constant-time version of the mbedTLS function called `get_zeros_padding` also presented a significant timing leak on QEMU translating from ARM32, as indicated in Tables 2a and b. The ARM32 binary is generated containing two conditional instructions with contrasting conditions: `moveq` and `orrne`, depending on the status flags generated by the same compare instruction. The QEMU's ARM32 front-end generates branches for each conditional instruction on the guest binary, even if subsequent instructions share the same conditional code. Because of the two previously instructions, QEMU generates a slightly different

---

[2] In fact, one of the usual phases of vectorization is the if-conversion pass, the process of converting control-flow dependencies, a conditional branch, to data-flow dependencies, a select.

CFG for the translated code regarding the original ARM32 binary CFG, compromising it. This demonstrates that the leakages are inserted in a instruction granularity, that is, for each conditional instruction a branch depending on a secret value is inserted and, hence an attacker could exploit the secret-material resulting after each conditional operations with suitable pos-processing analysis. By exploring this timing leakage, the number of zeros in the pad could be inferred.

### 5.3   The BigDigits Compare Case

The BigDigits Compare implementation also uses conditional instructions in its constant-time implementation. Similarly to the previous cases, it also presents a timing leakage, that is inserted by emulating condition codes in QEMU, as shown in Tables 2a and b. The comparison algorithm is generated with 4 conditional operations on ARM32: movcs, movls, andcc, and andhi. The QEMU TCG then disassembles the block and maps the conditional instructions to 4 branch instructions (brcond_i32) in the QEMU intermediate language. All the TCG branch instructions are translated to conditional branches on generated code and the leakages causes a severe impact on the execution time.

### 5.4   Other Cases

By observing the results, we note that all RFTs behave identically, as illustrated by the Conditional Select Case (x86). When forming different regions, LLVM still optimizes the LLVM select instruction by lowering to a conditional branch in both architectures: x86-64 and AArch64. In fact, LLVM select instruction can always be lowered to a conditional branch, but LLVM aims to generate a code where branches are executed unconditionally, and all the parameters used in the branches are assigned conditionally, since they does not suffer for branch misprediction penalty. In this way, we cannot expect LLVM to generate a constant-time code for implementations that results in a LLVM select instruction.

The QEMU TCG instead provides the movcond_i32 operation in its intermediate language. By examining the QEMU backend and our experimental results, we noted that this operation is always lowered to conditional (predicated) instructions on the investigated host platforms, due the QEMU simplicity and the lack of other powerful analysis passes.

## 6   Countermeasures

Since Dynamic Binary Translators such as QEMU introduce a branch that depends on a secret-value when emulating the status Flags, it can be mitigated stripping the branch out.

## 6.1   QEMU

On QEMU, the `brcond_i32` operation in its intermediate representation is always translated to a host branch instructions. The simplest way to eliminate the forward branch generated from a guest's conditional instruction is by transforming the `brcond_i32` to a `movcond_i32` operation. The `movcond_i32` operation, conditionally select a desired value depending on a predicated value (flags, in this case) and is always translated to a conditional instruction on the host platforms (for the four investigated architectures). Since the QEMU already generates the code to be used when the evaluation is true, the result of the same can be saved to a QEMU temporary that later can be selected by generating the `movcond_i32` operation in QEMU front-end. The value of the temporary is selected if the desired condition is true or it just discard otherwise, maintaining the older value.

We implemented this transformation in the QEMU ARM front-end in the function `disas_arm_insn`, which is responsible to disassemble the guest basic block and to map it to the corresponding QEMU TCG operations. With this transformation, all the aforementioned implementations that diverge from the native execution have the branch controlled by the secret data removed and translated to conditional instructions on the host platforms, mitigating the leakage. In fact, our statistic analysis show that this transformation removes the timing leakage points inserted by the QEMU translator. By stripping out the `brcond_i32` and replacing with a `movcond_i32` all the tested algorithms remained with their *t*-test values below 4, denoting a constant-time execution. By using the `movcond_i32` operation, branches that were inserted to skip the conditional instructions when the flags are evaluated to false were all translated to predicated instructions on the host platforms and presented a constant-time execution.

This approach is simple and effective to mitigate this side-channel. Other approaches may involve map the `brcond_i32` to another set of TCG operations that executes in constant-time or perform changes in ARM's back-end to always generate conditional instructions.

## 6.2   HQEMU

In the LLVM, however, we cannot rely on the `select` instruction for its intermediate language, since it's not always lowered to a conditional instruction on the host system. Also, using the `movcond_i32` instruction from the QEMU intermediate representation does not resolve the problem, since the same gets translated by HQEMU to a `select` instruction in the LLVM IR. Instead, LLVM provides an if-conversion transformation Pass that performs the if-conversion efficiently, converting conditional branches to predicated instructions. As this Pass is architecture-dependent, this must be attached to a Machine Function Pass, and cannot operate on LLVM IR directly. This means that changes in LLVM backends must be performed and compiled for mitigations to work.

## 7   Conclusion

In this work, we analyzed the impact of Cross-ISA emulation on binaries with and without timing leakage using QEMU and HQEMU, two popular multiple-target dynamic binary translators. Differently from High Level Languages Virtual Machines, Dynamic Binary Translators also address different challenges, such as instruction discovery during indirect jumps, status register emulation, among others, which can lead to different emulation mechanisms. By using a statistical method to evaluate timing leakages we asserted the feasibility of timing side-channels in dynamic generated code. Although side-channel analysis was also performed in High Level Languages Just-in-Time scenarios [4,7,24], this is the first work of its kind in analyzing a multiple-target dynamic binary translator impact on side-channel leakage. Given the growing importance of emulators in heterogeneous computing environments with multiple Instruction Set Architectures, this problem will become even more important.

In summary, the results show that dynamic binary translators maintain the constant-time property in several implementations and also leak information through timing-channels when emulating non constant-time implementations. However, translating conditional instructions may lead to a break in the constant-time property. Even if conditional instructions assure a constant-time execution in modern systems, dynamic binary translators such as QEMU may modify the Control Flow Graph from a binary, inserting non constant-time constructions, compromising the aforementioned property. This leakage compromises several constant-time implementations, including cryptographic codes used in popular known libraries, such as mbedTLS. We investigated these issues, showed the root cause and implemented a countermeasure for mitigation. The implemented transformation was able to convert branches controlled with secret data to conditional instructions on the host platform, mitigating the timing channels inserted by the emulation mechanisms and maintaining the constant-time property of the application.

**Acknowledgments.** We would like to thank CNPq (Grant #: 313012/2017-2), Intel Corporation, and the Sao Paulo Research Foundation, FAPESP (Grants #:2014/50704-7 and 2013/08293-7), for supporting this research.

## References

1. Becker, G., Cooper, J., DeMulder, E., Goodwill, G., et al.: Test vector leakage assessment (TVLA) methodology in practice. In: International Cryptographic Module Conference, p. 13 (2013)
2. Bellard, F.: QEMU, a fast and portable dynamic translator. In: USENIX Annual Technical Conference, FREENIX Track, p. 46 (2005)
3. Brennan, T., Rosner, N., Bultan, T.: JIT Leaks: inducing timing side channels through just-in-time compilation. Technical report, UC Santa Barbara, Computer Science (2018)
4. Cauligi, S., et al.: FaCT: a flexible, constant-time programming language. In: 2017 SecDev, pp. 69–76. IEEE (2017)

5. Chen, J., Venkataramani, G.: An algorithm for detecting contention-based covert timing channels on shared hardware. In: HASP, p. 1. ACM (2014)
6. Cleemput, J.V., Coppens, B., De Sutter, B.: Compiler mitigations for time attacks on modern x86 processors. TACO **8**(4) (2012). Article no: 23
7. Coppens, B., Verbauwhede, I., De Bosschere, K., De Sutter, B.: Practical mitigations for timing-based side-channel attacks on modern x86 processors. In: 2009 30th IEEE Symposium on Security and Privacy, pp. 45–60. IEEE (2009)
8. Davis, D., Hazelwood, K.: Improving region selection through loop completion. In: ASPLOS, vol. 4, p. 7-3 (2011)
9. Duesterwald, E., Bala, V.: Software profiling for hot path prediction: less is more. ACM SIGOPS **34**(5), 202–211 (2000)
10. Gianvecchio, S., Wang, H.: An entropy-based approach to detecting covert timing channels. TDSC **8**(6), 785–797 (2011)
11. Goodwill, G., Jun, B., Jaffe, J., Rohatgi, P., et al.: A testing methodology for side-channel resistance validation. In: NIST Non-Invasive Attack Testing Workshop, vol. 7, pp. 115–136 (2011)
12. ARM Holdings: ARM mbedTLS
13. Hong, D.Y., et al.: HQEMU: a multi-threaded and retargetable dynamic binary translator on multicores. In: CGO, pp. 104–113. ACM (2012)
14. Ireland, D.: BigDigits multiple-precision arithmetic source code (2016)
15. Renner, J., Cauligi, S., Stefan, D.: Constant-time webassembly (2018)
16. Käsper, E., Schwabe, P.: Faster and timing-attack resistant AES-GCM. In: Clavier, C., Gaj, K. (eds.) CHES 2009. LNCS, vol. 5747, pp. 1–17. Springer, Heidelberg (2009). https://doi.org/10.1007/978-3-642-04138-9_1
17. Kaufmann, T., Pelletier, H., Vaudenay, S., Villegas, K.: When constant-time source yields variable-time binary: exploiting curve25519-donna built with MSVC 2015. In: Foresti, S., Persiano, G. (eds.) CANS 2016. LNCS, vol. 10052, pp. 573–582. Springer, Cham (2016). https://doi.org/10.1007/978-3-319-48965-0_36
18. Napoli, O.O., do Rosario, V.M., Aranha, D.F., Borin, E.: Evaluation of timing side-channel leakage on a multiple-target dynamic binary translator (2018)
19. Payer, M., Gross, T.R.: Generating low-overhead dynamic binary translators. In: Proceedings of the 3rd Annual Haifa Experimental Systems Conference, p. 22. ACM (2010)
20. Reparaz, O., Balasch, J., Verbauwhede, I.: Dude, is my code constant time? In: DATE, pp. 1697–1702. IEEE (2017)
21. Rijmen, V., Bosselaers, A., Barreto, P.: Optimised ANSI C code for the Rijndael cipher (now AES). Public domain software (2000)
22. Smith, J.E., Nair, R.: Virtual Machines: Versatile Platforms for Systems and Processes. The Morgan Kaufmann Series. Morgan Kaufmann Publishers Inc., San Francisco (2005)
23. Standaert, F.X.: How (not) to use Welch's T-test in side-channel security evaluations. In: IACR, vol. 2017, p. 138 (2017)
24. Van Cleemput, J., De Sutter, B., De Bosschere, K.: Adaptive compiler strategies for mitigating timing side channel attacks. TDSC **17**(1), 35–49 (2017)
25. Wu, M., Guo, S., Schaumont, P., Wang, C.: Eliminating timing side-channel leaks using program repair. In: Proceedings of the 27th ACM SIGSOFT International Symposium on Software Testing and Analysis, pp. 15–26. ACM (2018)

# A GPU-Based Parallel Reduction Implementation

Walid Abdala Rfaei Jradi$^{(\boxtimes)}$ [ID], Hugo Alexandre Dantas do Nascimento [ID], and Wellington Santos Martins [ID]

Instituto de Informática, Universidade Federal de Goiás, Goiânia, Goiás, Brazil
walid.jradi@gmail.com, {hadn,wellington}@inf.ufg.br

**Abstract.** Reduction operations aggregate a finite set of numeric elements into a single value. They are extensively employed in many computational tasks and can be performed in parallel when multiple processing units are available. This work presents a GPU-based approach for parallel reduction, which employs techniques like *loop unrolling*, *persistent threads* and *algebraic expressions*. It avoids thread divergence and it is able to surpass the methods currently in use. Experiments conducted to evaluate the approach show that the strategy performs efficiently on both AMD and NVidia's hardware platforms, as well as using OpenCL and CUDA, making it portable.

**Keywords:** GPU · Parallel reduction · Portable

## 1 Introduction

Reduction is a basic step in many algorithms, including classical ones such as Stream Compaction [1], Golden Section and Fibonacci Methods [14] and Count Sort and Radix Sort [4]. A *reduction operation* can be formally defined as follows [20]: given a set $X$ of $n$ elements, $X = \{x_1, x_2, ..., x_n\}$, compute $x_1 \otimes x_2 \otimes ... \otimes x_n$, with $\otimes$ (also known as a *combining function*) being an associative and commutative operator. Examples of $\otimes$ when $X$ is composed by numbers are the operators $+, \times, \max$ and $\min$. Algorithm 1 illustrates a reduction process through the summation of a set of values.

A parallel version of a reduction consists of computing the $\otimes$ operator concurrently for the set of elements using multiple processing units. At a first glance of Algorithm 1, it may seem that the reduction operator sum $(+)$ is inherently sequential since the variable *accumulator* depends on values computed in previous steps. However, it is possible to parallelize that operator because of its associative property. In fact, the associativity of $\otimes$, sometimes combined with

This study was financed in part by the Coordenação de Aperfeiçoamento de Pessoal de Nível Superior – Brasil (CAPES) – "Finance Code 001". We also thank the research supporting agency FAPEG – Fundação de Amparo à Pesquisa do Estado de Goiás for scholarships provided to researchers involved with the project.

C. Bianchini et al. (Eds.): WSCAD 2018, CCIS 1171, pp. 168–182, 2020.
https://doi.org/10.1007/978-3-030-41050-6_11

---

**Algorithm 1:** *Summation(X)*

---

**Input**: Set $X = \{x_1, x_2, \ldots, x_n\}$ of numeric elements
**Output**: The sum of all elements
$accumulator \leftarrow 0$
**for** $i \leftarrow 1$ **to** $n$ **do**
$\quad \lfloor \quad accumulator \leftarrow accumulator + x_i$

**return** *accumulator*

---

the commutative property, allows one to divide the calculations hierarchically into subproblems that can be solved in parallel and then having their partial computations combined to produce the final result. The order in which the partial reductions are combined does not affect the final result[1].

Since the arrival of general programmable GPUs (GPGPUs), strategies to accelerate reduction operations on such devices have been developed. Two famous ones are described by Harris [11] and Catanzaro [2]. More recently, Justin Luitjens [15] presented improvements to the strategies described in [11]. Unfortunately, the approaches in [11] and [15], although very efficient, are limited to the hardware and software provided by NVidia. The proposal of Catanzaro [2], on the other hand, is based on the open standard OpenCL [8], adopted by a myriad of manufacturers, which makes it portable. However, the code presented in [2] does not utilize some strategies that could significantly improve its performance.

In the present work, we describe a new parallel implementation for reduction operators that provides both portability and good performance. It adequately combines strategies that were used in the approaches mentioned above.

The remainder of this article is organized as follows: Sect. 2 briefly describes previous work on GPU-based parallel reduction; Sect. 3 presents some of the optimizations commonly used in GPU codes; Sect. 4 explains our approach; Sect. 5 details the experiments performed for testing the approach; Finally, Sect. 6 draws our conclusions and points to future investigations in this area.

## 2    Parallel Reduction in GPUs

The basic idea for parallelizing a reduction task is to "split" it into smaller pieces that will be performed in parallel and then aggregated. The GPU hardware,

---

[1] Although, mathematically, the associativity is true for numbers in any set, in computational terms this is more complicated. For instance, that property holds for the set of integers, but the same does not happen for the floating point numbers due to the inherent imprecision that arises when combining (adding, multiplying, etc.) numbers with different exponents, which leads to the absorption of the lower bits during the combining operation. As an example, mathematically the result of $(1.5 + 4^{50} - 4^{50})$ is always the same, no matter the order the terms are added, whereas the floating point computation can result in 0 or 1.5, depending on the sequence in which the operations are performed [7,12,17].

however, has specific features such as the number of processing units, how the units are grouped together in processing blocks and a memory hierarchy with different sizes and speed values. These aspects, in addition to the nature of the computational task, need to be considered in order to maximize the *speedup* of a parallel code [23]. Table 1 summarizes the basic GPGPU terminology for both OpenCL and CUDA programming paradigms. In the present article, we adopt the OpenCL terminology for describing most of our work, except when mentioning Harris and Luitjens' approaches [11,15].

**Table 1.** Basic GPGPU terminology.

| OpenCL | CUDA | Meaning |
|---|---|---|
| Device | GPU | In OpenCL, any compatible device able to run parallel code. In CUDA, a NVidia GPU |
| Stream Processor (SP) | CUDA Core | Execution – or computing – units able to run generic algorithms, synchronously with other SPs/CUDA Cores |
| Processing Element (PE) | Scalar Core | The same as Stream Processor/CUDA Core |
| Streaming Multi-processor (SM) | Compute Unit (CU) | Tightly coupled multiprocessor blocks that group SPs/CUDA Cores. It also provides a way of communication through a shared memory mechanism |
| Kernel | Kernel | A function executed in parallel by threads/work-items |
| Wave-front | Warp | A group of 32 (NVidia) or 64 (AMD) parallel threads |
| Work-item | Thread | An instance of a kernel, ready to be executed |
| Work-group | Thread-block | Group of Work-items/Threads that can be executed in parallel |
| NDRange | Thread-grid | A container for a certain number of Work-groups/Thread blocks |
| Global memory | Global memory | Read/write space, accessible by all Work-items/Threads. It is the only way SPs grouped in different SMs can communicate |
| Constant memory | Constant memory | As well as the global memory, this kind of memory is available to all SPs and is physically located in the device's main memory. However, it can be used more efficiently than the first one if the executing units are equipped with hardware that supports constant memory cache |
| Local memory | Shared memory | Read/write space, accessible by all Work-items/Threads inside a SM |
| Private memory | Local memory | Available only within each SP during kernel execution; it correspond to GPU's registers |

One of the aspects to observe is the number of elements to be reduced in relation to the size of the GPU's local/shared memories. If that amount is sufficiently small to be stored in the local memory of each SM, then the reduction becomes simple. In [2], Catanzaro presents strategies for this case and conducts performance comparisons between them. After describing how reductions can be efficiently performed in small sets, the author shifts the focus to the discussion of cases in which a large volume of data must be handled. Three strategies are presented and a winner, called *"Two-Stage Parallel Reduction"*, is elected. Harris [11] deals only with reduction of large datasets.

Our approach is mainly based on the proposal of Catanzaro [2]. Therefore, a more detailed description of it is presented. First, however, we explain the strategies employed by [11] since some ideas for speeding up the computation come from that work. We also comment about the research of [15], because it is another way of dealing with this problem.

## 2.1  Mark Harris' Work

The work presented by Harris [11] focuses on techniques for performing reductions on large data volumes. The author shows, through successive versions of the same algorithm, how bad decisions or an incorrect way of mapping the problem to the target platform can negatively impact the application performance.

Harris performed experiments using a G80 GPU. That video card has a 384-bit memory interface, with a 900 MHz DDR memory, which leads to a theoretic $384 * 1800/8 = 86.4$ GB/s of memory bandwidth. All tests were conducted using a vector with $2^{22}$ (4M) integer values.

Problems like shared memory bank conflict, lack of communication between thread blocks (making it impossible for a kernel to reduce a large array at once) and highly divergent warps are addressed. Starting with a naive version, step by step improvements are described. Harris tested strategies such as: (1) Replacing conditional commands by new instructions that avoid divergent branching; (2) Keeping all threads active, doing work as much as possible; (3) Unrolling loops until maximum efficiency is reached; (4) Using CUDA C++ template parameters on device and host functions for the specification of the block size, so that only the necessary amount of threads are launched; and (5) Allowing each thread to individually compute as many reduction operations sequentially as possible in order to reduce synchronization between threads, among other benefits. As a result of applying all these optimizations, the final version of the code ran in 0.268 ms (30.04x times faster than its initial version) and reached a memory bandwidth of 62.671 GB/s. In our work, we use all strategies proposed by Harris except the fourth one.

## 2.2  Justin Luitjens' Work

In [15], Luitjens shows how the shuffle (SHFL) instruction, a feature of the NVidia's Kepler (and newer) GPU architecture, could be employed in order to make reductions even faster when compared to the strategies presented in [11].

Usually threads inside the same *Compute Unit* – CU (See Table 1) use their shared memory when they need to communicate. This involves a three-step process: writing the data to the shared memory, perform a synchronization barrier and then reading the data back from the shared memory. Kepler and newer architectures implement the *shuffle* instruction, which enables a thread to directly read private data from another thread in the same warp. According to the author, there are four main advantages for using this instruction:

- It ultimately allows threads inside a wave-front to collectively exchange or broadcast data;
- It replaces the three-step process by a single instruction, effectively increasing the bandwidth and decreasing the latency;
- It does not use the shared memory at all;
- A sync barrier is implicit in the instruction and, hence, a synchronization step inside a block is not necessary.

Several versions of the reduction process were proposed, implemented and compared by Luitjens with the SHFL instruction. It is important to note that, although Luitjens states that the adopted strategies lead to faster reductions than those described by [11], no comparative studies between the two approaches were conducted.

### 2.3 Bryan Catanzaro's Work

Now, we describe Catanzaro's two-stage parallel reduction approach for large datasets, as presented in [2]. This is illustrated for the sum (+) operator.

The first stage consists of three steps. The technique is based on dividing the data set into $p$ pieces (or "*chunks*"), where $p$ is large enough to keep all GPU cores busy. It is also necessary to limit the number of *work-items* to the maximum amount that the GPU can handle in total without having to switch between them (from now on, that maximum will be called $GS$ – or *global size*). Each chunk is then processed by a work-group. Since the sum operation has the properties of associativity and commutativity, each *work-item* can perform its own reduction in parallel. In the first step, every work-item takes, as the starting point, its global identifier and accumulates its partial sum in a private variable. It reads the data from a vector stored in the GPU's global memory, intercalating the access to the values with the other work-items in a sequential order. Basically, work-item $i$, $i = 0, 1, \ldots, GS - 1$, starts reading the position $i$ and skips $GS$ positions at every iteration.

After having completed a pass through the dataset, the second step is to have the *work-items* writing the result of their reductions in a scrap vector located at the local/shared memory of their work-group. Then, as the third step, the work-items in a same work-group (for all work-groups) perform a parallel reduction over their related local memory. At the end of this process, each work group will have the partial result of its reduction at the position 0 of its scrap/local memory. This partial result is then copied to another vector, this time stored in the GPU global memory, whose size must be equal to the number of work-groups ($|SM|$). The first stage is then complete. Its source code, for a sum operator ($+$), extracted from [2], is presented in Listing 1.1 with small adjustments.

**Listing 1.1.** Catanzaro's two-stage parallel reduction – stage 1

```
__kernel void reduce(__global float* buffer,
               __local float* scratch,
               __const int length,
               __global float* result) {

  int global_index = get_global_id(0);
  float sum = 0;
  //Step 1 - Loop sequentially over chunks of input vector
  while (global_index < length) {
    sum += buffer[global_index];
    global_index += get_global_size(0);
  }
  //Step 2 - Store partial computation in local memory
  int local_index = get_local_id(0);
  scratch[local_index] = sum;
  barrier(CLK_LOCAL_MEM_FENCE);
  //Step 3 - Perform parallel reduction
  int iLS = get_local_size(0);
  for (int offset=iLS/2; offset>0; offset=offset/2) {
    if (local_index < offset) {
      scratch[local_index] += scratch[offset];
    }
    barrier(CLK_LOCAL_MEM_FENCE);
  }
  if (local_index == 0) {
    result[get_group_id(0)] = scratch[0];
  }
}
```

The second stage is simpler. Since now there is a vector with $|SM|$ elements in the global memory – with the result of a partial sum in each position – just the first $|SM|$ *work-items* of the first SM copy their corresponding value to an array allocated in the local memory (for this, we are assuming that the number of processing units in a work-group is greater or equal to the number of work-groups). Then, the *work-items* perform a new parallel sum of the elements in the vector. After that, the position 0 of the local memory will have the final result. This is copied back to the global memory and the reduction finishes.

The overall approach of Catanzaro is the underlying architecture of our work. Nevertheless, we improved it with the extensive usage of the advanced techniques described in the next section.

## 3   Optimization Techniques

This section details some advanced techniques to further explore parallelism and that were extensively used in the present work.

### 3.1   Loop Unrolling

*Loop Unrolling* (also known as *Loop Unwinding* and *Loop Unfolding*) is an optimization technique – performed by the compiler or manually by the programmer – applicable to certain kinds of loops in order to reduce (or even prevent) the occurrence of execution branches and to minimize the cost of instructions for controlling the *loop* [5,13,21]. In general, it optimizes the program's execution speed at the expense of increasing the size of the generated code (*space-time tradeoff*). It is easily applicable to loops where the number of executions is previously known, like routines of vector manipulation where the number of elements is fixed.

Basically the technique consists of reusing the sequence of instructions within the loop, so as to include more than one iteration of the code every time the *loop* is repeated, reducing the amount of these repetitions.

The reuse is done by manually replicating the code inside the *loop* a certain number of times or through the "*#pragma unroll n*"[2] positioned immediately before the beginning of the loop. The number of times the loop is unrolled is called *Unrolling Factor* and, with the pragma directive, it is given by the parameter "*n*".

It is worth noting that with the pragma directive we leave the decisions of how the loop should be unrolled to the compiler, which may lead to a not so optimized code. In the experiments performed as part of this work, the best results were always achieved using manual loop unrolling.

Unrolling, when applicable, offers several other advantages over non-unrolled code. Besides the decrease in the number of iterations, an increase occurs in the amount of work done each time through the loop. This opens ways for the exploration of parallelism by the compiler in machines with multiple execution units, since each instruction within the *loop* can be handled by an independent thread. These are only the most easily perceivable benefits. Fog [5] lists several others, as well as some observations about when this technique should be avoided. Such factors (advantages and disadvantages) must be considered when deciding to use loop unrolling.

## 3.2 Persistent Threads

All the current programmable GPUs follow the "*Single Instruction Multiple Thread*" (SIMT) and "*Single Program Multiple Data*" (SPMD) paradigms, hiding the details of the underlying *hardware* where the code runs in an attempt to ease the development task.

Some authors [9] argue that the usage of these paradigms greatly limits the actions of the programmer, because the execution flow is entirely under the control of the video card's *scheduler*. They claim that, while such abstractions reduce the effort for new developers in the GPGPU field, they also create obstacles for experienced programmers, who normally face problems for which workload is inherently irregular, therefore making it more difficult to efficiently parallelize when compared to tasks which parallelism is more regular.

---

[2] A *pragma* is a language directive that provides additional information to the compiler, specifying how to process its input. This additional information usually is beyond what is conveyed in the language itself.

They argue that this uncovers a serious drawback of the current programming styles, which is not able to ensure *order*, *location* and *timing*. In addition, it does not allow the software developer to regulate these three aspects without completely avoiding the GPU scheduler. Thus, to overcome such limitations, developers have been using a programming style called *Persistent Threads ("PT")*, which low level of abstraction allows performance gains by directly controlling the scheduling of work-groups.

Basically, what the PT style changes is the *lifetime* of a *work-item* [19], by letting it to run longer and giving it much more work to do than in the traditional "non-PT" style [22]. This is done by circumscribing the kernel logic (or part of it) in a loop, which remains running while there are items to be processed.

Briefly, from the point of view of the developer, all work-items are active while the kernel is running. As a direct consequence of PT, a *kernel* should be triggered using only the amount of *work-items* that can be executed concurrently by each Streaming Multiprocessor. All these actions will prevent constant return of control to the host and the cost of new kernel invocations [19].

Gupta et al. [9] acknowledge, however, that the PT technique is not a panacea, and that its use should be carefully evaluated. In particular, the technique fits well when the amount of memory accesses is limited (i.e., few reading/writing to global memory and a large volume of computation) and the problem being solved has not many initial input elements or the growth in the number of elements in the input set is fairly limited. Beyond these conditions, the traditional non-PT style tends to outperform the PT style.

### 3.3 Thread Divergence

Current GPUs are able to deliver massive computational power at a reasonably low cost. Still, due to the way they are constructed, some obstacles must be overcome for the effective use of such power. One of the main and hardest obstacles to avoid is the presence of conditional statements [24] potentially leading to branches in the execution flow of the various work-items [10].

By default, GPUs try to run all the work-items inside the wave-fronts in the SIMD model. However, if the code being executed has conditional statements that lead to divergences in program flow, the divergent work-items will be stalled and its execution will only happen after the non-stalled work-items have completed their runs, which ultimately compromises the desired *speedup*. This phenomenon is called *Thread Divergence* [3,18].

Some strategies have been proposed in order to minimize or even eliminate the effects of such phenomena. Among them, we cite [3,6,10,16,18,24].

The strategy adopted in the current paper is detailed at the end of Sect. 4.

## 4   The New Approach

The improvements proposed in our work focus on Steps 1 and 3 of the first stage of the reduction presented in Sect. 2.3. The improvements employ the same strategies described by Harris [11] to increase the performance of Catanzaro's original approach [2] but with appropriately chosen interventions.

In step 1 of the original implementation, the vector in global memory containing the data to be reduced is entirely traversed by the *work-items*, each one performing its own reduction.

This step already uses the "Persistent-Thread" strategy, but its performance can be improved by adopting loop unrolling (Sect. 3.1). As it can be seen, instead of doing the unroll when the data is in local memory, as proposed by [11], our improvement performs the unroll in the global memory.

The code presented in Listing 1.2 shows the modified loop (now using a sum operator), assuming an unrolling factor (F) equals to 4, *iGlobalID* as the *work-item* global identifier and *iLength* as the number of elements to be reduced.

**Listing 1.2.** Unrolling the step 1

```
for (iPos = iGlobalID*iUnrollingFactor; iPos < iLength;
     iPos += iGlobalSize*iUnrollingFactor)
{
  i0 = iPos;    i1 = iPos+1; i2 = iPos+2; i3 = iPos+3;
  accumulator +=
  ((i0<iLength)*(aVector[i0])+
   (i1<iLength)*(aVector[i1])+
   (i2<iLength)*(aVector[i2])+
   (i3<iLength)*(aVector[i3])));
}
```

Special attention must be given to how the data is brought from global (*aVector*) to private memory (*accumulator*), through the use of algebraic expressions that prevent reading from invalid memory locations, thus avoiding the usage of "ifs" and potential divergences in the execution flow. The expression $i_n < iLength$ expands to integers 1 or 0 whether it is, respectively, true or false. In the first case $(i_n < iLength)*(aVector[i_n])$ is interpreted as $(1)*(aVector[i_n])$, adding the value stored in location $i_n$ to the partial sum (*accumulator*). In the second case, the expression is interpreted as $(0) * (aVector[i_n])$, ensuring that – regardless of the data stored in the position $i_n$ of the vector – the value 0 is added to *accumulator*, keeping the partial sum correctness.

Just before the beginning of Step 3, the resulting values of the previous sums are stored in local memory (Step 2). Then, each SM performs its own local reduction with its work-items.

In the solutions presented by [11] and [2], in this step, all *work-items* are kept synchronized through the use of barriers. However, with minor conceptual changes, it is possible to completely eliminate the overhead caused by the barriers, not only in the last 6 iterations of the loop, as proposed by [11].

Our strategy is to use algebraic expressions to keep all the *work-items* in the same execution step, maintaining its desired behavior and algorithm correctness, as can be seen in Listing 1.3. Here, the conditional statement is completely eliminated but yet the function returns the right result of the comparison.

**Listing 1.3.** Algebraic "if-then-else"

```
int smallestValue(int a, int b)
{ return (a < b) * a + (a >= b) * b; }
```

Note that the two boolean operations (($a < b$) and ($a >= b$)) are mutually exclusive, being interpreted internally by the compiler as 0 (false) or 1 (true). So, assuming that *a* is smaller than *b*, the result of the algebraic operation is *(1) \* a + (0) \* b* which, ultimately, will return only the value of *a*.

The same strategy can be applied to lines 19 to 23 of Listing 1.1, that represent the third step of the first stage. The new code is shown in Listing 1.4, where *iLocalSize* stores the number of active local work-items and *iLI* represents the *work-item's* local identifier.

Here, in each iteration of the loop, *iPos* is divided by 2 (*iPos >>= 1*) and *bFlag* is expanded to either 1 or 0, thus reducing by half the number of *work-items* doing a useful job. If, for the current *work-item*, the expression $iLI < iPos$ becomes true, then the expression in the last line will be interpreted as $scratch[iLI]+ = (1) * (scratch[iLI + (1) * iPos])$, ensuring that the value stored in position $iLI + iPos$ will be added to the value in position $iLI$. On the other hand, if the expression becomes false, it will be interpreted as $scratch[iLI]+ = (0) * (scratch[iLI + (0) * iPos])$, ensuring that the value in position $iLI$ will not be considered. Since all *work-items* are always in the same step of computation – doing exactly the same job (useful or not), independently of being in the same wavefront – sync barriers are unnecessary.

**Listing 1.4.** Avoiding Divergences

```
for (iPos = iLocalSize/2; iPos > 0; iPos >>= 1)
{
  bFlag = iLI < iPos;
  scratch[iLI] += (bFlag)*(scratch[iLI + (bFlag)*iPos]);
}
```

## 5  Computational Experiments

In this section we compare the new approach against the proposals of Catanzaro, Harris and Luitjens. Their original codes were publicly available and, therefore, used in the current study. All algorithms, the existing ones and our proposal, are in C++ language. Catanzaro's code uses OpenCL, as previously described. Harris and Luitjens are in CUDA. We performed experiments for comparing the performance of the codes in two GPU platforms: an AMD GPU and a NVIDIA GPU. For this aim, two versions of our approach were implemented: one in OpenCL and the other in CUDA.

For the first platform, we used a computer with an AMD FX-9590 Black Edition Octa Core CPU, with clock ranging from 4.7 GHz to 5.0 GHz, 32 GB of RAM and running Ubuntu 16.04 64-bits operating system. The computer had a Radeon SAPPHIRE R9 290X GPU video card, with 4 GB of memory. The architecture of the video card provides 2816 stream processing units and an enhanced engine clock of up to 1040 Mhz. Its memory is clocked at 1300 MHz (5.2 GHz effectively). At such speed, the theoretical GPU memory bandwidth is 332.8 GB/sec. The programming codes for this platform used OpenCL 1.2 with the Software Development Kit 2.9.1.

For the second platform, we used an Intel Xeon CPU E5-2650 computer, with 20 Cores (40 visible cores using hyper thread, each clocked at 2.3 GHz), with 128 GB of RAM and running Ubuntu 16.04 64-bits operating system. The computer was equipped with a NVidia Tesla K40m GPU with 11 GB of memory. This GPU architecture has 15 Multiprocessors with 192 CUDA Cores per MP, summing up 2880 CUDA cores. Each core has a clock of 745 MHz and the GPU's memory is clocked at 3.0 GHz. We ran only CUDA codes at this hardware, which were compiled using CUDA SDK 7.5.

For both platforms, we used the GNU g++ compiler version 4.8.2 and the compilation parameters "`-O3 -mcmodel=medium -m64 -g -W -Wall`".

All tests were run on two types of vectors, one of integers and one of single precision floating points. There were no measurable differences, regarding the execution times, between these types. We refer to vectors with 5,533,214 elements[3], except when another size is explicitly mentioned in the text.

Table 2 and Figs. 1 and 2 depict the speedup gains achieved by our OpenCL code against the code presented by Catanzaro at [2]. The performance of Catanzaro's approach is shown at the first data line of the Table. The results for our code appear in the next lines, for increasing values of the unrolling factor $F$. The values were obtained with the OpenCL CodeXL profiler version 2.0.12400.0, and are the averages of five consecutive executions for each test case.

As can be seen in the table, our implementation for $F = 1$ is already faster than Catanzaro's code. This is due to the optimization strategies implemented at steps 1 and 3, as described in Sect. 4. Our approach performs even better when the unrolling factor increases, reaching a *speedup* close to 2.8x when $F = 8$. It can also be noted that the *speedup* stabilizes around this value (for $F = 16$, the gain is around 1.5% when compared to the result for $F = 8$)[4].

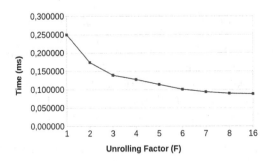

**Fig. 1.** Chart of the parallel reduction execution time.

---

[3] Reduction operations on vectors with millions of values are common when computing cost function in some real-life optimization problems. For instance, traffic assignment computation for large urban networks involves such vectors.

[4] The ideal unrolling factor strongly depends on the GPU model. In preliminary tests, performed in older hardware not listed here, the highest gains were obtained when $F$ was defined as 6.

**Table 2.** Parallel reduction execution times. New approach compared against Catanzaro's original code.

| F | Time (ms) | Speedup | Memory bandwidth (GB/s) | Bandwidth usage (%) |
|---|---|---|---|---|
| – | 0.294679 | – | 75.1083585868 | 22.57 |
| 1 | 0.249780 | 1 | 88.6094002722 | 26.63 |
| 2 | 0.173930 | 1.4360949807 | 127.2515149773 | 38.24 |
| 3 | 0.139260 | 1.7936234382 | 158.9318971708 | 47.76 |
| 4 | 0.127700 | 1.955990603 | 173.3191542678 | 52.08 |
| 5 | 0.113930 | 2.1923988414 | 194.2671464935 | 58.37 |
| 6 | 0.100810 | 2.4777303839 | 219.5502033528 | 65.97 |
| 7 | 0.093740 | 2.6646042245 | 236.1089822914 | 70.95 |
| 8 | 0.089490 | 2.7911498491 | 247.3221142027 | 74.32 |
| 16 | 0.088160 | 2.8332577132 | 251.0532667877 | 75.44 |

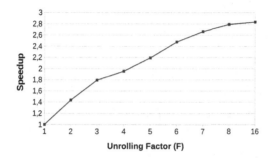

**Fig. 2.** Chart of the parallel reduction speedup.

Furthermore, the version of our approach implemented in CUDA was compared against Harris' Kernel 7 and Luitjens' code, in the second platform. The experiments also employed the two aforementioned vectors. Several values of the unrolling factor $(F)$ were tried in our code, in order to find the optimal value for the K40m video board. It was determined that up to $F = 6$ the performance gains are substantial and, with $F \geq 8$, the gains are very discrete. According to this, all experiments were conducted using $F = 8$, including the one presented by [11].

Table 3 shows the running time (in milliseconds) of the three approaches and the percentage of performance (given by the formula $100 * (1 - \frac{T}{T_H})$, where $T$ is the execution time of the method in the given line and $T_H$ is the execution time of Harris' code, as a reference. Our CUDA implementation runs in almost the same time of Harris' code. Luitjens approach, using the SHFL instruction in CUDA for the K40m GPU, outperforms Harris' code by 25.98%.

**Table 3.** Parallel reduction execution times in the K40m.

| Approach | Exec. time (ms) | % of Gain |
|---|---|---|
| Harris (Kernel 7) | 0.19032 | 0 |
| New Approach (CUDA. F = 8) | 0.18009 | 5.37 |
| Luitjens | 0.14086 | 25.98 |

Table 4 illustrates how the running time of the algorithms (also in milliseconds) change as the size of the vector doubles. For all cases the new approach is slightly better than Harris' method. Luitjens outperforms both methods, constrained to use a hardware with the SHFL instruction.

**Table 4.** Evolution of the execution times in the K40m.

| Vector size | Harris (Kernel 7) | New approach (CUDA. F = 8) | Luitjens |
|---|---|---|---|
| 2766607 | 0.18515 | 0.17941 | 0.07626 |
| 5533214 | 0.19032 | 0.18009 | 0.14086 |
| 11066428 | 0.29604 | 0.28219 | 0.24311 |
| 22132856 | 0.57268 | 0.53652 | 0.46887 |
| 44265712 | 1.13165 | 1.05426 | 0.91617 |
| 88531424 | 2.25516 | 2.09966 | 1.81140 |
| 177062848 | 4.51196 | 4.20577 | 3.60514 |

## 6    General Remarks

All parallel reduction techniques currently in use suffer from some basic issues. Many of them only reach their peak performance by employing proprietary strategies/technologies. That limits their use to the platforms for which they were designed. Others, although generic, do not adopt certain procedures that could increase their performance without loss of generality.

In the present work, we explored a combination of strategies that could improve the performance of the original Catanzaro's code for parallel reduction. One highlight should be made to the employment of attributions with algebraic expressions instead of conditional statements, in order to minimize or eliminate the phenomenon of thread divergence and to avoid the use of synchronization barriers.

The strategies presented in this paper are generic enough to be used with both CUDA and OpenCL and can run on hardware of the two major GPU manufacturers with minimal changes, just being adapted to the particularities of each platform.

The experiments that were carried out showed that the execution times of our approach and of Harris' are very similar. Therefore, we assume them to be equivalent. It was also possible to verify that Luitjens' proposal is more efficient than the other approaches. We advise to choose Luitjens' method if support to the SHFL instruction is available. For GPUs with no SHFL support, the new implementation described here is more advantageous, since it provides equivalent performance to Harris' approach [11] but with a code that is easier to implement and works for both CUDA and OpenCL.

It is worth mentioning that the discussed techniques are of general use, being reduction only one of its applications.

For future work, we intend to explore the benefits of SHFL-equivalent instructions that appear in recent AMD GPUs in our new OpenCL code.

# References

1. Billeter, M., Olsson, O., Assarsson, U.: Efficient stream compaction on wide SIMD many-core architectures. In: Proceedings of the Conference on High Performance Graphics 2009, HPG 2009, pp. 159–166. ACM, New York (2009). https://doi.org/10.1145/1572769.1572795
2. Catanzaro, B.: OpenCL optimization case study: simple reductions, August 2014. http://developer.amd.com/resources/documentation-articles/articles-whitepapers/opencl-optimization-case-study-simple-reductions/. Published by Advanced Micro Devices. Accessed 05 Jan 2014
3. Chakroun, I., Mezmaz, M., Melab, N., Bendjoudi, A.: Reducing thread divergence in a GPU-accelerated branch-and-bound algorithm. Concurr. Comput.: Pract. Exp. **25**(8), 1121–1136 (2013)
4. Cormen, T.H., Leiserson, C.E., Rivest, R.L., Stein, C.: Introduction to Algorithms, 3rd edn. The MIT Press, Cambridge (2009)
5. Fog, A.: Optimizing subroutines in assembly language: an optimization guide for x86 platforms. Technical University of Denmark (2013)
6. Fung, W.W.L., Sham, I., Yuan, G., Aamodt, T.: Dynamic warp formation and scheduling for efficient GPU control flow. In: 2007 40th Annual IEEE/ACM International Symposium on Microarchitecture, MICRO 2007, pp. 407–420, December 2007. https://doi.org/10.1109/MICRO.2007.30
7. Goldberg, D.: What every computer scientist should know about floating-pointarithmetic. ACM Comput. Surv. **23**(1), 5–48 (1991). https://doi.org/10.1145/103162.103163
8. Khronos OpenCL Working Group, et al.: The OpenCL specification. Version 1(29), 8 (2008)
9. Gupta, K., Stuart, J.A., Owens, J.D.: A study of persistent threads style GPU programming for GPGPU workloads. In: Innovative Parallel Computing (InPar), pp. 1–14. IEEE (2012)
10. Han, T.D., Abdelrahman, T.S.: Reducing branch divergence in GPU programs. In: Proceedings of the Fourth Workshop on General Purpose Processing on Graphics Processing Units, GPGPU-4, pp. 3:1–3:8. ACM, New York (2011). https://doi.org/10.1145/1964179.1964184
11. Harris, M.: Optimizing Parallel Reduction in CUDA (2007). https://docs.nvidia.com/cuda/cuda-samples/index.html#cuda-parallel-reduction. Published by NVidia Corporation. Accessed 10 Sept 2018

12. Higham, N.: Accuracy and Stability of Numerical Algorithms, 2nd edn. Society for Industrial and Applied Mathematics, Philadelphia (2002)
13. Huang, J.C., Leng, T.: Generalized loop-unrolling: a method for program speed-up. In: Proceedings of the IEEE Symposium on Application-Specific Systems and Software Engineering and Technology, pp. 244–248 (1997)
14. Kiefer, J.C.: Sequential minimax search for a maximum. Proc. Am. Math. Soc. **4**, 502–506 (1953)
15. Luitjens, J.: Faster parallel reductions on Kepler. White Paper, February 2014. http://devblogs.nvidia.com/parallelforall/faster-parallel-reductions-kepler/. Published by NVidia Inc., Accessed 25 July 2014
16. Meng, J., Tarjan, D., Skadron, K.: Dynamic warp subdivision for integrated branch and memory divergence tolerance. SIGARCH Comput. Archit. News **38**(3), 235–246 (2010). https://doi.org/10.1145/1816038.1815992
17. Muller, J., et al.: Handbook of Floating-Point Arithmetic. Birkhäuser, Boston (2009)
18. Narasiman, V., Shebanow, M., Lee, C.J., Miftakhutdinov, R., Mutlu, O., Patt, Y.N.: Improving GPU performance via large warps and two-level warp scheduling. In: Proceedings of the 44th Annual IEEE/ACM International Symposium on Microarchitecture, MICRO-44, pp. 308–317. ACM, New York (2011). https://doi.org/10.1145/2155620.2155656
19. Nasre, R., Burtscher, M., Pingali, K.: Data-driven versus topology-driven irregular computations on GPUs. In: 2013 IEEE 27th International Symposium on Parallel Distributed Processing (IPDPS), pp. 463–474 (2013). https://doi.org/10.1109/IPDPS.2013.28
20. Parhami, B.: Introduction to Parallel Processing Algorithms and Architectures. Plenum Series in Computer Science. Plenum Press, London (1999). http://books.google.com/books?id=ekBsZkIYfUgC
21. Sarkar, V.: Optimized unrolling of nested loops. Int. J. Parallel Program. **29**(5), 545–581 (2001). https://doi.org/10.1023/A:1012246031671
22. Steinberger, M., Kainz, B., Kerbl, B., Hauswiesner, S., Kenzel, M., Schmalstieg, D.: Softshell: dynamic scheduling on GPUs. ACM Trans. Graph. **31**(6), 161:1–161:11 (2012). https://doi.org/10.1145/2366145.2366180
23. Wilt, N.: The CUDA Handbook: A Comprehensive Guide to GPU Programming. Pearson Education, White Plains (2013)
24. Zhang, E.Z., Jiang, Y., Guo, Z., Shen, X.: Streamlining GPU applications on the fly: thread divergence elimination through runtime thread-data remapping. In: Proceedings of the 24th ACM International Conference on Supercomputing, ICS 2010, pp. 115–126. ACM, New York (2010). https://doi.org/10.1145/1810085.1810104

# Power and Energy

# Evaluating Cache Line Behavior Predictors for Energy Efficient Processors

Rodrigo Machniewicz Sokulski$^{(\boxtimes)}$ (ID), Emmanuell Diaz Carreno(ID), and Marco Antonio Zanata Alves(ID)

Federal University of Paraná, Curitiba, PR, Brazil
{rms16,edcarreno,mazalves}@inf.ufpr.br

**Abstract.** The ever-increasing size of cache memories, nowadays achieving almost half of the area for modern processors, and so essential to the performance of the systems, are leading into a crescent static energy consumption. In order to save some of this energy and optimize its component performance, many techniques were proposed. Cache line reuse predictors and dead line predictors are some examples. These mechanisms predict whenever a cache line shall be dead, in order to turn it off, also applying other policies on them, such as replacement prioritization or bypassing its installation inside the cache. However, not all mechanisms implement all these policies, that directly affect the cache behavior in different ways. This paper evaluates the impacts of the priority and bypass policies over two dead line predictors, the Dead Block and Early Write Back Predictor (DEWP) and the Skewed Dead Block predictor (SDP). Both mechanisms turn off dead cache lines using Gated-Vdd technique in order to save their static energy, thus analyzing how each policy (Priority replacement and cache Bypass) affects the energy savings and the system performance.

**Keywords:** Cache memory · Energy efficient · Cache usage predictor

## 1 Introduction

As technology advances and processors run faster, the performance gap between CPUs and DRAMs increases, further increasing the relevance of cache memories. These tiny and fast memories between the processor and the DRAM memory act attenuating the high delay of DRAMs, being critical for computers efficiency. In order for the processor to achieve higher performance, these cache memories need to maintain the necessary processor data for the majority of accesses, thus avoiding accessing to slower memory levels. Following this logic, the caches grew in size, and nowadays occupy about 50% from processors chip, also leading to increases in energy consumption.

The energy consumption in CMOS circuits such as SRAM and DRAM memories can be divided fundamentally into two sources. The dynamic energy used to perform circuits gating, and the static energy, also called leakage energy, which is

C. Bianchini et al. (Eds.): WSCAD 2018, CCIS 1171, pp. 185–197, 2020.
https://doi.org/10.1007/978-3-030-41050-6_12

spent even when there are no interactions. This second source is directly related to this component size. The bigger its storage capacity, the more static energy it spends. Therefore, the cache memories growth leads to a higher static energy consumption, increasing the importance of methods to save it.

Many cache line behavior predictors have already been proposed [2,6,10, 12,13,15]. Most of these mechanisms try to predict when a cache line content receives its last access, in order to apply a static energy saving technique over it. Regarding energy saving techniques, there are multiples proposals in the literature, where the most commonly used technique is called Gated-Vdd technique [22]. The Gated-Vdd consists in turning off a cache line in order to save almost all the static energy used to maintain it. This technique is applied whenever the processing core associated with a cache line is disabled, then we can disable the whole cache lines. Such gains may increase by using these techniques together with the cache line usage predictors, helping predicting the cache usage with cache line granularity. Despite the high savings, these shutdowns can directly increase the applications execution time.

Besides the cache line shutdowns, dead cache line predictors also allow cache line installation and replacement improvements, producing higher cache hit ratios. Whenever a cache line is predicted to be dead-on-arrival (i.e., the line is predicted to receive only a single access), that cache line can be bypassed, not being installed inside the cache, thus reducing the cache pollution [4]. For the cases where the cache line is predicted to have multiple accesses, whenever a cache line is predicted to be dead (i.e., it is not going to receive any further access until its eviction) the cache eviction policy can increase its eviction priority, in order to keep for longer the live ones. Nevertheless, during wrong predictions, these modifications in the installation and replacement policies may have a negative influence on energy consumption and the execution time from the programs, because data that should be kept in the cache is going to be fetched again from the main memory.

In this paper, our objective is to evaluate the influence caused by the early cache line eviction and the bypass techniques in the last level cache when using information from cache line predictors. We evaluate two cache dead line predictors, the Dead Block and Early Write Back Predictor (DEWP) [2] and the Skewed Dead Block Predictor (SDP) [13]. Our focus is to assess and understand the impact of these two techniques in the base implementation of each one of the cache line usage predictors evaluated, in terms of energy consumption and execution time. Our main contributions are:

**Implementation:** we present the idea of merging the DEWP and SDP mechanisms with the dead line priority eviction and the bypass policies.

**Energy Impact:** we evaluate different combinations of mechanism and policies that save from 30% to 60% of the energy consumed by a traditional cache and DRAM memory sub-system with performance variation of ±2%, offering an interesting trade-off between energy savings and performance.

## 2    Motivation

The increase of static energy consumption in cache memories [1] leads to the research of many dead line predictors [2,8,13–15]. These mechanisms try to predict when a cache line receives its last access in order to turn it off. In addition to this, the predictions can be used to change the cache lines install and replacement policy, prioritizing dead lines and making bypass from dead-on-arrival lines. According to each application's memory access pattern and the predictor accuracy, these policy change can lead to gains or losses in an execution.

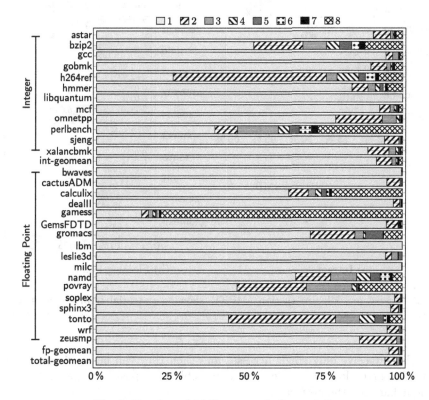

**Fig. 1.** Number of LLC accesses before eviction

We designed two main experiments using all the 29 applications from the SPEC-CPU 2006 benchmark suite, to understand the possible impact when prioritizing dead lines and performing bypass from dead-on-arrival lines. Further methodology details are present in Sect. 4.

In the first experiment, we evaluate the number of accesses per cache line before it gets evicted from the LLC. Figure 1 shows a histogram that counts the number of accesses each cache line from a 2 MB LLC received before it was invalidated. We can observe that on average more than 95% of the last level

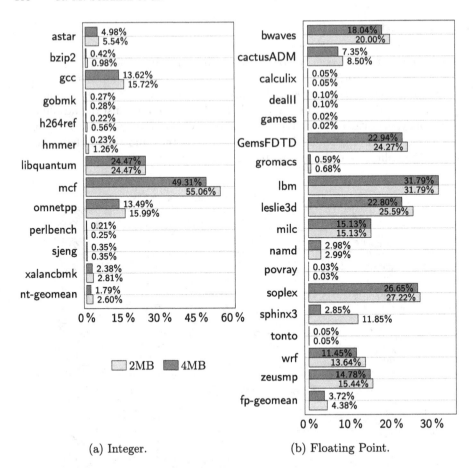

(a) Integer.                    (b) Floating Point.

**Fig. 2.** Misses per kilo instruction (MPKI) showing potential improvements when increasing the cache size.

cache lines receive only single accesses and then they can be considered dead. From this first plot, we can learn it is possible to bypass multiple cache lines without harming the performance.

In the second experiment to motivate this work, we executed the same applications with two different LLC sizes, 2 MB, and 4 MB as can be seen in Fig. 2. Considering that both techniques, bypassing and prioritization of dead cache lines, will virtually increase the cache memory size, by reducing the number of dead cache lines inside the LLC, this second experiment aims to show the possible reduction in the MPKI (misses per kilo instruction) metric whenever the cache memory gets its size increased. We can see that MPKI reduces on average 14% when doubling the LLC size, showing the potential to achieve performance improvements.

Our results from previous work [17,18] showed that for half of applications tested, more than 75% of the time, the circuit wasted static energy because the cache lines already received its last access and are waiting for its eviction. For most of the applications, a perfect mechanism could turn-off the cache lines for more than 40% of the execution time, with potential to save a high portion of static energy.

It is important to note that performance and energy consumption results will suffer significant influence from the dead cache line predictor accuracy. Whenever the mechanism correct predicts the cache line behavior, energy and time can be saved. On the other hand, during miss predictions, two different things can occur: (1) the system will consume extra time and energy to bring the cache line from the DRAM; or (2) the system will lack the opportunity to save energy and time.

Thus, we aim to evaluate the influence of dead lines priority and the bypass policy using two different dead cache line predictors, SDP and DEWP, in order to understand how each policy affects these dead line predictors.

# 3  Mechanisms and Techniques

This section details the dead cache line predictors DEWP and SDP, the gated-Vdd technique and the cache policies evaluated in this paper.

## 3.1  DEWP

The DEWP mechanism uses an access history table (AHT) with 512-entries, in order to store the number of reads and writes that a cache line content received before its last eviction. Based on historical data stored in the AHT, the predictor can determine when a cache line received its last access, declaring the line as dead. Moreover, it can reduce the memory controller pressure by detecting when the cache lines received their last write and performing early write-backs. Besides AHT, this predictor requires some additional information stored in each cache line, in order to make specific predictions to them.

Figure 3 illustrates the components requires by our DEWP implementation [17]. Unlike its original version, the read and write counters were replaced with an access counter, with the view to simplify the mechanism operation and analyze only its dead line predictions influence over the improved LRU and the bypass policy. The DEWP operations are triggered by some cache events; these events and its consequences are described below:

**During a cache line hit:**

- If the cache line and its *training* flag are on, the *access counter* from the AHT entry pointed by the *AHT pointer* in the cache line is incremented.
- If the cache line is on and the *training* flag is off, the *access counter* from the cache is decremented, denoting that one of the predicted accesses was performed.

- If the cache line is off and there is an AHT entry pointed by the cache line, the accesses counter from the entry is incremented, the cache line *training* flag is set and the cache line data is restored.
- If the cache line is off and there is no AHT entry pointed by the cache line, the line content is restored.

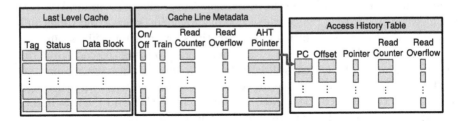

**Fig. 3.** Components necessary for DEWP.

**During a cache line miss:**

- If there is an AHT entry indexed by the PC from the instruction address that caused the cache miss and the Offset from the data accessed, the AHT entry information is copied to the cache line metadata. The *training* flag is disabled. If the AHT entry *pointer* flag is off, the flag is set and the cache line *AHT pointer* starts to point to this entry.
- If there is no matching AHT entry, a new entry is selected using the LRU policy, its entries are cleaned, and it is linked to the cache line. Furthermore, the *training* flag is set, causing new accesses to update the AHT entry.

**During a Cache Line Eviction:** If there is an AHT entry pointed by the cache line, the entry *access counter* is decremented with the line *access counter*; thereby if the predicted access number has not occurred, this information is updated in the entry.

**During Every Cache Line Access:** After each cache line accesses its *access counter* and *overflow* bit is verified and if both hold a 0 value, the line is considered as dead. In this case, it is turned off with the Gated-Vdd technique.

The *access counters* from the cache metadata and the AHT entries are 2-bit saturated counters. When they reach their maximum value, the *overflow* bit is set, indicating that number of accesses received is greater than the mechanism can hold and thus avoiding mispredictions due to big numbers of accesses.

## 3.2   SDP

The Skewed Dead line Predictor (SDP) uses the addresses from instructions that accessed a cache line in order to produce a trace. This trace is used to index prediction tables using skewed functions [23]. Then the indexed values are used to discover the instruction that makes the last access to each cache line content.

Our SDP implementation is illustrated in Fig. 4. We used 2 tables with 16 K 2-bit saturated counters each. Beyond that, the threshold determines if the cache line dead. We set the threshold equals 2, the same used on previous work [13]. The SDP mechanism also requires the inclusion of a 15-bit entry and a flag indicating the cache line state for each cache line. This 15-bit entry stores a history of the instructions that lead to the current cache line access. For each instruction that accesses the cache line, an XOR from the 15 least significant bits with the next 15 bits of its address is computed. Then this result is summed with the current cache line trace in order to update it.

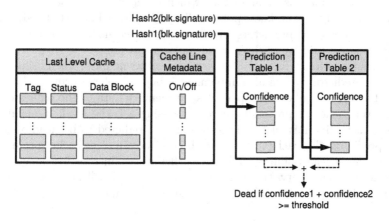

**Fig. 4.** Components necessary for SDP.

This mechanism operation is related to some cache events. These events and its related operations are described next.

**During a Cache Line Hit:** If the cache line was turned off, its content is retrieved. The tables lines indexed with the cache line trace are decremented. Then, the trace gets updated. If the sum from the new indexed entries is greater than 2, the line is considered as dead and turned off.

**During a Cache Line Miss:** The data is brought into the cache line and the line trace is updated with this single access. After that, this new trace is used to consult the prediction tables. If the sum from the indexed entries is greater than 2, the line is turned off.

**During a Cache Line Eviction:** The indexed entries are incremented before the cache line eviction.

### 3.3 Gated-Vdd

Gated-Vdd technique was developed in order to turn off the unused sub-circuits, consequently eliminating the leakage energy of these. The main idea behind this technique is the usage of an extra transistor in the supply voltage (Vdd) or ground path (Gnd) wire. By turning on this transistor, we can normally use the circuit, and whenever we turn off this transistor (gated), the circuit will be disabled. Thus, the gated-Vdd technique keeps the normal circuit behavior, but it can reduce most of static energy consumption if correctly used [5].

### 3.4 Cache Line Installation and Replacement Policies

The cache line policy is what defines which cache line shall be evicted when installing a new line. Well know policies like LRU (Least Recently Used), can be improved by dead line predictors. For instance, the cache line if predicted to be dead can receive priority in the normal replacement policy.

Besides the priority for early eviction of dead cache lines, when using a dead cache line predictor we can also implement a bypass policy during cache installation. The bypass policy shall permit send memory data to the requester (i.e., higher level caches or processing core) bypassing a cache level. It means that during a cache line miss if the data brought is predicted to be dead-on-arrival by the predictor, this cache line will not be installed in some cache specific level, reducing thus cache pollution, allowing other cache lines to live longer inside the cache. For simplicity, these two policies presented will be referenced to as *priority* and *bypass*, respectively, in the rest of this paper.

## 4   Methodology and Results

The most common objective when using dead cache line predictors is to reduce the static energy consumption from cache memories through the shutdown of its dead cache lines. However, there is a collateral effect in this reduction, the increase in the number of misses in the cache level where is applied, therefore raising the execution time and the memory hierarchy dynamic energy spend. In this section, our analysis contemplates the last level cache (LLC) and the DRAM energy consumption, and the execution time with each mechanism variation.

Our results were obtained using an in-house simulator, that models all the cache hierarchy, considering that non-memory instructions execute in a single cycle (IPC = 1), nevertheless the error rates when compared to a cycle-accurate simulator is maintained below 5% [16].

The tests were made using real execution traces which contains 2 billion instructions from each one of the 29 SPEC_CPU2006 applications [7]. The execution trace represents the most representative slide from each application and

**Table 1.** General parameters for the baseline cache model.

| Cache memory level | Size | Associativity | Cycles | Idle power | Dynamic energy |
|---|---|---|---|---|---|
| L1 | 32 KB | 8 Ways | 4 | Not modeled | Not modeled |
| L2 | 256 KB | 8 Ways | 8 | Not modeled | Not modeled |
| L3 | 4 MB | 16 Ways | 26 | 309 mW avg | 0.294 nJ avg |
| RAM | 1 GB | – | 200 | 8 mW avg | 3.760 nJ avg |

was obtained using PinPoints [20]. Table 1 shows our memory hierarchy configuration, that is base on the Core i7 processor design. We used the CACTI 6.5 [19] to model the power consumption for each of these memory components.

### 4.1 Energy Consumption and Performance Results

In order to better compare the results in terms of energy consumption and execution time, we generate a simple plot illustrated in the Fig. 5. It shows the energy consumption compared to a baseline without any dead cache line predictor. Thus our baseline corresponds to a traditional processor with a simple LRU replacement policy.

In the left of the figure we present the results for DEWP mechanism, and in the right, we show for the SDP mechanism. On each line, we have a different approach, turning on or off of the techniques (Priority and Bypass). We use $P$ or $NP$ when using or not the Priority policy, respectively. We also use $B$ and $NB$ to denote when we are using or not the Bypass policy. Thus, we obtain 8 combinations from two mechanisms (DEWP, SDP) with 4 policies (NP+NB, P+NB, NP+B, P+B). In the horizontal axis, there is the energy consumption and the performance in the vertical axis, both compared to the baseline system. This energy consumption presents the full cache memory sub-system and the DRAM, considering both dynamic and static energy.

Considering the first pair of results (DEWP and SDP, both executing NP+NB), we can observe that alone the dead cache line predictors with gated-Vdd technique only reduces energy consumption. However, during under predictions (predicting the cache line as dead before its last access), the system losses performance, because the extra DRAM accesses that are required to retrieve the discarded data. This negative effect cannot be avoided in this approach because the predictors are not providing tips for the internal policies of the cache.

Considering the second and third pairs of results (DEWP and SDP, when only P or B is enabled), we can notice that for DEWP, B leads to the best performance and energy improvements. Nevertheless, for SDP, only P could improve the performance, while B enabled energy savings on more applications. Based on the results, we can infer that reducing the cache pollution using Bypass present higher potential for energy savings. Nonetheless, the Priority enabled higher gains in terms of performance.

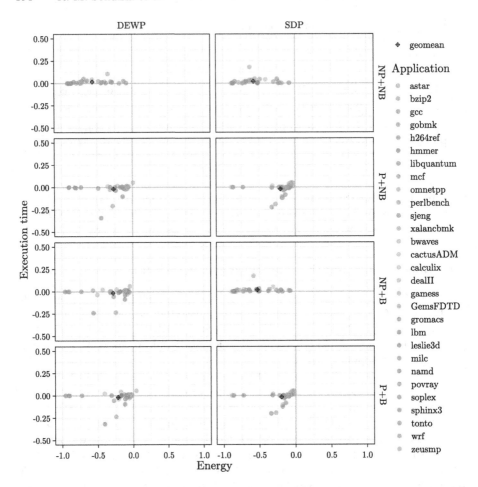

**Fig. 5.** Energy consumption and performance comparing each mechanism and policy to the baseline.

Considering the fourth pair of results, (DEWP and SDP, with P+B), we can observe that results look similar to NP+B although the energy savings could be pushed further for some applications. It is easy to understand why the bypass achieves almost the best results when used alone if we consider the motivation results, that showed that 95% of cache lines receive only single access.

We can see that for applications such as *gamess* with the highest number for cache lines with 8 or more accesses and lowest number of single accessed cache lines, that none of P or B can improve the performance nor the energy savings. This improvement happens because the dead cache line predictor alone obtain the most energy savings. Looking in a different perspective, we can infer that cache friendly applications tend to present lower gains when using any of these mechanisms, reinforcing the importance of good programming practices. We also note that for some applications, there is no direct correlation between the energy savings, caused by turning off dead lines, and the execution time It means that, even using new policies the application performance does not benefit from the mechanisms. This can be explained by the fact that not all the applications benefits from a bigger cache memory (see Fig. 2 from Sect. 2).

## 5  Related Work

Most of the line usage predictors implement just the replacement policy priority improvement or this improvement associated with the bypass technique. Table 2 shows some of the mechanisms that implement each of these options. Some of these mechanisms utilize some already complex cache replacement policies as RRIP, although, the use of these improved policies could mask our evaluations, thus the perfect LRU replacement policy was used in our experiments. Besides that, some of the mechanisms as Multiperspective reuse prediction technique

**Table 2.** Related mechanisms with their implemented policies.

| Mechanism | Priority | Bypass |
|---|---|---|
| Hawkeye [8] simulates the Belady's optimal solution for past cache accesses in order to discover the optimal behavior of each cache line content. Then the lines are classified in cache-friendly and cache-averse, adjusting the RRIP [9] counters | ● | |
| In [3] EVA, an algorithm that tries to calculate a coast to maintain each cache line content. With the expected remaining cache line lifetime and its access probability within this time, the benefit to maintain each cache line is estimated | ● | |
| The mechanism proposed by [21] analyze the relations between the cache compressed blocks size and its reuse predictions. It is able to determine which cache block or compressed cache blocks should be prioritized in the cache eviction, being able to apply eviction, insertion and promotion over the base replacement policy | ● | |
| Expected Hit Count (EHC) [25] is a mechanism that calculates the number of accesses that each cache line is expected to receive until its eviction based on the average number of accesses received in the last times the block was in the cache | ● | ● |
| Perceptron predictor [24] uses a sampler and the perceptron learning algorithm in order to train feature indexed tables and detect the moment when a cache line content receives its last access. This information is used to drive the replacement and bypass algorithms over the tree-based PseudoLRU replacement policy [11] | ● | ● |
| Multiperspective Reuse Prediction technique [10] is based on the Perceptron idea, although this predictor contains some many improved new features and a new training method | ● | ● |

and Perceptron predictor are very dependent to their configurations, generating a wide range of possible results. Therefore, our experiments were performed over DEWP and SDP, since its priority and bypass implementation were straight.

## 6   Conclusions

Despite the great effort to maintain the high processor performance, the growth of the cache memories is leading into an increase in its static energy expenditure, which is directly proportional to its size. Several mechanisms, called cache dead line predictors, have already been proposed as an alternative to curb these expenditures by detecting and applying optimization techniques on cache lines that have already received their last access. Each technique applied by these mechanisms affects both the cache and the predictor itself differently. This paper sought to understand how two optimization techniques, the dead line prioritization and the bypass of dead-on-arrival lines, affect two dead line predictors, the Skewed Dead Block predictor (SDP) and the Dead Block and Early Write Back Predictor (DEWP), both implementing the Gated-Vdd, in order to evaluate its effects regarding to energy consumption and execution time in each predictor.

Our results showed that for SDP, the Priority was the determinant factor affecting its energy consumption and execution time, whereas for DEWP, both techniques achieved similar performances. Furthermore, our experiments discovered that when combining both policies (P+B), the best performance results were achieved, with performance gains of 2.60% (DEWP) and 2.18% (SDP). Although the bypass technique did not significantly affected the SDP mechanism. This demonstrates that not always a particular technique or combination will produce positive effects with any predictor, showing the importance of evaluations over each combination of techniques prior to their adoption in a new predictor mechanism.

## References

1. Alves, M.A.Z.: Increasing energy efficiency of processor caches via line usage predictors. Ph.D. thesis, UFRGS, Porto Alegre (2014)
2. Alves, M.A.Z., Villavieja, C., Diener, M., Navaux, P.O.A.: Energy efficient last level caches via last read/write prediction. In: International Symposium on Computer Architecture and High Performance Computing, pp. 73–80 (2013)
3. Beckmann, N., Sanchez, D.: Maximizing cache performance under uncertainty. In: International Symposium on High Performance Computer Architecture, pp. 109–120 (2017)
4. Chi, C., Dietz, H.: Improving cache performance by selective cache bypass. In: International Conference on System Sciences, pp. 277–285 (1989)
5. Powell, M., Yang, S.H., Falsafi, B., Roy, K., Vijaykumar, T.: Gated-Vdd : a circuit technique to reduce leakage in deep-submicron cache memories. In: International Symposium on Low Power Electronics and Design, Digest of Technical Papers, pp. 90–95 (2000)

6. Faldu, P., Grot, B.: Leeway: addressing variability in dead-block prediction for last-level caches. In: International Conference on Parallel Architectures and Compilation Techniques, pp. 180–193 (2017)

7. Henning, J.L.: Spec cpu2006 benchmark descriptions. SIGARCH Comput. Archit. News **34**(4), 1–17 (2006)

8. Jain, A., Lin, C.: Back to the future: leveraging Belady's algorithm for improved cache replacement. In: International Symposium on Computer Architecture, pp. 78–89 (2016)

9. Jaleel, A., Theobald, K.B., Steely Jr., S.C., Emer, J.: High performance cache replacement using re-reference interval prediction (RRIP). ACM SIGARCH Comput. Archit. News. **38**, 60–71 (2010)

10. Jiménez, D.A., Teran, E.: Multiperspective reuse prediction. In: International Symposium on Microarchitecture, pp. 436–448 (2017)

11. Jiménez, D.A.: Insertion and promotion for tree-based PseudoLRU last-level caches. In: International Symposium on Microarchitecture, pp. 284–296 (2013)

12. Kaxiras, S., Hu, Z., Martonosi, M.: Cache decay: exploiting generational behavior to reduce cache leakage power. In: International Symposium on Computer Architecture, pp. 240–251 (2001)

13. Khan, S., Burger, D., Jiménez, D.A., Falsafi, B.: Using dead blocks as a virtual victim cache. In: International Conference on Parallel Architectures and Compilation Techniques, pp. 489–500 (2010)

14. Khan, S.M., Tian, Y., Jimenez, D.A.: Sampling dead block prediction for last-level caches. In: International Symposium on Microarchitecture, pp. 175–186 (2010)

15. Kharbutli, M., Solihin, Y.: Counter-based cache replacement and bypassing algorithms. IEEE Trans. Comput. **57**(4), 433–447 (2008)

16. Lee, H., Jin, L., Lee, K., Demetriades, S., Moeng, M., Cho, S.: Two-phase trace-driven simulation (TPTS): a fast multicore processor architecture simulation approach. Softw. Pract. Exp. **40**(3), 239–258 (2010)

17. Sokulski, R.M., Carreno, E.D., Alves, M.A.: Evaluating dead line predictors efficiency with drowsy technique. In: Brazilian Symposium on Computing Systems Engineering, pp. 250–255 (2018)

18. Sokulski, R., Carreno, E., Alves, M.: Introducing drowsy technique to cache line usage predictors. In: Brazilian Symposium on Computing Systems, pp. 259–265 (2018)

19. Muralimanohar, N., Balasubramonian, R., Jouppi, N.P.: Architecting efficient interconnects for large caches with cacti 6.0. IEEE Micro **28**, 69–79 (2008)

20. Patil, H., Cohn, R., et al.: Pinpointing representative portions of large intel ® itanium ® programs with dynamic instrumentation. In: International Symposium on Microarchitecture, pp. 81–92 (2004)

21. Pekhimenko, G., et al.: Exploiting compressed block size as an indicator of future reuse. In: International Symposium on High Performance Computer Architecture, pp. 51–63 (2015)

22. Powell, M., Yang, S.H., et al.: Gated-Vdd: a circuit technique to reduce leakage in deep-submicron cache memories. In: International Symposium on Low Power Electronics and Design, pp. 90–95 (2000)

23. Seznec, A.: A case for two-way skewed-associative caches. In: International Symposium on Computer Architecture (1993)

24. Teran, E., Wang, Z., Jimenez, D.A.: Perceptron learning for reuse prediction. In: International Symposium on Microarchitecture, pp. 1–12 (2016)

25. Vakil-Ghahani, A., Mahdizadeh-Shahri, S., et al.: Cache replacement policy based on expected hit count. IEEE Comput. Archit. Lett. **17**(1), 64–67 (2018)

# Author Index

Printed in the United States
By Bookmasters